Sports Collectors Digest

Mickey Mantle
MEMORABILIA

BY RICK HINES, MARK LARSON AND DAVE PLATTA

Published by

**krause
publications**

700 E. State Street • Iola, WI 54990-0001
Telephone: 715/445-2214

Library of Congress Catalog Number: 93-77548
ISBN: 0-87341-261-3
Printed in the United States of America

Contents

Acknowledgements

This book's cover photo, designed by Tom Mortenson, originally appeared on the cover of the Nov. 29, 1991, Sports Collectors Digest. Kevin Huard supplied memorabilia for the photo.

Rick Hines and Dave Platta were contributing writers for Chapters 1 and 2.

Several other writers have had their SCD stories reprinted in this book in the remaining chapters. They have been given credit; the dates at the end of the story are when the story was originally published. Back issues of SCD have also been used for pricing information and auction results. Auction houses have been credited if photos were used from their auction catalogs.

Kelly R. Eisenhauer compiled a Mickey Mantle memorabilia checklist which first appeared in the October 1984 Baseball Cards Magazine. Updated versions appeared in the December 1988 issue, the Nov. 29, 1991, SCD, and in this book, mainly using data from the third edition of the Standard Catalog of Baseball Cards, the seventh edition of the Sports Collectors Digest Baseball Card Price Guide and issues of Krause Publications' Sports Card Price Guide.

The second edition of the Sports Collectors Digest Baseball Autograph Handbook, by Mark Allen Baker, and the Sports Collectors Digest Team Baseballs book, also by Baker, have been used, as has the Sports Collectors Digest's Complete Guide to Baseball Memorabilia, by Mark K. Larson.

The book Everything Baseball, by James Mote, published in 1989, by Prentice Hall Press, New York, N.Y., was used as a source for Chapter 9.

Those at Krause Publications who helped make this process run smoothly include Mary Sieber, Barb Lefeber, Jeanette Sawall, Patsy Morrison, Tom Nelsen, Kathy Hines and Marge Larson.

Introduction

Mantle sees them (Baby Boomers), too. "I sit here whenever I'm doing a card show and a guy will come by. You know, you can tell he's like a president of a company or something. And, he'll have his kid with him and he'll say, 'There he is, son.'

"Almost everyone of them will say, 'I've waited 30 years for this.' They'll shake hands. It really makes you feel good. I played for 20 years; retired in '68 and to have people still remember you and feel like that about you, it's really great. I have a lot of people say, 'Don't you get tired of it?' Hell, no! I don't get tired of it. It's flattering to me." - Mickey Mantle, as told to Pete Dobrovitz during a card show in New York, and published in the Sept. 9, 1988, Sports Collectors Digest.

In this day of prima donna athtletes signing mega-buck contracts, perhaps the previous quote is the perfect example of why Mickey Mantle remains so popular - he's still flattered by all the attention he receives, and he accepted his role as "public property." He also provided us with a lot of terrific, wonderful memories...

Chapter 1

Baseball's greatest switch-hitter

Courtesy Leland's Inc.

The Mick's on deck at Yankee Stadium.

By Dave Platta

There's nothing tougher in sports than living up to hype. Once you're labeled a "man of destiny," or the next this or the second that, you're living under a microscope, trying to be the first version of yourself. Yes, it's difficult dealing with all that hype. But what do you do when you're named after a Hall of Famer? If you're Mickey Charles Mantle, you make everyone forget the guy for whom you were named. Mickey Cochrane? Who's he?

Mickey Mantle was born Oct. 20, 1931, in Spavinaw, Okla. Life was tough in northeastern Oklahoma in the 1930s — the Great Depression was reaching its depths, and Oklahoma was the great Dust Bowl, in the midst of the great drought that drove thousands, in their dilapidated Model T's, from their farms west to California, hoping for a land of milk and honey but willing to settle for a job and just enough money to get by.

Mantle's father, Elvin "Mutt" Mantle, worked for Eagle-Picher Zinc and Lead Co., one of many mining companies operating in northeastern Oklahoma, southwestern Missouri and southeastern Kansas. Mantle did everything — from shoveling ore, to breaking boulders and working as a mule skinner — until he was promoted to ground supervisor.

The elder Mantle, a switch-hitter who could run and had a good arm, also loved baseball. Although he never had a chance to move past playing for the town team, his baseball influence on Mickey was one of the best things he could have done for the youngster — he made him switch-hit from the first time he picked up a bat. Mutt would pitch to Mickey, who would hit left-handed.

When Mickey's left-handed grandfather, Charlie Mantle, pitched, Mickey would hit from the right side. The gentlemen would alternate pitching to Mickey, who became so comfortable hitting from both sides that he enhanced his progress to the major leagues.

Times were tough in Commerce, an Oklahoma mining town. Not only was the pay low, but the mine's dust caused illnesses among the miners and their families. By the time Mickey was 13, his grandfather and two of his uncles were dead of Hodgkin's Disease, a form of cancer of the lymph nodes. Whether it was caused from working in the mines, or if it was just hereditary in the Mantle family, was uncertain. But it scarred Mickey's outlook on life, especially when the disease claimed his father a decade later.

Certainly, Mutt Mantle recognized the hazards and problems of being a miner. At the first opportunity, he moved his family away from Commerce, trading the deed to his house for a tractor, a horse, some cattle and the right to work as a sharecropper on a farm owned by a local doctor. The farm provided room for the five Mantle kids to run. Besides Mickey there were twins Roy and Ray, who both had shots at pro ball, Barbara, the only daughter, and Butch, the youngest.

Despite all the hard work the family did, life on the farm didn't last — Mutt's dreams were destroyed by the same problem that drove "Okies" off their land during the Dust Bowl days — the weather. But it wasn't a lack of rain that did them in; ironically, a fall flood cost the Mantles their farm.

After several days of rain just before harvest time, the Neosho River overflowed its banks, filling the creek on the farm. Crops were ruined and the family was driven from its home, forced to move to a two-room shack just outside Commerce that didn't even have inside plumbing. Getting two adults, five children and all their possessions into two rooms took some ingenuity.

When you're living in poverty, there has to be an escape hatch. For young Mickey, that escape was through sports. He was big, quick, strong and fast, an athlete who could set the heart of any football, baseball or basketball coach racing. During his sophomore year at Commerce High, Mantle was convinced by a friend to go out for the football team, despite his father's objections that he'd get hurt and ruin his budding baseball career. Events later showed that Mutt Mantle knew what he was talking about; Mickey, a running back, didn't make it through his first season on the gridiron.

Things were going well until Mickey sustained an injury during a practice, nearly bringing his fledgling athletic career to an untimely end. Mickey was carrying the ball when a tackler kicked him in the left shin. At the time, the injury didn't look all that serious, so the coach, who thought it was a sprain, told Mickey to go home and soak his leg.

It wasn't a sprain, but more likely a deep bone bruise with internal bleeding. The day after the injury, Mickey woke up with a raging fever. His left ankle was swollen to twice its normal size. When doctors at the nearby Picher hospital examined the leg, they concluded the wound was superficial, but they were worried about the high fever. They lanced the ankle and treated it with compresses and liniments, hoping to slow the swelling. Nothing seemed to work.

Finally, osteomyelitis set in. Osteomyelitis, a bacterial infection of bone which can deteriorate it enough so that the bone tissue dies, is what ended Bo Jackson's football career. Jackson had his hip replaced with plastic. Doctors in Oklahoma in 1946 were thinking in similar terms for young Mickey — but the surgery they considered was amputation; osteomyelitis was then considered a deadly disease which claimed many lives due to its bacterial nature.

Mickey's parents objected strenuously to the idea of amputation. Lovell Mantle, not about to let her son get sliced up, went to a lawyer in nearby Miami, Okla. He drew up papers that transferred Mickey to the state hospital for children in Oklahoma City. There, the doctors used a new drug to control the inflammation in Mickey's leg. Six daily penicillin injections into the injured limb led to dramatic improvement. Mickey left the hospital soon after, but, because he was down to 110 pounds, he was carried out by one of his brothers.

A long stretch of rehabilitation was ahead for Mantle, mainly because the osteomyelitis could flare up again, as it later did throughout his baseball career. However, the resilient 15-year-old was soon running around playing basketball and baseball in between flare-ups of the disease.

It didn't prevent Mantle from showing his abilities in the Ban Johnson League, an amateur league one step up from the sandlots. He hooked on with the Baxter Springs Whiz Kids, based in Baxter Springs, Kan. Major League scouts kept an eye on the league, especially the Whiz Kids, the class of the league.

The team was run by Barney Barnett, who, like most men in the area, worked in the mines. Away from the mines, Barnett's life revolved around the baseball team. He worked as promoter, manager, recruiter, groundskeeper, and even owned the lighting system used by the team for weekday night games. To pay the light bills, Barnett would pass the hat to spectators, who'd contribute whatever they had to keep the team in business.

Barnett also passed the hat for other reasons. In his autobiography, Mantle told of hitting three homers in a game. Barnett passed the hat and collected more than $50 in change. Although it was a hardship to return the money — $50 was two weeks' pay for most miners — Mantle did so because he was still in high school; he would have lost his amateur status and eligibility to play sports at Commerce High.

In the summer before his senior year, Mantle caught the eye of a New York Yankees' scout, Tom Greenwade, who came to Baxter Springs to watch the Whiz Kids' third baseman, Billy Johnson. That day, Mickey hit two home runs that landed in the river behind the outfield, more than 400 feet from home plate. Mickey's performance convinced Greenwade that he should watch Mantle, not Johnson.

That night, Greenwade talked to Mickey about possibly playing for the Yankees. Since Mantle was still in high school, the talk couldn't progress any further, but Greenwade made a vague promise or two to talk about signing with the Yankees after graduation. The Mantles were definitely interested in the Yankees; the Bronx Bombers had been THE team for nearly three decades.

The Yankees had the House that Ruth Built, Lou Gehrig, Joe DiMaggio, 15 American League pennants and 11 World Championships in the 27 seasons since 1921. Nothing epitomized "excellence" more than the guys in pinstripes. There wasn't a kid in America who wouldn't give his left arm for a shot to add his name to the honor roll list of greats who had passed through the portals of Yankee Stadium.

Mickey finished his senior year at Commerce High, but didn't attend his graduation ceremony. Greenwade persuaded the school to let Mantle skip it so he could play for the Whiz Kids that night. Mickey lit it up on that early summer night of 1949. He homered from both sides of the plate, gaining a final stamp of approval from Greenwade.

What a prospect Mickey was! He was what would be considered a five-tool player in current scouting parlance. He could hit for average, hit for power, run, throw and field. With all that, Mantle was given a hefty signing bonus and a nice deal with the Yankees, right?

Wrong. Greenwade was a seasoned veteran in negotiating contracts with young prospects. The Yankee scout admitted that young Mickey hammered everything thrown at him, but, after all, these guys weren't pros. Could he hit big-time pitching? Maybe, maybe not. Besides, Mickey was small, at 5'9" and perhaps 160 pounds, his arm was erratic, and his fielding at shortstop was pretty lousy.

But Greenwade was willing to take a risk on Mickey. He offered a salary equal to what Mickey could make working in the mines and playing ball on the weekends. To clinch the deal, Greenwade included a signing bonus of a little more than $1,000. Thus, Mickey Mantle became a member of the New York Yankees organization.

Of course, Greenwade, in talking to the press about the young phenom he'd just signed to a contract, called Mantle the best prospect he'd ever seen. Mantle, he predicted, would set all kinds of records at Yankee Stadium. Mickey, a 17-year-old shortstop, didn't worry about it; he needed to show he could meet those lofty expectations.

Mantle's first stop was Independence, Kan., the Yankees' Class D affiliate in the Kansas-Oklahoma-Missouri League, the equivalent of today's Appalachian League or Pioneer League. Mickey, fresh out of high school and away from home for the first time, was pretty typical among players in the K-O-M League. Homesickness was a common problem for kids trying to cope with the responsibilities of being on their own while also learning their new profession. Baseball was very different — it wasn't just a game anymore. It was their job. Either they did well, or they were gone.

Harry Craft, a former outfielder for the Cincinnati Reds, managed the Independence team. In his six-year major league career, Craft, a starting outfielder for the Reds' pennant-winning teams in 1939 and 1940, hit .253 in 566 games. Craft returned to the minors to begin working his way up the ladder as a manager.

He eventually returned to the big leagues, managing the Kansas City Athletics from 1957 to 1959, the Chicago Cubs in 1961 (as part of the ill-fated "college of coaches" concept of then-Cubs owner Philip K. Wrigley), and the National League expansion franchise in Houston, as the team's first manager, from 1962 to 1964.

Craft, who had been handling younger players for some time, knew when to be patient, and when not to put up with anything. Mantle was obviously the brightest young star on his ballclub, so Craft spent hours with Mickey, helping him adjust to life as a pro baseball player. Mantle, it was clear, was intense and hated to lose.

In fact, like many young players who were used to being stars on the sandlots, Mantle was having trouble coping with the idea that even if he made seven outs for every three hits, he was still doing very well. An attitude like that was not only hazardous to water coolers or anything else breakable in the dugout, it could break a young player's spirit until he learned to cope with failure.

Another problem Mickey had was his fielding. He was undoubtedly a gifted athlete, but he had throwing problems which were so bad that a chicken-wire fence was erected behind first base to protect the fans. For an intense player like Mantle, it was torture. But Craft encouraged Mickey, telling him to forget about the most recent error and concentrate on the next play or the next at bat.

Apparently it worked well enough; Mickey compiled some pretty decent numbers in his first professional season. In just 89 games, he had 101 hits, 29 for extra bases, and a .313 batting average. He also scored 54 runs and had 63 RBI, leading Independence to the K-O-M League pennant. The only negative stat on the books was on the fielding side of the ledger.

Mickey had 47 errors at shortstop, and a depressing .886 fielding percentage. But the Yankees weren't worried about his fielding; they were thrilled with his adjustment in playing professional ball and hitting professional pitching. As far as the brass in New York was concerned, Mickey's future looked bright.

Mantle played Class C ball in Joplin.

In that off-season, Mantle passed two milestones. First, he met a young girl, from nearby Picher, named Merlyn Johnson, who would later become his wife. Second, he was summoned by the local draft board. But, after X-rays were taken of his injured leg, he was classified 4-F; the bone disease he suffered from was a permanent condition.

The 1950 season was a watershed year for Mickey. The Yankees moved him up one classification, from Class D ball to Class C, where he was assigned to play for the Joplin Miners of the Western Association. Over the winter, Mickey grew stronger, adding an inch in height and 10 pounds in weight. He was happy about moving up the ladder, since his previous manager, Harry Craft, would be joining him. If he impressed the Yankees in 1949 with his first-year play, Mantle had their eyes popping out with his performance at Joplin.

Mantle dominated Western Association pitching right from the start. His timing and power improved, and he hit over .400 for most of the season. He would also start hitting home runs in great numbers for the first time in his pro career, winding up with 26 dingers in just 137 games. Mickey led the league in runs with 141, hits with 199, total bases with 326, and a .628 slugging percentage. He tailed off just a bit in the season's final month and wound up with a batting average of .383, still by far the best in the league. He also earned the nickname "The Commerce Comet."

Those statistics convinced the Yankees that Mantle was their top prospect — tops in the organization for power, speed and throwing. His only problem remained in the field. Mickey had another brutal year at shortstop, committing 55 errors and winding up with a fielding percentage of just .908. He was the first to admit that things weren't going well at short.

Mantle started in the Western Association All-Star Game, and committed four errors. In his autobiography, Mantle said that not only did he commit those four errors, but after the fourth miscue, the pitcher struck out a batter. When they started throwing the ball around the infield after the out, he got nailed square in the face.

The Yankees were more than willing to overlook their phenom's fielding deficiencies at shortstop for one simple reason: they planned to follow Harry Craft's suggestion that Mantle be moved to the outfield to take advantage of his natural abilities. His speed, quickness and arm strength seemed tailor-made for the outfield, and more specifically, center field, where there was more ground to cover. The stats proved Craft right. Any organization that racked up pennants and World Championships like the Yankees did during the previous quarter century couldn't be accused of making bad decisions. So, Mickey became an outfielder.

He was also called up to the big leagues in September after Joplin's season was over. But Mickey wasn't put on the roster, nor was he going to play in a game. He was sent to Yankee Stadium for the season's final week to soak up a little major league atmosphere, to gain exposure to the big time. The Yankee manager and coaches worked with him and observed his work habits. Mantle was given a taste of what it would be like if he would continue to work hard and improve.

It was an awe-inspiring experience for a 19-year-old kid. The Yankees, in the middle of winning five consecutive American League pennants, won five straight World Championships, too. Mantle, watching Phil Rizzuto, Joe DiMaggio and Yogi Berra go through their paces, was able to dream what it would be like to play with these superstars.

Mantle wasn't alone. The Yankees had signed another young talent, Bill "Moose" Skowron, and were giving him the same treatment. Skowron, a star at Purdue University, joined Mantle to see how the big leaguers did it. Both, of course, would become key parts of the dominating Yankee ballclubs in the American League in the 1950s and early 1960s.

But it was back to reality for Mantle after he tasted the major leagues. He returned to working in the mines because the family needed the money. About this time, Mutt Mantle began looking haggard. He insisted there was nothing wrong and told Mickey there was nothing to worry about. Then the good news came.

Mickey was instructed by the Yankees to report to the team's training camp in Phoenix in mid-February 1951. But then the confusion started. Mickey thought they'd send a ticket and expense money so he could get to Arizona, so he forgot about the matter.

When February rolled around, newspaper reporters were asking him why he wasn't already in Arizona, training with the Yankees. After dismissing the reporters with a few jokes and a quick photograph of him in his mining hard hat, Mantle figured he'd better find out what was happening in Phoenix. Yankee General Manager Larry McPhail told Mantle he didn't know how to reach him, since the Mantles didn't have a phone. Eventually, Tom Greenwade, the scout who had signed Mickey, showed up in Commerce with a train ticket and spending money. Finally, Mantle was off to join the big league club for spring training.

Mickey reported to the Yankees training camp nominally as a shortstop. Longtime Yankee shortstop and coach Frank Crosetti worked with him on his fielding; Mantle needed all the help he could get with his glove work. But the Yankees were still pondering Harry Craft's advice.

Mickey and his family playing cards, 1951.

The final convincer came during the first week of camp. By chance, Manager Casey Stengel put Mantle in a group of the team's fastest players running sprints. When Mantle won the race by a wide margin, Stengel was astounded. He had Mickey run again, and again, to prove it wasn't a fluke. When he timed Mantle running the bases, his time was 13 seconds, which is a good speed for a world class sprinter.

Within a week, Stengel had Mantle working in the outfield. Tommy Henrich, who had retired that winter, was coaching for the Yankees. Mantle, who became Henrich's main project, learned there was a lot more to playing the outfield than meets the eye.

The slick-fielding Henrich worked with him on fundamentals such as positioning, reacting to the sound of bat on ball, footwork, judging speed, height, and distance of fly balls, learning how to judge the location of the wall while chasing the ball, and throwing from the outfield.

None of these fundamentals bears a resemblance to playing in the infield. Even sunglasses can give a new outfielder problems. In his first exhibition game as an outfielder, Mantle settled under a fly in right field, flipped down the glasses, lost the ball in the darkness, and got conked on the head.

But that was about the only problem Mantle had that spring. He was a terror with the bat, crushing the ball from both sides of the plate all through March. Rookies were slowly returning to the minors. Mantle, originally expected to wind up with the Yankees farm club in Binghamton, was hoping he'd stay in Beaumont to play for Harry Craft.

But his outstanding play kept Mantle from traveling to either club. Stengel spent the entire spring talking about the new phenom in camp. Toward the end of spring training, the Stengelese versions of Mantle's exploits were getting top billing, even crowding out news about future Hall-of-Famer Joe DiMaggio's heel injury, which would end DiMaggio's career after the 1951 season.

Some impressive spring performances in front of rather large crowds helped Mantle gain some publicity. In an exhibition game in Los Angeles, Mantle destroyed pitchers from the University of Southern California. He had four hits, including two homers and a double, against the Trojans. In a scene that would become associated more with Elvis Presley or the Beatles, Mantle gained his first taste of adulation from the USC students and fans attending the game. Mantle didn't particularly care for the attention, but he would have to get used to it over the years.

After a short detour home to Oklahoma for a re-examination by the draft board to reconfirm his 4-F status due to the osteomyelitis in his leg, Mantle returned for the final spring exhibition game. He had four hits off Brooklyn Dodgers pitching, including a homer over the scoreboard at Ebbets Field, and wound up hitting .402 for the spring. After just 1 1/2 years in the minors, Mantle had earned a spot in the big leagues.

It was quite a jump for a 19-year-old kid. Mantle, who had never played a game beyond Class C, was penciled into the starting lineup of the two-time defending World Champions, batting third to boot against the Washington Senators. The Yankee brass thought three games on the road to open the 1951 season would give Mickey a chance to get his feet wet and prepare him for what would be a zoo in the Bronx when they returned for their home opener.

So, of course, it rained three straight days in Washington, and the only way Mantle could possibly get his feet wet was sloshing through mud puddles in D.C. Thus, he'd make his major league debut in Yankee Stadium, with all the attending hoopla, with the crowd expecting big things right from the start from that kid the papers had labeled "the next Babe Ruth." It wasn't an easy way to begin a career.

In his first game, Mantle singled in the sixth inning off Boston's Bill Wight. In his first month, Mantle hit fairly well from the right side of the plate, but had serious trouble as a lefty. Major league right-handers gave him absolute fits, throwing fastballs up and in while he chased that high heat with little success.

That wasn't the only heat Mantle faced. Fan expectations were so high for Mantle that inevitably they would be disappointed, and they let him know how disappointed they were that the "New Babe" wasn't living up to his press clippings. He finally hit his first homer on May 1, a titanic shot off of Chicago's Randy Gumpert that carried about 450 feet at Comiskey Park, a ballpark notorious for being a tough place to hit the long ball.

But those moments were few and far between for Mantle, who slowly worked his way from the starting lineup to the bench. The pressure on him was intense; the media scrutiny of his problems never really let up. Eventually, it affected his fielding. After Mantle struck out five straight times against Boston, he was relegated into sharing right field with second-year player Jackie Jensen.

Finally, the inevitable happened. Right after the All-Star break, the Yankees sent Mantle back to the minors to rediscover the hitting abilities that brought him to the big leagues so quickly. Mickey, sent to Kansas City of the American Association, had trouble readjusting. In his first game back, he missed what should have been an easy fly ball that turned into a ground-rule double.

That was just the start of it all. Again, he got no relief from the fans, who booed him unmercifully. The huge heaping of abuse everywhere he went started to eat away at him, resulting in an 0-21 mega-slump. Mantle, thinking his dreams were history, was ready to quit and go home, feeling thoroughly defeated. But that's when the family stepped in. Mutt Mantle, looking even more drawn and tired, drove to Kansas City from Commerce. Fresh off a five-hour drive, he glared, yelled and finally got the point across to his son that he should stay with it, since it was either that or go work in the lead mines.

From then on, Mickey got the lead out, as it were. He found strength and inspiration in his father's words, and he found his stroke. In his first game after nearly hanging it up, Mickey hit a double, a triple and two massive homers against Toledo. Within a month, Mickey raised his batting average to .361, pounded 11 homers and drove in 50 runs in just 40 games. His slugging percentage was .651, and he was doing what the Yankees knew he could do.

By the end of August, Mickey was in the big leagues again, just in time to help the Yankees in their stretch drive for a third straight American League pennant. Since the Yankees were rolling, and Stengel wasn't going to mess with his successful combination, Mantle spent most of this time on the bench, pinch-hitting and playing occasionally. But he had the best seat in the house as the team won the pennant again.

Across town, the New York Giants were staging the greatest comeback in baseball history, capped by the Miracle at Coogan's Bluff — Bobby Thomson's ninth-inning homer off Ralph Branca, giving the Giants the National League pennant. The upcoming World Series would be the first of 12 for Mantle, but it would also be the shortest.

In Game 1, Mantle was a surprise starter in right field. It was a less-than-memorable start for what would be an outstanding run of World Series appearances. Mantle, batting lead off, went hitless, but walked twice, as the Giants beat the Yankees 5-1.

Game 2 was very memorable, but for all the wrong reasons. Mantle again led off and started in right field. In the third inning, he finally got his first World Series hit, a drag bunt single, and scored on Gil McDougald's single. That was Mantle's highlight; the sixth inning was the lowlight, not only of the day, but of the season.

Since Joe DiMaggio's oft-injured heel was bothering him again and he wasn't at full speed, Casey Stengel told Mantle to help him out. In the sixth, Willie Mays, leading off for the Giants, hit a short fly ball to right center field. Mickey, mindful of DiMaggio's

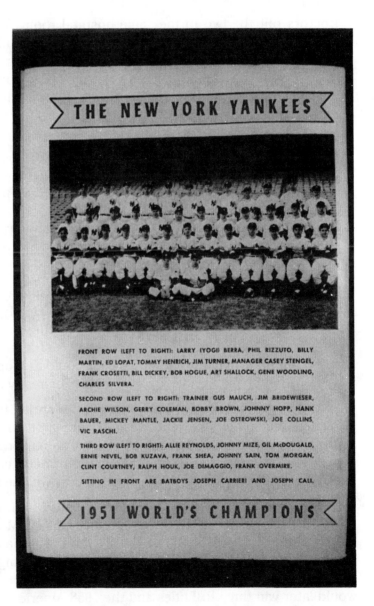

THE NEW YORK YANKEES

FRONT ROW (LEFT TO RIGHT): LARRY (YOGI) BERRA, PHIL RIZZUTO, BILLY MARTIN, ED LOPAT, TOMMY HENRICH, JIM TURNER, MANAGER CASEY STENGEL, FRANK CROSETTI, BILL DICKEY, BOB HOGUE, ART SHALLOCK, GENE WOODLING, CHARLES SILVERA.

SECOND ROW (LEFT TO RIGHT): TRAINER GUS MAUCH, JIM BRIDEWIESER, ARCHIE WILSON, GERRY COLEMAN, BOBBY BROWN, JOHNNY HOPP, HANK BAUER, MICKEY MANTLE, JACKIE JENSEN, JOE OSTROWSKI, JOE COLLINS, VIC RASCHI.

THIRD ROW (LEFT TO RIGHT): ALLIE REYNOLDS, JOHNNY MIZE, GIL McDOUGALD, ERNIE NEVEL, BOB KUZAVA, FRANK SHEA, JOHNNY SAIN, TOM MORGAN, CLINT COURTNEY, RALPH HOUK, JOE DiMAGGIO, FRANK OVERMIRE.

SITTING IN FRONT ARE BATBOYS JOSEPH CARRIERI AND JOSEPH CALI.

1951 WORLD'S CHAMPIONS

Baseball's 1951 World Champions.

problems, broke for the ball, but DiMaggio called him off. When Mantle sheared off to avoid colliding with DiMaggio, he caught his spike on a drain cover buried, but not buried deeply enough, in the outfield grass.

Mickey went down almost as if he'd been shot. As he laid motionless in the outfield, there was a stampede into right field, led by trainer Gus Mauch. The outfielder was carted off on a stretcher with a badly injured knee, which was wrapped and taped with splints on both sides of the leg. That night, Mantle had to remove the bandages from the leg because the knee had swollen so much.

The next morning, Mickey re-wrapped the knee, and, accompanied by his father, took a cab to Lenox Hill Hospital. What followed made the knee injury seem minor. Mantle had trouble getting out of the cab and into the hospital, so he leaned on his father for support. When Mickey put his full weight on Mutt's shoulder, his father crumpled to the sidewalk.

Doctors put the two in the same hospital room. Mickey had surgery on his right knee to repair torn ligaments. The doctors fitted Mantle with a special cast with steel weights at the bottom and told him to use the weights to rehabilitate the knee over the winter. To spur the healing process so he'd be ready by opening day, Mantle could add to the weights as time went on. But Mantle later admitted he never used the weights, one possible reason his productivity tailed off so drastically in the final years of his career.

But Mickey's problems paled compared to what was happening to his father. Mutt Mantle underwent tests to determine why he had lost 30 pounds over the past year, and what might have contributed to his collapse on the sidewalk in front of the hospital. After Mickey's knee surgery, Mutt was diagnosed with Hodgkin's Disease, the same cancer that had killed his father and two brothers. The disease was so far advanced that medical science at that time could do almost nothing to stop it from spreading and killing him.

Just before Christmas, Mickey married his fiancee, Merlyn, but his father's illness made the 1951-52 winter a rather joyless time. Finally, Mickey and Merlyn took Mutt Mantle on a long drive to Rochester, Minn., hoping doctors could do something at the world famous Mayo Clinic. The doctors did test after test, and even did exploratory surgery. But ultimately they admitted they couldn't stop the cancer from spreading further in the lymph nodes and worsening Mutt's already fragile condition.

Spring finally came, and Mantle reported to spring training in St. Petersburg as one of two contenders for the vacant center field spot. Joe DiMaggio had retired over the winter, hanging up his spikes mainly due to his nagging heel injury. Jackie Jensen was actually the favorite to earn the starting job in center, since Mickey was coming off knee surgery and the Yankees didn't know how well he had healed.

Mantle didn't start running close to full speed until two weeks into spring training. Casey Stengel, not about to take any chances, eased Mantle into the lineup, alternating him in center with Jensen. When the season began, Jensen was in center, with Mantle flanking him in right. When Jensen started slowly, going just 2-19, the Yankees gave up on him and traded him to the Washington Senators for center fielder Irv Noren. Jensen would later win three RBI titles and the 1958 American League MVP award while playing for the Boston Red Sox.

But Jensen's departure didn't immediately give Mantle the center field job. Two weeks after the trade, Mantle started in center against the Chicago White Sox. He pounded out four singles, raising his average above the .300 mark. Mickey was off and rolling.

But that month also brought tragedy. On May 6, he got the call he'd been dreading. His father had died that day, killed by the same cancer that claimed so many members of the Mantle family. Mutt Mantle was just 39 when he died; the memories of his father's early death would haunt Mickey for years.

There were other distractions, too. Mickey and Merlyn shared an apartment in New York with Billy Martin and his wife. Martin lived his life off the field the same way he played the game on the field — loud and flashy, with a wry sense of humor. He also liked to party, and the Mantle-Martin combination became legendary around New York and the American League.

Jackie Jensen's trade paved the way for Mantle.

The wisecracking city boy from the West Coast and country kid from the mining towns of Oklahoma hit it off from day one. Mantle admits to living the high life, especially on road trips, where he and Billy tended to be the life of the party.

They were certainly the life of the party on the field, as well. Martin's intensity and Mantle's bat helped lead the Yankees to their fourth straight pennant. Mantle, in his first full season in the majors, posted some pretty incredible numbers for a 21-year-old outfielder who'd had a rough year off the field. He hit .311, had 171 hits, a career best 37 doubles, 87 RBI and, with 23 homers, started a streak of what would become 11 seasons topping the 20-homer mark.

But Mantle led the American League in one statistic he'd just as soon forget; he led all outfielders with 14 errors. However, it was hardly a disaster, considering it was only Mantle's second season playing the outfield. He did, after all, tie for the league lead in double plays, participating in five. Two years later, Mantle, showing the talent that would eventually distinguish him as one of the finest-fielding center fielders in the game, would lead the league in assists, with 25.

His prowess would continue — in 1959 he'd lead the league in fielding percentage, .995, committing just two errors in 375 fielding chances; in 1962, he'd win a Gold Glove as one of the American League's top fielders; in 1966, he'd go errorless in 108 games in the outfield.

Mantle shined even more with his bat, especially in the 1952 World Series, when he was 10-29 off Brooklyn Dodger pitching. He hit .345, ripped two homers, scored five runs and drove in three, helping the Yankees beat the Dodgers in seven games to capture their fourth straight World Championship.

Each of the homers were clutch hits. In Game 6, his eighth-inning homer gave the Yankees a 3-2 victory. In Game 7, Mantle's homer off Dodger rookie right-hander Joe Black in the sixth inning broke a 2-2 tie, giving the Yankees the lead for good.

Mantle also managed one of the finest defensive plays in the Series in that final game. He liked to nail runners who rounded first base a little too far after singles to center. The Dodgers' Jackie Robinson, one of the finest baserunners in history, was well aware of Mantle's abilities. Robinson singled to center and purposely took a wide turn at first, trying to get Mantle to throw behind him so he'd have a chance to take the extra base. But Mickey faked the throw, and when Robinson took off for second, Mantle instead threw to Billy Martin covering second base. Robinson was out by a mile.

Mantle's exploits in a Yankee uniform earned him the highest honor possible — his hometown of Commerce honored him with a parade down main street. Hundreds of people lined the streets as Mickey and Merlyn waved and smiled from an open convertible. Later, a banquet followed in Mantle's honor. A tickertape parade down Broadway is one thing, but to be honored in your hometown is a whole different ball game.

1953 would be a whole different ball game for Mickey, too. Mantle, no longer the brash newcomer, entered spring training as the Yankees' regular center fielder, the offensive leader expected to carry the bulk of the load as the Yankees went for an unprecedented fifth straight American League pennant and fifth consecutive World Championship.

The 1952 American League Champion New York Yankees.

Mantle showed the world he could live up to those expectations in the final spring exhibition game. The Yankees, scheduled to play the Cincinnati Reds April 9, were then going to Pittsburgh to play the Pirates the next day. After the game against the Reds, Mickey, Billy Martin, and the third member of their good-time party animal group, Whitey Ford, left for that well-known capital of suburban Cincinnati night life, Covington, Ky. The trio, supposed to be back at the train station by 10 p.m. for the all-night ride to Pittsburgh, missed the train.

Plan B was to catch a plane for Pittsburgh, which would get them to the ballpark in plenty of time. But that night a winter storm moved in, and the resulting blizzard grounded all planes in the Cincinnati area. Their last hope was to convince a cabdriver into driving them to Pittsburgh. $500 and hours later, the three arrived at the ballpark. Mantle and Martin missed batting practice, which angered Casey Stengel, who told the two exhausted ballplayers that they were going to play nine innings that day even if it killed them. The unspoken thought was that Stengel hoped it would.

But, given all that, Mickey didn't have a miserable day. In his first at bat, he crushed one that went clear over the right field stands, an estimated 550 feet. Stengel, who couldn't argue with success, or with a Ruthian shot, especially hit under classic Ruthian conditions that included a near-sleepless night with an attendant hangover, gave Mantle the rest of the day off for good behavior.

That was only the first of the mammoth home runs to come in 1953. A week later, Mickey hit one that not only is in the record books, it resulted in the coining of a new baseball cliche. The Yankees were playing the Washington Senators in Griffith Stadium when left-hander Chuck Stobbs served one up that Mantle hit just right.

The ball not only went over the left field fence, it cleared the bleachers and went halfway up the football scoreboard in left. It nicked the edge of a beer advertisement on the board and left the ballpark, landing across the street in someone's front yard. After the game, Red Patterson, the Yankees public relations man, grabbed a tape measure and paced off the distance of the blast. The figure he announced was 565 feet, longer and farther than any known home run in baseball history. The concept of the tape-measure home run was born.

Mantle missed a few games that year because of a mysterious rash. Shortly before the season, Merlyn gave birth to their first son, Mickey Elvin. The new dad developed a mysterious and annoying rash that just wouldn't go away. It got so bad Stengel told Mickey to go home to Oklahoma for a few days, see the baby, and relax, figuring the skin problem would clear up. Sure enough it did — on the flight home.

Mickey thought he should take a few days off anyway, so he went fishing. A photographer snapped a picture of him with a fishing pole, relaxing and looking happy. He promptly received a phone call from New York telling him to get his rear end on the first plane out and to get back in uniform immediately.

For the rest of the season, the only ones getting nervous rashes were pitchers who had to throw to Mantle. His numbers weren't quite as outstanding as the past season, but he played in 15 fewer games and had 89 fewer at bats. Mickey wound up with 24 doubles, 21 homers and 92 RBI. His average dropped to a still impressive .295, and his slugging percentage was .497.

During the World Series, Mantle continued to shine. He homered in Game 2 as the Yankees jumped out to a commanding 2-0 lead over the Brooklyn Dodgers. Chuck Dressen's crew won the next two games, but in Game 5 Mickey ripped a grand slam in an 11-7 Yankee win that broke the Dodgers, and paved the way for the Yankees' unprecedented fifth consecutive World Championship.

Mantle displays the ball he hit 565 feet.

During the 1953-54 winter Mickey picked the wrong sport to occupy his time; he worked with Harold Youngman, a Kansas highway and asphalt contractor. Mickey's PR job was to make contacts and win road-paving contracts for Youngman's company. Mantle, just a bit bored, formed a basketball team named after Youngman's company.

With a few local athletic stars, including his twin brothers Roy and Ray, Mantle began playing exhibitions, including a few with the Harlem Globetrotters. Things were just fine until Mantle, making a cut on a fast break, blew out his knee.

Mickey wound up in a Springfield, Mo., hospital, where doctors removed some cartilage from his right knee, the knee he'd damaged after his mishap with the drain cover in 1951. Mantle left the hospital three days after the operation but never properly rehabbed the knee. He admitted he was still limping by spring training, favoring the leg, resulting in a strain on his left knee and muscle pulls and spasms elsewhere. Unquestionably, his failure to rehabilitate himself after his two knee injuries severely shortened his playing career.

Meanwhile, Ray and Roy, who had just graduated from Commerce High, joined Mickey in the Yankee organization. Mantle, who thought they might have the necessary talent, persuaded Casey Stengel into letting them work out at Yankee Stadium. When the twins ripped liners during batting practice and impressed Stengel with their speed, the die was cast. Tom Greenwade, the same scout who signed Mickey, signed

20

the twins, who were assigned to the Yankees Class D affiliate at McAllister, Okla., in the Sooner State League.

Both hit over .300, then really opened eyes in Instructional League that winter; Roy hit over .400 while Ray outran everyone except Mickey. The twins moved up to Class C, but one wound up in the Army, and the other injured his leg. The possibility of an all-Mantle Yankee outfield, a thought that had some sportswriters in New York in a frenzy, diminished.

But Mickey was still around. Despite his injuries, he played in all but six games in 1954. For the first time, but not the last, he led the American League in runs scored (129), while posting double figures in doubles, triples and homers. The 12 triples would be a career high, and the 27 home runs were his best power output to date. He also topped 100 RBI (102) for the first time in the majors, and coaxed his batting average back up to .300.

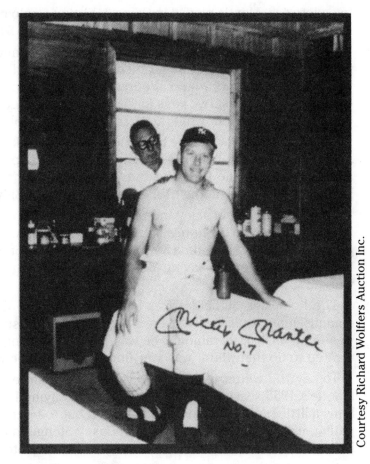

Mantle visited the trainer more than he preferred.

Those numbers were all right, but 1954 was the first time in six seasons the Yankees didn't win the pennant, despite posting 103 victories, the most they would ever win under Casey Stengel. For the first time in 13 seasons the team exceeded the 100-win mark, but Al Lopez guided the Cleveland Indians to an amazing 111 wins, the all-time American League record. Although the Indians were swept in the World Series by Willie Mays and the New York Giants, it was of little consolation to the Yankees.

1954 would be an aberration; the Yankees returned to the World Series in 1955. Mantle offered a dress rehearsal of future feats. For the first time in his career, Mickey won the American League home run title, with 37, and added 25 doubles and 11 triples, which tied him for the league lead. His .611 slugging percentage led the league, the first of four slugging titles he'd win. Mantle also scored 121 runs, second best in the league, had 99 RBI and hit .306, posting these impressive numbers despite being pitched around, as indicated by his league-leading 113 walks.

Although the Yankees reached the World Series, it wasn't their year. The Brooklyn Dodgers, apparently weary of "wait 'til next year," beat the Yankees in seven games, giving the borough of Brooklyn its only world title. The Series was frustrating for Mickey, who sat out the first two games due to injuries. After the Yankees cruised to two victories, Mantle played in Game 3, hitting a solo home run off Johnny Podres. But the Yankees got hammered 8-3, and lost Game 4 too, 8-5. Mickey's lone hit was a single.

At this point, Mantle's leg was bothering him so much that he only appeared in one more game, popping out as a pinch hitter against Podres in Game 7. He could only watch as the Dodgers won on Podres' eight-hit shutout, aided by Sandy Amoros' great catch to save at least two runs in the sixth inning. The Yankees headed into the winter quietly, thinking about what they had to prove the following season.

The commissioner's office had scheduled the Yankees to play an exhibition series in Japan against the local professional teams. The trip, however, looked less appealing after the loss to the Dodgers, but everything was already set. Most of the players brought their wives on the trip, except Mickey and Billy Martin.

After the novelty of saki (and perhaps the sushi) paled, Mickey was desperately trying to find a way to get home. Merlyn was seven months pregnant, which kept her from going to Japan, so long-time Mantle friend Harold Youngman suggested someone back home send a telegram saying Merlyn was about to give birth and having problems. It worked.

The homesick outfielder was happy to return to Oklahoma, until someone in the commissioner's office discovered David Mantle wasn't born until December. Mickey was fined $5,000, the amount he was paid for playing in Japan. He didn't care; all he wanted to do that winter was stay home, relax and be with his growing family.

To say the winter of 1955-56 was the calm before the storm is misleading. Calling Mantle's 1956 season a storm would be like saying Hurricane Andrew made the wind blow a little harder than normal. It turned out to be the year everyone had been anticipating, especially Mantle. For years, Casey Stengel had been saying Mickey would be Babe Ruth, Lou Gehrig and Joe DiMaggio all rolled into one.

In a spring training interview, Mantle even set goals to win the batting title, lead the league in RBI, win the home run crown and lead the Yankees to the World Championship. Although they were bold statements, they were taken seriously; Mantle had the potential to accomplish these feats. Now, it was time to do it. And he would.

On the season's first day Mantle offered a sign of things to come; his bold statements might not be so bold after all. The Yankees opened against the Washington Senators at Griffith Stadium, three years to the date after Mickey hit his legendary homer against Chuck Stobbs. In the first inning, Camilo Pascual threw a pitch that Mantle ripped to center field. Not only did it clear the 31-foot high wall, it left Griffith Stadium, cleared Fifth Avenue and landed on the roof of a building across the street. Since Mickey was the tape-measure king, fittingly they measured the homer at 455 feet. In the sixth inning, he did it again. This time, the ball cleared the center field wall and landed in a clump of trees outside the stadium.

After taking two of three from the Senators, the Yankees returned to New York for the home opener against Ted Williams and the Boston Red Sox. Not only did they sweep the Sox three straight, but Mickey hit homers in the first two games, giving him four round-trippers in five games. His hot start was aided by Yogi Berra's hot streak, too. Berra, batting behind Mantle in the cleanup spot, hit four homers in the first seven games. With Berra having a good season, opposing pitchers couldn't pitch around Mantle as easily as they had before.

Berra was the type of hitter pitchers hated to face. At least with Mantle, things were up front and obvious. If you threw one just a little bit too good to Mantle, you had to be ready to either duck or watch it sail out of the ballpark. Berra, however would swing at just about anything, and, even worse from the pitcher's viewpoint, he would hit it, too. The three-time American League MVP was famous for swinging at pitches over his head and ripping them for homers.

Late in April, Mickey pulled a ligament in his right knee. Stengel wanted to bench him until the knee was fully healed, but Mantle insisted on playing. It was that kind of year: no major injuries, and the minor ones didn't worsen into something that would cause problems.

Mantle and Berra weren't alone in their fast starts. The Yankees went 8-3 in April. In May, Mantle exploded at the plate. On May 1, he hit a solo homer off Detroit's Steve Gromek. The next day, he homered off Frank Lary. When Kansas City arrived for three games, Mantle homered in each, giving him nine homers in just 16 games.

Suddenly, the writers were dusting off reference books. Back in 1927, Babe Ruth hit his ninth homer in the season's 29th game, which put Mantle 13 games ahead of the Ruth's pace when he hit 60 homers. Mickey's chase was on for Ruth's single-season homer mark.

It wasn't just home runs. Mantle was also hitting .433 at that point. But it would get even better before the month was over. From May 8-18, Mickey teed off six more times — twice off Bob Lemon and once each off Early Wynn, Billy Pierce, Bud Daley and Dixie Howell. He also mixed in enough other hits, including one 3-for-4 game, to raise his league-leading batting average to .446.

Mickey ripped five more home runs before May ended, including shots off Pedro Ramos and Camilo Pascual during a doubleheader against Washington May 30. For the fourth time that season Mantle had hit two homers in one day. He hit 16 homers in May, and, after six weeks and 41 games, had scored 45 runs, ripped 65 hits and had 50 RBI. He was hitting a league-leading .425, and had an incredible .882 slugging percentage. The Yankees had already opened up a six-game lead over the Chicago White Sox and Cleveland Indians.

Although things were incredibly good in May, the first two weeks of June were incredibly bad, as the Yankees slumped, losing their first four games and six of eight. Mantle managed just one homer during that stretch and Cleveland cut the lead to just 2 1/2 games. But Johnny Kucks shut out the Indians to snap the Yankees out of their slump. Mickey rediscovered his stroke and homered in three consecutive games, raising his total to 24.

On June 18, Mantle helped stretch the Yankee's winning streak to five when he hit homer number 25 off the Tigers' Paul Foytack. It was another cannon-blast hit into the teeth of a strong wind that was blowing straight in from center field. The ball cleared Tiger Stadium's 110-foot-high roof in right field and landed in the middle of Trumbull Avenue, nearly nailing a car that was driving down the street. Two days later, Mickey helped the Yankees sweep the Tigers in three games when he hit two solo homers off Detroit's Billy Hoeft. He now had 27 homers.

Opposing managers were now pulling out all the stops, wondering how to deal with Mantle. Kansas City's Lou Boudreau developed the "Mantle Shift," based loosely on the defensive alignment he invented while managing Cleveland to deal with Ted Williams. Boudreau put three infielders on the right side of the infield and shifted the outfield in a similar fashion.

Williams refused to hit to the opposite field, too stubborn to let the shift tamper with his style at the plate. Mantle, however, tried to hit grounders to the opposite field or attempted to bunt his way on base. He did, that is, until Casey Stengel noted the shift was doing just what it was intended to do — neutralize Mantle's power.

July 1, Mantle had another two-homer day, his sixth of the season, and the second time he'd ever hit homers from both sides of the plate. Mantle would accomplish this feat 10 times in his career, a major league record. His two homers gave him 29, putting him eight games ahead of Ruth's 1927 pace, and gave him 100 hits for the season.

Three days later, the Yankees played a holiday doubleheader against Boston. In the first game, the score was 6-6 when the Red Sox threatened in the ninth. The Sox had a man on second when someone singled to center. Mantle, thinking he could nail the runner trying to score, somehow strained his right knee while making the throw. But by mid-July, his knee healed enough so he could play in the All-Star game. For the second straight year, Mickey homered in the game.

The Yankees, who had won five straight before the All-Star game, kicked it into high gear after the break, extending the streak into double figures and knocking the White Sox out of the pennant picture. Then, while playing Kansas City, Mickey outfoxed the "Mantle Shift" by bunting for a base hit. His next time up, Boudreau put the Athletics in a more conventional alignment, so Mantle put one where they couldn't get it — in the seats for his 32nd home run.

With the White Sox already history, Mantle and company focused on the Indians in a similar fashion. In the opening game of the series, a 13-6 Yankee victory, Mantle drove in six runs and ripped homers off future Hall-of-Famers Bob Lemon and Bob Feller. The Yankees' lead stretched to 10 games over the Indians, and Mickey remained in the homer record hunt, with 34 after 97 games, slightly ahead of Ruth's pace.

But the team's cushion disappeared when the Indians won the final three games of the series, moving to within seven games of first place with slightly over 50 games left to play. The Yankees losing streak stretched to six games, but, fortunately for them, the Indians lost three straight too, and couldn't cut into the seven-game deficit. Then the Yankee bats woke up and Mantle started ripping homers again, hitting number 41 against the Orioles' Don Ferrarese on Aug. 12. The hot streak put Mantle 11 games ahead of Ruth's record pace, kept his batting average at .371 and put the Yanks 8 1/2 up on Cleveland.

On Aug. 14, the Red Sox came to Yankee Stadium, as did Mickey's good-luck charm — President Dwight Eisenhower, who had seen the Yankees open at Washington. Mantle liked Ike; it seemed every time he came to a game, Mickey would homer. He did so in the series' opening game, too, hitting number 42 to move 13 games ahead of Ruth's pace. His three-for-three effort raised his average to .374.

However, mid-August was anything but Ruthian for Mantle. He went a week and a half without a homer, and his average fell to the low .360s. Ted Williams was now challenging Mantle for the batting title, which would ultimately ruin Mantle's chance to become only the 10th player in modern major league history to lead his league in batting average, homers, RBI and win the Triple Crown. Williams, the last player to accomplish the feat (he hit .343 with 32 homers and 114 RBI in 1947), won the A.L. Triple Crown in 1942 and led the majors in all three categories.

In the final week of August, Mantle's bat once again woke from its slumber. He hit two homers against the White Sox, then two more against Kansas City, for 46. Mickey, still in the hunt for 60 home runs, also raised his batting average back up to .367, giving him a relatively comfortable lead in the batting title race.

Then, his good luck charm showed up again when the Yankees went to Washington. President Eisenhower told Mickey he hoped he would hit a homer, but that the Senators would win the game. Ike was half right. Mantle hit homer number 47, but the Yankees won the game, despite three homers by Washington outfielder Jim Lemon.

Mantle entered the homestretch with a chance at Ruth's record, but it wasn't going to be easy. He needed 13 homers in 25 games, but judging the rest of the season by Ruth's pace was misleading. Ruth had 17 roundtrippers in the final month to reach 60. The combination of a pennant drive and the attention from fans and the media could make September 1956 a pressure cooker for Mantle.

The heat never got turned on, whether you're talking about media attention, or about Mantle's hitting. Mickey went stone cold for two solid weeks. Not only could he not hit for power, he could barely hit at all. Forget about Ruth — the Triple Crown was now in serious jeopardy. After 1-for-11 and 0-for-12 stretches, his average dropped to .352, just three points ahead of Williams. The Tigers' Al Kaline had also cut Mantle's RBI lead, moving within two, at 116 to 118.

On Sept. 13, Mantle's stroke returned and he ripped two hits, including his 48th homer, against Kansas City. Five days later, the Yankees clinched the pennant, the fifth time Mantle played on an American League champ in his six years. In the clincher, Mickey had the game-winning hit against the White Sox at Comiskey Park.

The game was 2-2 in extra innings when Billy Pierce made a mistake. Mantle hit it onto the left field roof at Comiskey, an estimated 550-feet — the longest home run ever hit there. It put Mantle in some select company; Mickey hit 50 home runs for the first time in his career, becoming only the eighth man in major league history to do so, joining Babe Ruth, Jimmie Foxx, Ralph Kiner, Hack Wilson, Hank Greenberg, Johnny Mize and Willie Mays.

Casey Stengel dubs Mickey with the Triple Crown in 1956.

Mantle had the homer title wrapped up, but the batting championship and RBI crowns were still undecided. With two weeks left in the season, Williams got hot and passed Mantle in the batting race, leading .355 to .350. When the Yankees went to Boston, Mickey regained the lead, going 5-for-7 while Williams went 2-for-8. There was one hitch, however. Mantle pulled a muscle in his right thigh, forcing him to sit out a few games. That might not hurt him in the batting race, but Al Kaline, healthy and hitting, was again threatening for the RBI title. With less than a week to go, and Mickey nursing his thigh injury, Kaline had 124 RBI to Mickey's 127.

Mantle missed several games in the final two weeks because of his leg injury. Although Mantle needed all the at bats he could get in his chase for the Triple Crown, when personal stats were ranked against the opportunity for a World Series title, the Series won, hands down.

Still, the magic number remained at four before the season's final three-game series in Yankee Stadium against the Red Sox. Mantle led Williams by four points in the batting race and Kaline by four for the RBI crown. When Williams tailed off in the final three games, Mickey won the batting title with a .353 average, best in both leagues.

Mantle's league-leading 52 homers were secure, but the RBI title was still undecided on the last day. Mickey, who drove in 130, had to wait for Kaline's final results. Kaline drove in only two that day, for 128 RBI. Thus, Mantle led the majors in RBI, too, and, in addition to winning the historic Triple Crown, became only the fourth player to lead all major leaguers in the big three stats, joining Williams, Lou Gehrig (1934) and Rogers Hornsby (1925).

Mantle had his Triple Crown. Now, it was time to pursue his last goal — a World Series title for the fourth time in six seasons. As he'd hoped, the Yankees opponents were the Brooklyn Dodgers, who'd beaten them in the previous Series.

President Eisenhower greets the 1956 World Series participants.

Game 1 was at Ebbets Field. President Eisenhower threw out the first ball and, once again, was Mickey's good luck charm. In the first inning, Mantle ripped a two-run homer off Dodger starter Sal Maglie. But it wasn't enough. The Dodgers came back to win the opener 6-3, taking the early advantage in the Series.

Game 2 was even worse for the Yankees. The Yankees jumped all over Don Newcombe early, with Yogi Berra's second-inning grand slam the big blow in knocking the Dodger ace out. But the Yankee's six-run lead evaporated. Gil Hodges hit two-run doubles in the fifth and sixth innings, and a 7-7 tie resulted in a 13-8 Dodger victory. Memories of 1955 made the Yankees feel even worse.

Mantle and company, facing do-or-die time, returned to familiar turf for the next three games. Enos Slaughter's three-run homer in the sixth inning powered the Yankees to a 5-3 win in Game 3. The Yankees took Game 4, too, 6-2, to tie the Series. Mantle contributed a solo homer to lead off the sixth.

Oct. 8, 1956, entered the record books as one of the greatest games in World Series history, thanks to Mantle and a journeyman pitcher who had his finest moment with the eyes of the world upon him. Although the Dodgers shelled him in Game 2, Don Larsen was Casey Stengel's choice to start Game 5. Larsen, part of an 18-player trade the previous season which brought him over from Baltimore, was 3-21 with the Orioles that season. But he'd found a home in the Bronx as a reliever and a spot starter, going 9-2 in 1955 and 11-5 in 1956. He'd adopted a no-windup delivery which, without a normal motion, tended to drive batters crazy.

Saying Larsen was on that day would be the all-time understatement. He handled the Dodgers easily through the first four innings. But Brooklyn's Sal Maglie was cruising too, until Mantle batted for the second time. Mickey pulled one down the right field line that just hooked around the foul pole. Although it was just 296 feet from home plate, it stayed fair just long enough to be a home run, and the Yankees led 1-0.

In the top of the fifth, Mickey supplied more heroics. Dodger first baseman Gil Hodges laced a Larsen fastball to left center field. Had Mantle not backed up a little bit and cheated toward left field just before the pitch, there was no way he would have caught the ball. But, somehow, he made a running catch in left center field, more than 400 feet from home plate. That was the closest the Dodgers would come to getting a hit all afternoon.

Larsen threw an unprecedented perfect game, getting Dale Mitchell on a called third strike to end it. It was unquestionably the greatest World Series pitching performance. Larsen retired all 27 batters he faced on just 97 pitches, and only went to three balls in the count once, against Pee Wee Reese in the first inning.

The Dodgers didn't throw in the towel, however. Game 6, back at Ebbets Field, featured another pitchers' duel, this time between the Yankees' Bob Turley and the Dodgers' Clem Labine. Only one run scored. It came in the 10th inning, when Enos Slaughter misjudged Jackie Robinson's liner, which fell for a double to bring home the winning run, Jim Gilliam, from second.

Appropriately enough, the Series went to Game 7, with all the chips on the table. Stengel, in a surprise move, started two right-handed hitters, Elston Howard in left and Moose Skowron at first, against the Dodgers' ace, Don Newcombe, also a right-hander. But when you're hot, you're hot. Howard and Skowron both homered, and drove in five runs between them, as the Yankees destroyed Brooklyn 9-0 to win the Series. Mantle had his wish — the Triple Crown and another World Series ring.

After the season, the awards started pouring in for Mickey. Baseball writers named him the Most Valuable Player in the American League. He was also chosen as player of the year by *The Sporting News* and won the Hickock Belt, presented to the Professional Athlete of the Year. It was a perfect end to a perfect season.

His accomplishments also allowed Mantle to cash in with business opportunities and endorsements. For a kid who grew up in poverty which only mining towns can truly appreciate, it was all rather mind-boggling. He bought a piece of a Holiday Inn in Joplin, was ripped off by an insurance scam artist, bought a bowling alley in Dallas, and moved his family to Texas.

Mantle also had trouble getting a new contract from Yankee General Manager George Weiss. Mickey made $32,500 in 1956; he wanted to double it to $65,000. Weiss acted as if Mickey wanted to own the club and handed Mickey a detective report, detailing his every move off the field during the 1956 season. Mickey threatened to retire to run his bowling alley; Weiss threatened to trade him to Cleveland. Finally, one of the Yankees owners, Del Webb, called to tell Mickey not to worry; Mickey got his $65,000.

The 1957 season provided its share of turmoil. The most famous incident happened May 15. Mickey, Whitey Ford, Hank Bauer, Yogi Berra and Johnny Kucks and their wives arranged a birthday party for Billy Martin. The six couples met for dinner and went to the famed Copacabana nightclub to watch Sammy Davis Jr., the featured singer that night.

The maitre d' at the Copa set up a special table for the Yankees. While the players were enjoying themselves and minding their own business, the people at an adjacent table started heckling the singer. Finally, a few of the Yankees asked them to cut it out. One of them stood up and said, "The Yankees are here. Big deal!"

Billy Martin finally piped up, politely telling them to relax and let the other people at the club enjoy the show. One of the hecklers invited Martin to step outside. The two left, along with Ford and Bauer. Suddenly, there was a loud crash; one of the drunks was laid out cold on the cloakroom floor. The bouncers at the Copa hustled the Yankees out the back door.

It didn't do much good. The papers the next day headlined the "Brawl at the Copa." The players ended up in George Weiss' office and had to pay for the damage at the nightclub. Meanwhile, the hecklers sued the Yankees. Mickey was called to the stand, where he testified he didn't see anything. When asked what he thought had happened, Mantle said he thought Roy Rogers must have come riding through; his horse Trigger must have kicked the guy in the head. The courtroom broke up in laughter. The Yankees won the court case.

There's been much speculation about what really happened that night. Mantle says neither Martin nor Bauer threw the punch; he thinks one of the bouncers smacked the drunken heckler. No matter what happened, Billy Martin was the fall guy for the incident. Weiss, who never liked Martin, seized the opportunity to get rid of Martin, who he thought was a troublemaker. At the trading deadline a month later, Weiss sent Martin and pitcher Ralph Terry to the Kansas City Athletics for pitcher Ryne Duren and outfielder Harry "Suitcase" Simpson.

Mantle and Ford were devastated by the trade. The three went out together one last time as Yankees and wound up crying. Since the Athletics were playing at Yankee Stadium, Ford told Martin that if they got far enough ahead the next day, he'd tip Martin on what he was throwing, if Billy promised not to hit a homer.

Ford was able to deliver as promised. He stood straight up and signaled a fast ball, which Martin whacked to left field for a homer. Martin circled the bases laughing; Ford glared. When Stengel asked Ford if he had let Martin hit it, Ford denied it with a smile, and knocked Martin down his next at bat.

During the season, Mantle faced a real dilemma, one that few major leaguers have incurred. What do you do for an encore after winning the Triple Crown? Mickey didn't lead the American League in homers, RBI, or batting average, but he did lead in runs scored for the second straight season. His homer total dropped just a bit, to 34, and he went from 130 RBI to 94, but a series of nagging injuries kept him out of 10 games.

Pitchers also began avoiding him. Mantle led the major leagues in walks with 146, one of only two big leaguers to receive more than 100 free passes. Mickey raised his batting average a dozen points to .365, but 38-year-old Ted Williams was making one last shot at hitting .400. He fell short in the final week to end at .388, becoming the oldest batting champ in major league history.

As for the pennant race, the Chicago White Sox were out of the gate fast. But the team, which would later become the "Go-Go Sox," was simply overpowered by the Yankees, who beat the Sox 14 of their 22 meetings while winning their eighth pennant in nine years. Mickey was joined by Yogi Berra, who had 24 homers, Moose Skowron, who hit .304, and rookie Tony Kubek, who hit .297.

The Yankees' World Series opponents were the upstart Milwaukee Braves. Game 3 would be a painful experience for Mantle. The teams had split the first two games, making Game 3 crucial. Milwaukee native Tony Kubek homered to start the game at County Stadium. Mantle and Berra followed with walks. Mickey took a good lead off second, hoping to help the Yankees blow the game wide open. When Braves pitcher Bob Buhl tried to keep Mantle close with a pickoff throw to second, it went wild.

Mantle dove headfirst into the bag. As second baseman Red Schoendienst went after the ball in vain to keep it from sailing into center field, he slipped and landed on Mantle's shoulder. Mickey pushed Schoendienst away and moved to third as the Braves chased the ball down in the outfield. Mantle later scored, but that night his shoulder stiffened up. It was so painful that in the 10th inning of Game 4, with the tying run on second, Mantle flagged the dugout. He removed himself from the game, believing he couldn't make a throw to the plate if needed to preserve the win.

That virtually ended Mantle's season. He would have a homer and 2 RBI in the Series in just 19 at bats, but he really wasn't a factor. Although the Braves pulled the upset and beat the Yankees in seven games, Mantle could ease the pain with thoughts of his second straight A.L. Most Valuable Player award.

George Weiss, however, apparently didn't see it that way. The Yankee GM sent Mickey a contract calling for a $5,000 pay cut. Although Mantle was the MVP for a second straight season, Weiss reasoned his statistics weren't as good as they were in 1956. Weiss refused to deal with agents. When Mantle refused to show up on time for spring training in St. Petersburg, Weiss told reporters Mantle would be traded. Mickey showed, and took a $12,500 pay raise for his second straight MVP season.

Mantle's shoulder gave him problems throughout spring training. He'd undergone surgery in the off-season but started slowly, unlike the rest of the team, which was streaking to yet another A.L. pennant. Finally, Mickey got rolling and posted another fine season. For the fourth time in his career, he led the league in runs scored, with 127, won his third home run title, with 42, and led the league in total bases for the second time and walks for the third time. He hit .304 with 97 RBI, fifth best in the league, helping the Yankees to their third straight pennant and another shot at the Braves in the World Series.

Mantle won two straight American League MVP Awards.

The Yankees, losing three of the first four games, seemed to be handing the Braves their second straight Series title. But then Stengel's crew woke up to sweep the final three games, taking their sixth World Championship of the decade, and fifth since Mantle joined the ballclub. Mickey had a triple, two homers, and 3 RBI in the Series. He was also a new father. His son Billy was born that winter.

The next season was frustrating for Mantle. Nothing went right for him in 1959. The injury bug hit Mantle twice in three days. First, he reinjured his right shoulder when he hurried a throw from center field. A few days later, he was hit on the hand by a pitch during batting practice; it chipped a bone in his right index finger. Things were not going well, and not just for Mickey.

Pitchers Don Larsen and Tom Sturdivant nursed sore arms to start the season. Middle infielders Andy Carey and Gil McDougald had hand injuries that kept them out of the lineup. First baseman Moose Skowron, who was dealing with the chronic back pain that would cut his career short, was in the most pain. Finally, as if to answer the age-old question "What else can go wrong?", the team suffered through an outbreak of the Asian flu.

The Yankees finished the season in third place, 15 games behind the pennant-winning Chicago White Sox. Mickey's year would have been outstanding for anyone but

Mickey Mantle: a .285 batting average, with 31 homers and 75 RBI. He lead the league in only two statistical categories; his .995 fielding percentage as an outfielder was fine, but being the league's strikeout king for the second time in his career was definitely less than exciting.

But even with the disappointing season, the Yankees were busy assembling the final pieces of a team that would win the next five pennants. In mid-1959, General Manager George Weiss traded pitchers Tom Sturdivant and Johnny Kucks and infielder Jerry Lumpe to the Kansas City Athletics for pitcher Ralph Terry and third baseman-outfielder Hector Lopez. Terry became the number two pitcher in the Yankees' starting rotation; Lopez became a top pinch-hitter.

After the season, the Yankees made another trade with Kansas City — the most important trade since Babe Ruth came from the Red Sox to the Bronx. It would impact Mantle's career more than any other move the Yankees would ever make. Pitcher Don Larsen, outfielder Hank Bauer and first basemen Norm Siebern and Marv Throneberry were sent to the A's for infielders Joe DeMaestri and Kent Hadley and outfielder Roger Maris.

Although Mantle and Maris would be forever linked in baseball annals, all Mickey knew about Maris came from his former minor league manager, Harry Craft, who managed Maris at Kansas City. Craft told Mantle that Yankee Stadium was made for Maris, who had the perfect left-handed pull-hitter swing to put plenty of homers in the right field porch, just 296 feet away from home plate. Craft also said Maris could be "another Mantle." How prophetic those flip, off-the-cuff statements would be two years later.

Mickey began the 1960 season in a horrible slump, totally lacking confidence. The problems began when George Weiss sent a contract calling for a $17,000 pay cut to $55,000, reasoning that Mantle had a bad year. Mickey held out nine days of spring training, then finally negotiated for a $10,000 pay cut. He admitted the contract squabbles messed up his head and ruined his concentration. He started making stupid plays and began doubting his abilities.

Mantle recalls being so disgusted with striking out one day, he didn't notice the ball got past the catcher and went all the way to the backstop. He was thrown out while he was still making his way to the dugout. Another time, he thought there were only two outs when he hit an infield grounder. As he jogged halfway to first, he realized there was only one out, and Roger Maris' hard slide into second base to break up an inning-ending double play was wasted. Casey Stengel then benched Mantle, played Bob Cerv in center, and left Mantle fuming mad at himself.

He finally turned things around the next night against Baltimore. In his second at bat, Mickey homered to right center field. As he circled the bases, the boos he'd heard during the first few innings were replaced by some applause and some cheering. In the eighth inning, the Orioles had retaken the lead, leaving Mantle one last chance to do something against Hoyt Wilhelm and his Cooperstown-bound knuckler.

Mickey swung feebly, missing the first knuckler. He popped the second knuckler up behind home plate, easy prey for catcher Clint Courtney. But Courtney somehow dropped the ball, giving Mantle new life. Mantle put the next knuckler into orbit, into the upper deck, for a game-winning homer. Mickey was back on the right track.

The team was beginning to jell, too, leaving the White Sox and Orioles in the dust. The Yankees won their last 15 games, finishing eight games ahead of Baltimore and winning their 10th pennant in 12 seasons. Mickey's rotten first half turned into a fine season. His average dropped to .275, but he led the American League with 40 homers, his fourth homer crown. He led the league with 119 runs scored, the fifth time he'd done so, and had a league-leading 294 total bases, the third time he led the A.L. in that category.

Teammate Roger Maris had a big year, too. He finished second to Mantle with 39 homers, led the league with 112 RBI and led in slugging percentage with .581, a preview of what was to come. As a team, the Yankees hit 193 homers, a new American League record that lasted only until next season's record-breaking onslaught.

However, the good feelings soured during the World Series against the Pittsburgh Pirates. Game 1 turned out to be crucial, not only for the Yankees, but for Casey Stengel's future, too. Stengel passed on Whitey Ford and instead started Art Ditmar in the opener at Forbes Field. Traditionally, teams start their best pitcher in Game 1, enabling them to start Games 4 and 7 if needed. Stengel never explained why he held Ford out. As with all controversial moves, managers are either heroes or bums. Stengel wound up a bum; the Pirates hammered Ditmar to win the game 6-4.

Yankee sluggers dominated the next two games, ripping Pirate pitching for 16-3 and 10-0 victories, the latter a four-hit shutout by Ford at Yankee Stadium. The Pirates then swept the next two games in the Bronx, 3-2 and 5-2, and forced the Yankees to win the final two Series games at Forbes Field.

In Game 6, Whitey Ford did his best to keep the Yankees alive. He tossed his second shutout of the Series, a seven-hitter, as the Yankees again scored in double digits, beating the Pirates 12-0.

Game 7 was anything but a pitchers' duel. The Pirates jumped to a 4-0 lead after two innings, but Moose Skowron and Yogi Berra homered, giving the Yankees a 5-4 lead. It was 7-4 in the eighth inning, when shortstop Tony Kubek met his match, thanks to a pebble in the infield. Pinch-hitter Gino Cimoli hit a double-play grounder that hit a pebble and struck Kubek in the throat. Kubek dropped to the ground and was forced to leave the game. The Pirates' rally continued and five runs scored, the big blow a three-run homer by Pirate backup catcher Hal Smith. Suddenly, the Yankees were down 9-7 going into the ninth inning.

The Yankees weren't about to go quietly. Bobby Richardson and Dale Long opened the inning with singles. Mantle then contributed his 10th hit and 11th RBI of the Series when he singled home Richardson, making it 9-8. Yogi Berra then drove home the tying run, keeping the Yankees' title hopes alive.

But the leadoff man for the Pirates in the bottom of the ninth was second baseman Bill Mazeroski, who sent Ralph Terry's second pitch of the inning high over the ivy-covered left field wall. The Pirates won 10-9, capturing an improbable World's Championship.

The best way to describe the Series is improbable, especially when you look at the cold, hard statistics. The Yankees batted an astounding .338 off Pirate pitching, with 11 home runs and 55 runs scored in seven games. In comparison, the Pirates hit just .256, with only 26 runs scored and four homers. Pirate pitchers posted some ugly numbers, too, compiling a 7.11 ERA for the Series. Four pitchers, including Bob Friend, had ERAs over 10. The Yankees, who scored 10 or more runs in four games, had at least 10 hits in six games. Whitey Ford, who tossed two shutouts, surrendered only 11 hits in 18 innings.

Mantle, who had a big Series, collected 10 hits, including three home runs, 11 RBI and a .400 batting average. Although it was his best performance in any of his dozen World Series appearances, it was of little consolation to Mantle. The Yankees lost the World Series, and, even worse in his mind, they lost to a lesser-talented team that they had outplayed.

Two days after the Series was over, the Stengel era ended. The Yankees fired Stengel, saying that at 70 years of age, the Ol' Perfessor just didn't have it anymore. All Stengel could say was "Most people are dead at my age, at the present time at least. I'll never make the mistake of being 70 again."

A month later, General Manager George Weiss retired too, completing the turnover in the Yankee front office. Roy Hamey, a longtime Yankee assistant general manager, and longtime Yankee catcher Ralph Houk, who took over Casey's spot in the dugout, were put in charge to keep the Yankee tradition alive.

It would be Mickey Mantle's task to lead the charge on the field just as he had done the past decade. Houk made that notion clear the first day of spring training, telling Mickey his job was to keep the faith through his actions on the field. Mantle, Ford and Berra, the veterans who provided the link from the DiMaggio era, would make or break the Yankees during this transition from Stengel to Houk.

In one of his first moves, Houk shifted Berra, who was showing his age behind the plate, from catcher to left field, finally getting Elston Howard in the lineup at catcher. Because he'd been an outfielder at the beginning of his career, Berra was willing to switch to help the team. Another big change was installing Whitey Ford as a regular starter to pitch every fourth day.

Previously, Stengel started Ford at most every fifth day or only against the league's top teams, mainly due to worries about Ford's slight stature at 5-foot-9, 160 pounds. Houk's final major move was to flip-flop Mantle, who hit third, and Maris, who hit fourth in the batting order.

The idea was to protect Maris and keep opponents from pitching around the Yankee right fielder. Although Mantle started quickly, the move didn't look all that hot in the season's first month. Mantle was hitting .455, with five homers and 11 RBI after just 10 games, but Maris had a horrible 5-for-31 start, hitting .161. A month and a half into the season, the Yankees were struggling, stumbling along with a 16-14 record, five games behind first-place Detroit.

Maris went on a tear with four homers and a .438 average in five games, but his batting average was still just .210. Unfortunately, those four homers were all Maris had hit so far. On May 22, he went to an eye doctor, figuring he might have vision problems. When his eyes blurred after he was given eye drops, Maris had to leave that night's game in the first inning. But then things became crystal clear and the team got sharp.

In a 17-game stretch, the Yankees hit 32 homers, including seven in one game against the Red Sox on Memorial Day in Boston. Mantle and Maris had two homers each in that game. The pair ended the month with 26 homers between them; Maris had a dozen.

In June, the Yankees really started rolling, going 22-10. The hot topic became Mantle and Maris and their quests to break Babe Ruth's home run record. The two continued to pile up the numbers. By August, Maris was leading the league with 40 homers; Mickey was on his heels with 39. As the inevitable game-by-game comparisons with Ruth's 1927 season occurred, papers across the country started conducting polls, asking fans if they wanted to see the record broken, and if so, by whom — Mantle or Maris?

There was little question about which slugger was more popular. Mantle, whose rags to riches story epitomized what America and baseball were all about, had been around for several years and had won four home run titles. Maris, relatively unknown, wasn't particularly popular with the sportswriters because he wasn't glib or very outgoing. When it came right down to it, he was downright shy around strangers; most writers were strangers to Maris, who wanted to keep it that way.

The M & M Boys — Mickey Mantle and Roger Maris.

Maris, who had toiled in relative obscurity before being dealt to the Yankees and winning the MVP award the previous season, wasn't used to the pressure cooker like Mickey was. He was popular with his teammates, but curt with the writers. He grew tired of the incessant questions, so the papers tagged him as surly. Naturally, stories started appearing about friction between Maris and Mantle, fueled by the supposed rivalry between the two who were pursuing the most prestigious record in baseball.

Nothing was further from the truth. Mantle and Maris had become friends quickly after Maris arrived. The two were a lot alike — incredible athletes, shy around strangers, but outgoing when they were around people they trusted. What no one knew was that in 1961, Mantle, Maris and backup outfielder Bob Cerv shared a New York apartment as a haven to escape from the madness that Yankee Stadium had become. The three outfielders used to laugh and joke about the ludicrous stories detailing the feud between Maris and Mantle. They would shout, "Didja hear? I hate your guts." Then they'd laugh at the insanity of it all.

It truly turned into an insane period. Since 1961 was the first year of American League expansion and the schedule increased from 154 to 162 games, several sportswriters asked the question: if someone had extra games to break the record, was it fair? The final decision was left to Commissioner Ford Frick, who, however, was hardly an impartial observer. Before serving as National League president and then commissioner, Frick had been a New York sportswriter. He became Babe Ruth's confidant and the ghost-writer of his biography.

Frick finally ruled that the record would stand unless Maris or Mantle broke it by the season's 154th game. The final eight games, Frick said, would give an unfair advantage to anyone chasing Ruth's record. Others argued that the Yankees actually played 155 games in 1927 because a game was called after five innings and ended as a tie. But all arguments fell on deaf ears at the commissioner's office. "Asterisk" became the new catch-word for the nation's baseball fans.

Papers sought new angles on the home run title chase. One commissioned a study of the baseball to see if the ball was livelier than in Ruth's day; several baseballs were sliced up and analyzed. Another paper dissected bats to determine if the lumber used in 1961 was better than in 1927. Finally, Mantle suggested that maybe the bat and ball were the same, but the players were livelier.

Other writers tried to show how wild things were getting. In one article, Dick Young of the *Daily News* mentioned Maris was still 25 games ahead of Ruth's pace; Clete Boyer, however, with his two homers, was but 80 games behind Ruth. But the levity was the exception, not the rule. The home run race was one of the biggest stories to ever hit baseball. The concept of the daily press conference didn't exist, so writers descended on Mantle and Maris, surrounding them at their lockers for hours after the game.

It was no big deal to Mickey, who'd been dealing with the media crush since his rookie season in 1951, when he was supposed to be Ruth, Gehrig and DiMaggio combined. Mantle, who had known most of the New York writers for most of the decade, had built a relationship with them. He willingly answered just about any question asked by the writers.

Maris, however, had no such experience with the media blitz. He'd played for the Cleveland Indians and Kansas City Athletics, two teams hardly known for setting records for media coverage. Maris grew tired of repeatedly answering the same questions, especially stupid questions (and there were plenty). Finally, he would snap, make some sort of comment and escape to the relative sanity of the showers.

The writers didn't appreciate that "treatment." Many wrote nasty stories, describing Maris as moody, uncooperative, uncommunicative and unpopular. They were right; he was all that — to sportswriters. But Maris, who was considered a complete ballplayer, always hustling and willing to do whatever it took to win, was popular with his Yankee teammates.

The pressure finally affected Maris in an obvious way. Early in September at their apartment in Queens, Cerv noticed white patches on Maris' scalp. Maris' hair was falling out in patches, and he was developing a skin rash. One doctor even advised Maris to avoid pressure situations until the rash went away and his hair grew back.

At the end of August, Maris had 51 homers; Mantle had 48. All eyes were on the two sluggers as they earnestly raced to catch the Babe. The one advantage Ruth had over others was that he got red hot in September, crushing 17 homers that final month. Unless a player had built up a big head of steam and was way ahead of Ruth's homer pace at the start of the season, he could forget about breaking the record. But Mantle, needing 13 home runs, and Maris, needing 10, were within range.

But the pennant race wasn't over just yet. During the Labor Day weekend, the red-hot Detroit Tigers, only 1 1/2 games behind the Yankees, came to Yankee Stadium for a crucial series. The Tigers, having won 11 of their last 14, were led by some pretty good ballplayers of their own — Al Kaline, Norm Cash and Rocky Colavito.

The first game was a pitchers' duel. Detroit's Don Mossi shut down the Yankees, as Whitey Ford did against the Tigers. Although Ford pulled a leg muscle in the fifth inning, Bud Daley and Luis Arroyo kept the Tigers at bay through nine innings, with some big defensive help from Yogi Berra to cool what could have been a game-winning rally.

After Bill Bruton walked with one out in the eighth, Al Kaline followed with a line drive smash off the left field wall. Berra, who played it perfectly, threw to second to nail a surprised Kaline. In the bottom of the ninth, the Yankees finally got to Mossi. After Maris and Mantle flew out and struck out to open the inning, consecutive singles by Elston Howard, Berra, and Moose Skowron brought home the game's only run.

In the second game, Maris hammered homers off Frank Lary and Hank Aguirre, leading the Yankees to a 5-2 victory. He now had 53 homers, putting him eight games ahead of Ruth's pace. Mantle, however, pulled a muscle in his left forearm trying to check a swing. He had to leave the game, so writers, figuring Mantle would miss at least a week with the muscle pull, counted him out of the home run race.

Mantle had other ideas. He told Houk he could play and then proved he could do the job even with a muscle pull. In the bottom of the first, he staked the Yankees to a 2-1 lead with a 400-foot cannon blast into the right field bleachers. His forearm was so sore he had to ice the arm between innings, but he didn't let it stop him. The Tigers regained the lead at 5-4, but Mantle led off the ninth inning with another homer, another 400-footer to right field, tying the game at 5-5. Elston Howard would later hit a three-run homer the ninth to give New York the 8-5 win. The Yankees' sweep over the Tigers, for all intents and purposes, sewed up their second straight American League pennant.

While the tally stood at 53 homers for Maris and 50 for Mantle, the Washington Senators arrived for four games in three days. Both sluggers hit a homer in the series. After the Yankees swept all four games, extending their winning streak to seven games, Cleveland came to town. In the first inning of the first game, Tony Kubek ripped a triple. When Maris brought him home with a bunt single, the writers went nuts. Why was Maris bunting when he was chasing Ruth's record? The answer was simple — he wanted to win. Of course, Maris shut everyone up in his next at bat; he hit homer number 55.

By Sept. 10, Maris had 56 homers, Mantle had 53. The Yankees had a 12-game winning streak. With an 11 1/2 game lead over Detroit, the team's magic number was eight. But Mickey, feeling lousy, was feeling the flu. Yankees broadcaster Mel Allen told Mantle he knew a doctor who specialized in giving vitamin shots which would fix Mickey up good as new.

It became known as "The Shot." Mantle went to see Dr. Max Jacobson, who had reportedly treated stars such as Eddie Fisher, Elizabeth Taylor and Tennessee Williams. Jacobson, who soon thereafter quit practicing medicine, gave Mantle a shot in the hip, but stuck the needle in higher than normal. He grazed the hip bone, causing Mantle, who was in much pain from the moment the needle went in, to nearly pass out walking back to the St. Moritz hotel.

Merlyn Mantle was coming in from Dallas the next morning. Mickey, who was running a big fever, couldn't even get out of bed. After he called the hotel manager to have someone pick up his wife at Union Station, he promptly passed out. Merlyn found him still in bed, sick and sweating, running a 104-degree fever. She took him to Lenox Hill Hospital, where doctors lanced the wound to drain an infection that had set in overnight. Doctors said the bone was bruised; Mickey would be incapacitated for a while, basically ending his run at Ruth's record ended.

Mantle hit one more homer in the final three weeks of the season, but "The Shot" basically ended Mantle's 1961 season. Mantle lead the league in three categories, attaining a .687 slugging percentage, tying Maris with 132 runs scored and drawing a major-league-leading 126 walks. Despite his injury troubles at the season's end, Mantle, who hit .317 with 54 homers and 128 RBI, missed only nine games.

On Sept. 20, in the 154th game of the season, Maris hit his 59th homer, blasting a fastball off Orioles starter Milt Pappas in the third inning in Baltimore's Memorial Stadium. Although he didn't make it before the artificial time limit set by Commissioner Ford Frick, Maris, asterisk or no asterisk, became the all-time single season major league homer king, hitting number 61 off Boston's Tracy Stallard in the third inning in the season finale.

Mickey wasn't at Yankee Stadium on the big day. He was in the hospital, battling the virus that originally drove him to the doctor and eventually ruined his season. He was in uniform for the World Series, but only played in two of the five games against the Cincinnati Reds. Mickey literally had a hole in his leg, an oozing sore packed with gauze to soak up blood and pus from the infection. The sight of the wound made Moose Skowron and Tony Kubek so nauseous they had to leave the trainer's room while team doctor Sidney Gaynor removed the packing from the wound.

Mantle sat out the first two games of the Series, but in batting practice before Game 3 in Crosley Field in Cincinnati he hit six homers in just 10 swings. Ralph Houk was persuaded to start Mantle the next night. He didn't do much in the game, going 0-for-4 and handling few chances in the field; Yogi Berra in left and Roger Maris in right handled everything they could to alleviate the pressure on Mickey's leg.

Mantle did, however, inspire the Yankees, who won Game 3 3-2, aided by a Maris homer in the top of the ninth inning. In Game 4, Mantle singled off Jim O'Toole in the fourth inning, but then he made a big mistake: he tried to break up a double play. His slide into second base ripped open the abcess on his leg, forcing him to leave the game. Mantle, his uniform pants soaked with blood from his waist to his knee, tried to convince Houk to leave him in the game. But enough was enough; he was through for the season. The Yankees, however, did reclaim the World Championship, beating the Reds in five games.

The 1962 season would be a big, big year for Mantle, although in May it looked like the season would be a disappointment. In a game against the Minnesota Twins, Mantle, trying to leg out an infield hit, pulled a hamstring so severely that he missed nearly a month of the season. But in his first at bat after coming off the disabled list, he ripped a pinch-hit home run off Cleveland's Gary Bell.

Despite playing in just 123 games, Mickey led the American League in walks with 122 and in slugging percentage at .605. Mantle was voted one of the league's top fielding outfielders and earned his only Gold Glove award. His statistics are truly astounding, considering he missed one-fourth of the team's games that year. Mickey ripped 30 homers, had 89 RBI, and batted .321, his best average in five seasons. If his power stats are projected to a full 162-game schedule, he would have had 40 homers and 120 RBI.

Mantle was especially consistent down the stretch, leading the Yankees to their third straight American League pennant. He capped the season by being named the A.L. MVP for the third time in his career.

The World Series was less than stellar for Mantle. The San Francisco Giants held him scoreless. He had no RBI and just two singles and a double in 25 at bats for a .120 batting average. Fortunately for Mickey, the Yankees won the Series anyway, clinching it with Bobby Richardson's leaping catch of Willie McCovey's liner with two out and two on in the ninth inning of Game 7, a catch that preserved a 1-0 victory and their third straight world championship.

Mantle started 1963 the same way he did 1962 — he got hurt. This time, however, the injury ruined his season; he broke a bone in his foot in June in the second game of a doubleheader against the Orioles. Mantle, chasing a fly hit by Brooks Robinson, tried to use the chain-link fence in center field at Memorial Stadium to get a little extra lift as he leaped to catch the ball. Instead of the lift he wanted, his foot caught in the fence.

Mantle was carried off the field on a stretcher. He didn't play again until August against Baltimore, when he ripped George Brunet's second pitch into the left field stands at Yankee Stadium. It was a sweet moment in a season that otherwise lacked sweet moments.

When the season was over, Mickey had missed nearly 100 games, watching most of the season from the bench. He played in 65 contests, hitting a solid .314 with 15 homers and 35 RBI in just 172 at bats. At that pace, had he played a full season, he would have had 45 homers and 115 RBI.

Although the Yankees won their fourth straight American League title, the World Series was another matter. Mickey played in all four games against the Los Angeles Dodgers, but had about as much success against them as his teammates did. The Dodgers pitching staff dominated the Series. Sandy Koufax, Don Drysdale, Johnny Podres and Ron Perranoski limited the Yankees to four runs and just 22 base hits in four games, holding them to a team batting average of .171. Mantle wound up 2-for-15, a .133 batting average, but one hit was one of the two homers the Yankees hit off Dodger pitching. Los Angeles swept the Series in four, the first time any team had done so against the Yankees.

Big changes occurred after the Series. Ralph Houk resigned as manager to become the team's general manager. In a move that surprised almost everyone connected with baseball, catcher Yogi Berra, one of the team leaders, was named manager. Although Yogi had a reputation for non sequiturs, most fans didn't realize he was one of baseball's best catchers at calling a game.

Many of the younger players were prone to ignore Berra, a low-key personality. In August, the team, in third place behind the Orioles and White Sox, was playing rather poorly when the famed harmonica incident happened. As the team bus slowly snaked its way through New York traffic, utility infielder Phil Linz was in the back of the bus playing a harmonica he'd just bought. Berra, in the front seat, was fuming after another close loss.

Finally, Berra, who'd had enough of Linz's poor playing, told Linz to put away the harmonica. He also suggested where he should put it. Linz didn't understand what

Berra said, so Mantle told him that Yogi had said to "play it fast." As Linz resumed his dirge-like rendition of "Mary Had a Little Lamb," Berra stormed to the back of the bus and slapped the harmonica out of Linz's hands. The harmonica hit Joe Pepitone in the knee, and the wise-cracking first baseman called for a medic. But the real call here was a wake-up call from Berra, letting his team know that he'd had enough.

Mantle, in the midst of what would be his last big season in the majors, didn't need that wake-up call. He compiled a .303 batting average, with 35 homers and 111 RBI, finishing third in the American League in both categories. He also scored 92 runs, seventh best in the A.L. To top it all off, the Yankees won their fifth straight pennant by winning 22 of their last 28 to edge the White Sox by one game and the Orioles by two.

The Yankees faced the St. Louis Cardinals in the World Series. The Cardinals, in fifth place in mid-August, made a September rush to win the National League pennant. Led by two mid-season acquisitions, outfielder Lou Brock and relief pitcher Barney Schultz, the Cardinals overcame the Philadelphia Phillies, who blew a 6 1/2 game lead in the final two weeks.

In his 12th World Series, Mantle hit .333, with three homers, eight RBI and eight runs scored in the seven games. But the Series belonged to the Cards. The Yankees homered three times off Bob Gibson in Game 7, but manager Johnny Keane stuck with the right-hander. The Cardinals won 7-5, handing the Yankees their second straight World Series loss and third defeat in their five-year string of A.L. pennants.

The fireworks started the next day. The Yankees fired Berra, citing the early season problems as the reason for the change. The same day, Johnny Keane resigned as Cardinals manager, citing the mid-season firing of the team's general manager, Bing Devine, and the rumors surrounding future managerial changes in St. Louis. Keane was then promptly hired as the new Yankee manager.

It wasn't a match made in heaven. The Yankees, a veteran club somewhat set in its ways, were used to Berra's easygoing style. Keane, however, had his rules, and everyone was going to follow them, even if his name was Mantle. The 1965 season wouldn't be one Mantle would want to write home about. Knees, legs, arms, hamstrings — you name it, Mantle injured it.

His injuries, combined with the problems he was having with Keane, made 1965 a miserable year. The Yankees slipped to sixth place, marking the first time they'd finished out of the first division in 40 years, and began a title drought that would last 12 seasons.

Mickey played in just 122 games that season. His .255 batting average was the first time he'd dipped below .300 in four years. Mantle, who had just 19 homers and 46 RBI, even considered retiring throughout the season.

But the frustrations in 1965 were only a warm-up for 1966. The Yankees completed the slide, finishing in last place for the first time since 1912. Mel Stottlemyre, who won 20 games in 1965, lost 20 in 1966. For Mantle, it was another forgettable season. He played in just 108 games, managing 23 homers but only 56 RBI and a .288 batting average.

The wear-and-tear and the injuries from 16 major league seasons were obviously taking a toll on the once fleet Mantle, so the Yankees moved him to first base to save his legs. The move gave Mantle two more seasons, but the three-time MVP was clearly about through. In 1967, he hit 22 homers, but hit only .245. In 1968, he hit 18 home runs, but his average dropped to .237.

Mickey takes a break from the wear and tear.

Mantle's final two seasons resulted in farewell tours throughout the American League. Fans gave him standing ovations nearly everywhere he went, finally giving him credit for his courage and ability. He kept hitting the home runs, and slowly moved up the all-time list.

In September 1968, Mickey was stuck on 534 career homers, tied with Jimmie Foxx for what was then fourth on the career home run list. Denny McLain, on his way to a 31-6 record and his second straight Cy Young Award while leading the Detroit Tigers to a World Championship, wanted to give Mantle a going-away present in his final at bat in Detroit.

Tigers catcher Bill Freehan let Mickey know that McLain was going to groove one to him. After letting a fastball pass right down the middle, Mantle, in disbelief, accepted McLain's offer and deposited the next pitch, in the same spot, into the upper deck at Tiger Stadium for home run number 535. When the next batter, Joe Pepitone, asked McLain for a pitch just like the previous one, McLain knocked him down with the first pitch.

Mickey added career homer 536 before the season concluded. That winter, he had a feeling his career was over. He could barely run and the ghosts of injuries past were still haunting him. After arriving in Fort Lauderdale a week early for spring training, he confirmed what he had feared all winter — it was time to hang it up. So, in an emotional press conference on March 1, Mantle announced his retirement.

The numbers Mickey compiled in his 18-year career with the Yankees were truly astounding. He played in 2,401 games, a Yankee record. Not only did he hit 536 homers, he drove in 1,509 runs, scored 1,677 runs, had 2,415 hits, and a lifetime batting average of .298. He won three MVP awards and played on seven World Champions. In World Series play, Mantle hit a record 18 homers, drove in 40 runs and scored 42 in 65 games. He was named to the All-Star team 20 times, won four home run titles, led the league in runs scored six times, and won the Triple Crown in 1956.

But sheer numbers don't really describe Mantle's contributions to the Yankees and the role he played in keeping the dynasty alive and kicking in the Bronx.

Mickey learned, as had countless other former major league stars, that there was life after baseball. But it wasn't nearly as much fun. His bowling alley in Dallas wasn't doing all that well, the motel in Joplin was long gone, and much of his money went down the drain in bad investments. Right after he retired, Mantle launched a restaurant chain called Mickey Mantle Country Cookin'. The restaurants seemed to cook along nicely for a while, but after 13 of them opened up, the corporation ran into trouble and it folded.

Mantle had part of his final year's salary deferred, but after the restaurant chain closed, he accepted a standing offer from Ralph Houk to join the Yankee's coaching staff. Mickey coached first base for the middle three innings of games for one week, but realized coaching wasn't for him; he had no real responsibilities and was there strictly to put more people in the stands. After that, Mantle had a stint as a color commentator for NBC's Game of the Week. He realized that wasn't working either, but finished out the season before calling it quits as a broadcaster.

Perhaps Mantle was having problems deciding what to do next, but the Yankees and baseball had no problems finding ways to honor him. In June 1969, the Yankees held a ceremony to retire Mantle's uniform number. Monuments were put up in center field to honor Mickey and Joe DiMaggio. In 1974, Mantle received the ultimate honor, becoming only the seventh player in history to be named to the Baseball Hall of Fame in his first year of eligibility. Mickey received 322 votes out of 365 ballots cast, or 88 percent, which, at the time, was the ninth highest percentage in four decades of voting.

The fact that his good buddy Whitey Ford was also elected, on just his second try, made it even better for Mantle. It was only fitting that the two inseparable buddies who carried the Yankees to pennant after pennant in the 1950s and 1960s would wind up in Cooperstown together.

Of course, there were some tough times, too. None has been tougher on Mickey than the battle his son Billy is wag-

A day to remember, in June 1969.

A Day To Remember handout

ing against Hodgkin's Disease. At the age of 19, Billy was diagnosed with the same cancer that claimed the life of Mantle's father, uncles, and grandfather. Billy Mantle has had some close calls, but at last report, he was still in remission.

The other bit of trouble came from a ruling by then Commissioner Bowie Kuhn. Mickey worked for the Claridge Hotel in Atlantic City, a hotel with a casino connected. Mantle's job was to do charity and public relations work strictly for the hotel, not the casino. He was to host golf tournaments, raise money for charities, present checks to worthy causes and smile a lot. It was similar to a public relations job held by Willie Mays at Bally's Park Place hotel, located across the street from the Claridge.

Mays was banned from baseball when he took the job, since baseball was touchy about being associated with gambling. Of course, the rule was applied selectively, since Mantle's boss at the Claridge worked for the Sahara Hotel in Las Vegas back when Del Webb owned not only an interest in the hotel/casino, but the Yankees, too.

Other owners, most notably John Galbreath of the Pittsburgh Pirates, owned race-tracks and racehorses, but apparently baseball owners owning gambling establishments didn't threaten the game. Two years later the new commissioner, Peter Ueberroth, lifted the ban and welcomed Mantle and Mays back to baseball.

Courtesy Richard Wolffers Auction Inc.

Casey Stengel and his two prized pupils, Hall of Famers Mantle and Whitey Ford.

Of course, to baseball fans, Mantle never left the game. At most, the game left Mantle. Mickey remains the most popular man on the baseball card circuit, although in recent years he has cut back his scheduled autograph appearances because, at 61, he doesn't quite have the resiliency of a teenager. His baseball cards remain the most sought-after cards in nearly every set he's in. The value of his first-ever Topps card is quickly reaching the point where the card is worth twice what he was paid to play the entire 1952 season.

The reasons why Mantle remains popular, even with those who never had the good fortune to see him play, are quite simple. Mickey has retained his down-home attitude and personality, despite decades of being in the spotlight in the world's media capital. He remains humble and friendly to everyone, spending time with anyone who comes seeking an autograph at shows. During card shows he even takes pride in getting those treasured autographs exactly right, worrying about his penmanship the same way he worried about playing the game.

It's a rare man who can handle the pressures of being a legend before he even plays a major league game. Even rarer is the man who can live up to the hype. And it's almost unheard of for a man to do all that and remain the kind of person he was before going through the wringer. Mickey Mantle is one of those unique individuals, and baseball is better for his contributions.

Mantle, Mickey Charles: (The Commerce Comet), bats both, throws right, 5'11 1/2" 195 lbs, born Oct. 20, 1931, Spavinaw, Okla. Hall of Fame 1974.

NY Yankees

Year	G	AB	H	2B	3B	HR	R	RBI	BB	SO	SB	BA	SA	TB	Pos.
1951	96	341	91	11	5	13	61	65	43	74	8	.267	.443	151	OF-86
1952	142	549	171	37	7	23	94	87	75	**111**	4	.311	.530	291	OF-141, 3B-1
1953	127	461	136	24	3	21	105	92	79	90	8	.295	.497	229	OF-121, SS-1
1954	146	543	163	17	12	27	**129**	102	102	**107**	5	.300	.525	285	OF-144, SS-4, 2B-1
1955	147	517	158	25	**11**	**37**	121	99	**113**	97	8	.306	**.611**	316	OF-145, SS-2
1956	150	533	188	22	5	**52**	**132**	**130**	112	99	10	**.353**	**.705**	376	OF-144
1957	144	474	173	28	6	34	**121**	94	**146**	75	16	.365	.665	315	OF-139
1958	150	519	158	21	1	**42**	**127**	97	**129**	120	18	.304	.592	307	OF-150
1959	144	541	154	23	4	31	104	75	94	**126**	21	.285	.514	278	OF-143
1960	153	527	145	17	6	**40**	119	94	111	125	14	.275	.558	294	OF-150
1961	153	514	163	16	6	54	**132**	128	**126**	112	12	.317	**.687**	353	OF-150
1962	123	377	121	15	1	30	96	89	**122**	78	9	.321	.605	228	OF-117
1963	65	172	54	8	0	15	40	35	40	32	2	.314	.622	115	OF-52
1964	143	465	141	25	2	35	92	111	99	102	6	.303	.591	275	OF-132
1965	122	361	92	12	1	19	44	46	73	76	4	.255	.452	163	OF-108
1966	108	333	96	12	1	23	40	56	57	76	1	.288	.538	179	OF-97
1967	144	440	108	17	0	22	63	55	107	113	1	.245	.434	191	1B-131
1968	144	435	103	14	1	18	57	54	106	97	6	.237	.398	175	1B-131
18 years															
	2,401	8,102	2,415	344	72	536	1,677	1,509	1,734	1,710	153	.298	.557	4,511	OF-2,019,
	(52nd)	(85th)	(79th)			(8th)	(22nd)	(34th)	(5th)	(8th)				(25th)	1B-262, SS-7, 3B-1, 2B-1

World Series
NY Yankees

Year	G	AB	H	2B	3B	HR	R	RBI	BB	SO	SB	BA	SA	TB	Pos.
1951	2	5	1	0	0	0	1	0	2	1	0	.200	.200	1	OF-2
1952	7	29	10	1	1	2	5	3	3	4	0	.345	.655	19	OF-7
1953	6	24	5	0	0	2	3	7	3	8	0	.208	.458	11	OF-6
1955	3	10	2	0	0	0	1	1	0	2	0	.200	.500	2	OF-2
1956	7	24	6	1	0	3	6	4	6	5	1	.250	.667	16	OF-7
1957	6	19	5	0	0	1	3	2	3	1	0	.263	.421	8	OF-5
1958	7	24	6	0	1	2	4	3	7	4	0	.250	.583	17	OF-7
1960	7	25	10	1	0	3	8	11	8	9	0	.400	.800	20	OF-7
1961	2	6	1	0	0	0	0	0	0	2	0	.167	.167	1	OF-2
1962	7	25	3	1	0	0	2	0	4	5	2	.120	.160	4	OF-7
1963	4	15	2	0	0	1	1	1	1	5	0	.133	.333	5	OF-4
1964	7	24	8	2	0	3	8	8	6	8	0	.333	.792	19	OF-7
12 years															
	65	230	59	6	2	18	42	40	43	54	3	.257	.535	123	OF-63
	(2nd)	(2nd)	(2nd)			(1st)	(1st)	(1st)	(1st)	(1st)					

Bold indicates league leader

Chapter 2

The Mantle Mystique

Mantle remains a barometer of the hobby, says Midwestern dealer

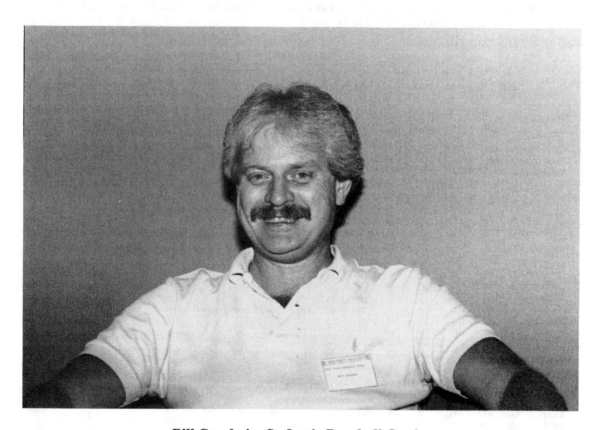

Bill Goodwin, St. Louis Baseball Cards.

By Rick Hines

Although he's not in Mickey Mantle country, one of the Midwest's leading sports card dealers says that as Mickey Mantle goes, so goes the hobby.

Bill Goodwin, of St. Louis Baseball Cards in St. Louis, Mo., specializes in pre-1970s cards. Goodwin, who has a big mail-order business, has set up at most major card shows since 1985. Thus, he's seen the peaks and valleys in the hobby and Mantle's role in it.

"Mantle has always been a barometer of how well the hobby's going. He's always been, I guess, the most popular player for a number of reasons. I suppose it's partly because his cards are available from the '50s and '60s, which is the era that most collectors we deal with are collecting from, and he's always been the most popular player, coming from New York, and the Yankees and playing in a lot of World Series," he said.

Goodwin thinks Mantle's celebrity status in the hobby will always remain high. "Part of it is the timing. He was at the top in the '50s and '60s when baseball cards were produced. I think that has a lot to do with it, and it also has a lot to do with the baby boomers who grew up with baseball during that era who are now collecting. He's by far the one superstar in the most demand and probably has the biggest increases in prices."

Although the recession slowed things down in the hobby, prices for most Mantle items remained stable for Goodwin. "Mickey Mantle cards are very popular now and seem to be going up in price and in demand, especially the higher grade ones," he said. "You see that reflected in the *SCD* price guide.

"One thing that fluctuates a great deal, but always winds up going up, it goes up and down, is the '52 (Topps) Mantle," Goodwin stated. "Maybe a little over a year ago, Mint copies were going in the $70,000 range. And now that card on a wholesale level is probably down to $30,000-$40,000. So that fluctuates a great deal. But it goes through periods of time when it goes up and down.

"I think at one time it got up to $3,000 and then went down to $600 around 1979 or 1980," he said, "but as you can see, from 1980 it's all the way up to $30,000, so it's always going up. I think that's a card that when the economy turns around, and that may be some time from now, but that's a card that's really going to shoot up."

A dealer who specializes in cards, Goodwin doesn't think Mantle card prices have peaked. "I wouldn't say they've peaked at all," he said. "There are some cards that just seem to level off because of the economy right now, but Mantle cards are still going higher."

Although most Mantle collectibles are out of the average collector's price range, Goodwin said there are still some very affordable Mantle items. "Everybody has a budget, but I'm sure you could buy, depending on what condition you want to get into, say, a '58 Mantle All-Star with corner wear. Let's say 25 percent of book is going to put you in around $25. Now $25 is still a lot of money, but it's still affordable if you want to buy it in a lesser grade. That card is $100 in Mint condition. And then you can even get into the match covers or match box covers. There's a lot of price ranges for Mantle."

There are thousands and thousands of Mantle collectors, but many of Goodwin's regular customers are investors. "Investors like Mantle because he's such a sure thing as

1958 Topps Mantle All-Star.

far as prices go. I think investors feel very comfortable with Mickey Mantle cards and memorabilia."

Goodwin wasn't a big fan of Mantle's until after he met him at a card show. "I guess I was a bigger fan after I met him than before, because I thought he was more down-to-earth and a nice guy to be around.

"I'm not an autograph person; I don't really relate well to it, it's just not my personality. I don't get a big kick out of sitting next to somebody when they sign autographs, although I know some people in the hobby who do. So I'm not really a guy who likes to rub elbows with them, any player, not just Mantle, but I do enjoy some of the Mantle stories."

As for the new Mantle products on the market, Goodwin said it's going to take a long time for new products to catch up with the old ones in price simply because everybody's putting things away, and there is a lot more produced. But he does like the new material because, "I like the idea of people looking back on the history of the game and things like that, so I have no problem with that."

"New York phenomenon" keys Mantle's status in hobby

By Rick Hines

Mickey Mantle will always be popular, as long as the New York market dictates hobby trends, says a Midwestern sports memorabilia dealer.

Pat Quinn, co-owner of Sports Collectors Store in LaGrange, Ill., deals in just about every kind of collectible, including sports cards, memorabilia, programs, publications and autographs, from the four major sports — baseball, basketball, football and hockey. His store has advertised in *Sports Collectors Digest* for several years, and they've been holding private auctions since 1968, the oldest running sports auction in the hobby.

Quinn said while Mantle items sell well for him, some Chicago athletes do better, specifically Michael Jordan. "Jordan would outsell anything around this area, as far as I'm concerned," stated Quinn. "I'm not talking price wise, I'm just talking about item wise. Mantle items around here are worth a fortune compared to anything else."

Quinn said the New York phenomenon is the reason Mantle is so popular. "Without a doubt," he said, "because it certainly wasn't people from this area, I'm sure of that. Or any other area for that matter, if you really want to be truthful about it. Who cares in Nebraska about Mickey Mantle outside of a handful of fans?

"You've got to sort of follow, in certain aspects," continued Quinn, "you've got to follow the New York market. If the New York market is bringing a lot of money on

The Mick — always a New York favorite.

a certain athlete, you've got to fall in line. So he'll (Mantle) always have this status as long as New York dictates hobby trends to the rest of the hobby."

Quinn feels Mantle's popularity will continue to grow "unless he did something drastic that ticked the nation off, which I doubt very much he would," said Quinn. "Why should he? He's in a perfect position to be loved and revered until the end."

Mantle's popularity, according to Quinn, has increased 10-fold, maybe 100-fold, over the years. "His popularity is evidenced by the fact that every time you go to an autograph show he's sold out. That says something for his popularity."

Quinn doesn't recall ever selling any real unusual Mantle memorabilia items. "I think personally I remember owning a jersey of his at one time that I think I sold for $1,000, or $2,000 at the most. I just haven't come across anything currently that is a high-ticket item."

Where do dealers come up with all of the Mantle cards and memorabilia? "Most of our Mantle or any other memorabilia comes from a handful of different sources," Quinn said, "collectors who are no longer interested, collectors who only own one or two pieces, people who have gathered up a few items and have now decided it's time to capitalize financially on those particular items, etc."

Quinn said he doesn't have any regular Mantle customers, but when he gets Mantle items in, he contacts dealer friends in New York to see if they're interested.

The prices for Mantle items will continue to go up, he thinks, if people don't get carried away. "I remember when we went down to New York City for a show at the Penta Hotel; I can't remember what show it was, but it had to be in the last 10 years, I know that. But at the Penta they were doing Mickey Mantle (autographs) for $5, and people were buying.

"Then other people started getting him into shows around the New York area and the price kept escalating and escalating and escalating. Now I understand, and I may be wrong, I think a baseball now is $50-$55 from him.

"It's getting to the point now, price wise, where you're getting out of a lot of people's pockets, away from them. I think one of two things may happen, or may not; it's pure speculation on my part. I think his stuff will become stagnant for a while because of the price, or it may even drop down. If it drops, I think it will continue to roll and it will pick up more customers. I think if you get to a certain point for a guy's autograph, especially a living guy, like Joe DiMaggio, the prices are outlandish. I don't see a lot of people buying Joe DiMaggio (autographs) unless it's in person.

"It's kind of ridiculous to pay $55 for a ball signed by a guy," continued Quinn, "but then again, I'm looking at it in a different light. Mickey Mantle and his people are looking at it in a whole other light. They're feeling that $55 isn't enough. But I don't think that's neither here nor there. I think everything's slowed down, so, in essence, a $55 ball does not become that important anymore to a person versus maybe something they can pick up for $15-$20."

As for affordable Mantle items to the average collector, Quinn doesn't think there are any. "To be truthful with you, I doubt if there are," he said.

"It's how you look at it. Like I say, the people that have the Mantle items and are selling them, whether they be Mantle himself or people who have dealt with Mantle, or people who have bought things from Mantle, of course, they're going to think more positive because they want to sell those items. But it's getting to the point where how many people have $50-$60 for a baseball.

"If you get into the cards, you can't get any cards for those prices. If you could buy a card of his, from during his playing days, for $55, you'd be getting a big steal. It just can't be done. So cards are basically out of a big majority of the collectors' field, out of their pocketbook range.

"The only thing they can afford now is an autograph, because I think that's the lowest thing on the totem pole as far as prices go. Except for maybe programs or something that he might be in, or pictures of him."

Older Mantle memorabilia continues to skyrocket in price

By Rick Hines

The higher values of older Mickey Mantle memorabilia is perhaps pricing some collectors out of the Mantle market, says a West Coast dealer who ranks Mantle among the elites in the baseball memorabilia hobby.

Steve Waibel is the assistant general manager of San Diego Sports Collectibles, which deals mainly in retail sports cards with three stores in the San Diego area. They also do a large mail-order business around the country.

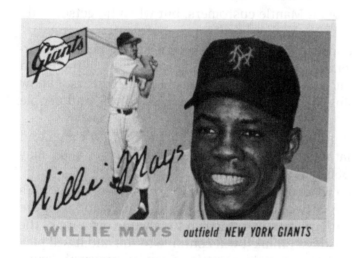

Willie Mays, another favorite in New York.

According to Waibel, Mantle memorabilia ranks in the top five in the hobby, along with "Ted Williams, DiMaggio, that kind of thing. He's right up there."

When you think of baseball from the 1960s, you think of Mickey Mantle, the player of that decade. "The main reason for his popularity," said Waibel, "is that he played in New York; he was high profile. Willie Mays had better career numbers, but didn't play in the same market for his whole career. I think that had an effect on his (Mays') popularity.

"I think Mantle's popularity will grow," continued Waibel. "I think he'll be god-like, Babe Ruth-like, 10, 20 years down the line. He's a legend. People buy his stuff and have never seen him play a game, (they buy it) just because of who he is."

Waibel said the most unusual Mantle item the business has sold was a movie poster of Mantle and Maris. "I can't remember the name of the movie, but that would be the most unusual Mantle item we've had."

Most of their Mantle items come from private collectors, Waibel said, except for items such as autographed balls and photos. As for Mantle buyers, he said, "I have a few people who do just Mantle. If a new Salvino statue or something like that comes out, they always pick it up. But they usually like the Yankees, more than just Mantle. They like the Mantle/Maris."

As for the future prices of Mantle items, Waibel forsees the older material continuing to skyrocket. "I think the original things, the game-worn jerseys, bats, balls, hats, that stuff is going to skyrocket, more than it already has. But I think that's true of any original stuff with anybody from the '60s or '70s.

"There's a lot of stuff that's manufactured now, a lot of manufactured memorabilia. You can find an autographed Mantle jersey, but it's not a real one, it's just a jersey with his signature on it. I think the real, true game-used stuff is going to be really hot.

"The new material tends to be overdone," Waibel continued, "but people still buy it. I'm not a believer in manufactured stuff, you know, like the (Joe) Montana jerseys. We don't even carry that stuff. It doesn't, to us, have real meaning."

Waibel said it's getting more difficult to find affordable Mantle items. "That's getting hard, because most of the cards and everything are priced above what the average guy can afford. There's a few things, a few of the cards, the non-regular issue cards, like the '59 Topps, they have a special card of Mantle in there.

"Some of the specialty cards are still under $100; those things sell like crazy. Anything with Mantle on it, that's out of a regular Topps set in the '60s, that isn't his regular card, that's under $100, they sell immediately."

Despite Mantle's popularity nationwide, Waibel is not a Mantle fan. "I'll have to say no," he said. "I am to an extent, but I think Mays was a better player. I always felt like he never got his due, and so that made me not like Mantle as much. The numbers that Mays put up were far greater, but I realize the effect Mantle has had on the industry."

There are still Mantle bargains around, says East Coast dealer

By Rick Hines

Interest in Mickey Mantle will never wane, says an East Coast card dealer who thinks there are some real bargains to be found regarding Mantle collectibles.

Angelo Accetturo, vice president of the Greg Manning Co., in Montville, N.J., says Mantle cards are the top seller for the company, which mainly sells cards from the 1950s and 1960s.

"Mantle is the best seller we have by far," said Accetturo, who also handles all cards, from tobacco on up, plus a little bit of memorabilia. "There's never been a problem with selling a Mantle card. It's just the easiest one to sell, that's for sure.

"We deal in all grades of cards," Accetturo continued. "If the cards are priced according to grade they sell no matter what, especially Mantle. You could say that for all cards, but the off-grade Mantle cards sell as quick as the high-grade Mantles."

Agreeing with most of the other dealers in this survey, Accetturo said Mantle's popularity stems in large part from the fact he played in New York. "It's a big market and I guess baby boomer-aged people remember him well. He's an American hero to them. The New York market would be, I would say, the number one reason."

Accetturo doesn't think Mantle's popularity will ever shrink. "I can only see it getting bigger. I have never seen him decrease in popularity; I've only seen it increase."

The company has regular Mantle customers who are called when Accetturo thinks something arrives that they might be interested in. "Usually though, we put things out for everybody to get a shot at," he said, adding most of his company's business is done through *Sports Collectors Digest* ads.

"I think prices for his items will always be up; I don't see them ever going down," he said. "I wouldn't say they've peaked because there's always going to be a demand for them," he continued.

"When new people come into the hobby, naturally they notice that the Mantle cards are always higher priced. They see the reasoning behind it after a while, and there's always interest in them. He's baseball. If you think baseball in his era, you think Mickey Mantle."

Babe Ruth is synonymous with the New York Yankees.

As for a younger base of Mantle collectors, Accetturo replied, "Yes, there is one, just like there's collectors today who collect Babe Ruth."

Accetturo said there are affordable Mantle items in the hobby. "Sure, the later year cards, off-condition cards, even the special cards in the sets, like the World Series cards. They're all real bargains compared to the regular-issue card.

"There's a lot of stuff, and then there's, of course, all the other different type of reprint sets out with the Mantles in them," he said.

A Mantle fan himself, Accetturo said his company doesn't deal much with the new Mantle items being produced.

There's still room for more Mantle autograph collectors

By Rick Hines

Only Nolan Ryan's signature is in greater demand than Mickey Mantle's, says one of the leading sports autograph dealers in the country.

Mark Jordan, of Bedford, Texas, also deals in memorabilia, almost any non-card item, but 70 percent of his business is autographs.

Mantle, he said, is probably the second-best seller he has behind only local favorite Nolan Ryan. "After him you would have Mantle, Ruth and then DiMaggio," said Jordan. "He's popular because he was the superstar that most of the guys in the '50s and '60s grew up liking. Most of those guys are the collectors who have the money right now.

"If you're a little kid, or a teen-ager, and you're following the game now, you may grow up with Kirby Puckett or somebody. But if you're collecting, Mantle is the easiest guy to pick up as a hero from the '50s and '60s. And he's much more popular than say, Ted Williams, who I would consider might be a better player. But Williams is extremely popular also."

One reason Mantle is so popular in the hobby is that he's been on the show circuit longer than anyone else, Jordan said. "I would say he regularly does 40 shows a year, or more, and he sells out at every show he goes to. People want to stand in line and meet Mickey Mantle, more than DiMaggio or anybody else.

"DiMaggio sells out and stuff, but people know he's a legend more and they're looking at it as an investment more. But I think people really want to meet Mickey Mantle."

As for Mantle's popularity, Jordan thinks it stays about the same. "It's just when the base of collectors increases, then more people are interested in Mantle. In that regard, it's increased. But proportionately, he's always the Mick.

"Even in the '70s, when the hobby was real small, his status is the same. There's just many more people collecting now, so that's driven up a demand for his signature and his appearance and everything else."

Dealers Mark Jordan (left) and Dick DeCourcy.

Jordan estimates he's sold more than 100 different types of Mantle items, everything from game bats to game jerseys. "But my staple is autographed balls and 8x10 photos of him, Hall of Fame plaques, nothing real unusual."

Jordan said he gets a lot of his material from other collectors, but he's had private signings with Mantle in the past (until Upper Deck signed Mantle to an exclusive contract). Thus, he has a good stash of Mantle signed items.

"Probably more than half my business is my staff and I calling people to fill want lists," Jordan said. "This is stuff that doesn't reach my ad or catalog. We try to give people good service and call them up when they send us want lists. The advertising (in hobby publications), the catalog and personal phone calls are the main ways we sell stuff."

Mantle items, he said, won't decrease in price. "There's fluctuations in the market right now, especially in cards, so maybe Mantle cards can go down somewhat, but we're talking about memorabilia. And people have asked me the question a lot, 'Doesn't Mantle sign too much? Don't people hoard his stuff? How can this stuff possibly continue to stay at the level it is or even have room to increase?'

"And I mean even when he dies, his stuff will go up and all. I'm not rooting for any bad luck for anybody, because I would like to see guys like Mantle and DiMaggio and Williams stay on the show circuit as long as they can because it helps fuel interest in the hobby.

"There's plenty of people who have come out to these shows just to meet these guys and have become either big collectors or small collectors. So I think it's good to have these guys show up at shows.

"The fact that Mantle still sells out tells you there's still a huge demand for his autograph, because he signed what? 300 a day. That's 600 a weekend, and even if he did 50 shows a year, that's what, 30,000 autographs a year? That's not many autographs considering how many millions of people there are in this country. Even if he signs that many autographs for 20 straight years, it's still one autograph for every 200 people in this country, or not even that much.

Mantle's autographs are still in demand.

"The point is there's a lot of people who casually might have a Mickey Mantle autograph or a Nolan Ryan autograph who wouldn't be a collector. I think with your superstars you have tons of casual collectors, which I call the same type of people who go to the stadium and watch ball games.

"I mean the Blue Jays or the Colorado Rockies will draw four million this year, and yet those four million people who go to those games, all are collectors a little bit. They'll buy programs, yearbooks, they'll want a couple of autographed balls of their favorite players, and then they'll buy a Mantle or Nolan Ryan or something to complement that.

"So I think the collector base is pretty big, and that's worn out by the fact also that you see how many cards the card companies sell. There's lots and lots of casual collectors, people that never heard of *SCD*, but yet they go to shows and stuff and they're part of the marketplace."

Jordan thinks Mantle items will continue to rise in price, although not dramatically. "The price of a game-used bat is lower this year than it was last year, but all that's based on speculation. And the price of his jersey is much cheaper than it was last year, but that's more what the marketplace is than what it says about Mantle.

"A lot of markets, such as bats and uniforms, I think, are very thin markets, and once you have one or two or three guys that have paid their $100,000 for a Mantle uniform, they're out of the marketplace for the moment in that item, so the next time a Mantle uniform may come up, it may only bring $75,000 or $50,000. That's a different area of the marketplace."

When asked if there are affordable Mantle items in the marketplace, Jordan replied, "I still think that anything that he'll sign at a show is not a bad deal, whether it's a ball or any 8x10. I'll tell you something that people don't think about, that I think are good values right now, are signed Hall of Fame plaques, or even 3x5 cards.

"There's not as many of those around, and I have people come up to my table at shows and have the 8x10s and balls and want Hall of Fame plaques and 3x5s. I can get more for a 3x5 right now than an 8x10 because of the supply of them.

"I think Hall of Fame plaques and Perez-Steele cards and stuff like that are excellent items to have signed. They're part of a finite set. Like in the Perez-Steele, the Satchel Paige and Lloyd Waner are very valuable; they're worth at least $2,000 each, when you can buy a Lloyd Waner autograph for $15. It's what it was signed on that makes it valuable."

Jordan isn't really a Mantle collector, but he realizes how popular he is in the marketplace. "I realize how important he is in the grand scheme of things. I certainly recognize him as the most popular player of his era and maybe even two or three eras, and that's saying a lot.

"A lot of people have knocked him for being drunk or doing this or doing that, but the one thing I'll say about Mickey Mantle — he's made lots of money off the hobby, but I think he gives collectors a quality product. He takes his time; every autograph is neat and legible.

"He shows up when he's supposed to. I think he's overall good for the hobby and I think he's a great player, but I look at him more in a business sense than in any fan sense, I guess."

Leland's Inc. obtains unusual Mickey Mantle items

Mantle's generosity contributes to abundance of memorabilia in the marketplace

By Rick Hines

Mickey Mantle memorabilia is abundant in the marketplace in part due to the player's own generosity, says a leading New York City auction house owner.

Joshua Leland Evans, owner of New York City's Leland's, said Mantle items are very popular in his company's million dollar auctions, which have included items such as Babe Ruth's uniforms and the infamous "Mookie" ball from the 1986 World Series.

"The market has an interesting phenomenon that the more modern players are more valuable than the older players. There are exceptions," Evans said.

"Babe Ruth stuff is great, and it will always be great, but take a guy like Harry Heilmann, who could be one of the greatest players who ever lived. Yet he could sell for a lot less than say, Mickey Mantle stuff, which is much more common and should be worth less. But Mantle's stuff is right up there. It's Ruth, Gehrig, DiMaggio and Mantle."

Besides the New York connection, Evans said one reason for Mantle's popularity is because many of today's collectors remember seeing him play. "The first game I ever went to I saw Mickey Mantle play; even me, I'm only 32. I saw the guy play, so there's like an out-of-sight, but still-in-the-mind phenomenon that exists with Mantle."

If nothing else, Mantle will always remain popular because of his name, said Evans. "They (fans) will remember a guy like Mickey Mantle because of his name. Just the fact that it's Mickey Mantle; that's a great name for a baseball player. It's got two M's and Mickey and all that. It's a great name for a baseball player. Even he said the best thing his father ever did for him was call him Mickey Mantle."

Leland's Inc. seeks unusual Mantle items.

Despite Mantle's popularity, Evans said prices for his items fluctuate; they don't always increase. "Everything in the sports memorabilia business is cyclical and stuff will always go up and down; nothing goes up continuously, things just don't work that way. Even if it's always going up, it's going to come down. It's just a matter of time. Maybe not down as much as it's gone up, but it will come down.

"The Mantle card," Evans continued, "the '52 Topps card, it went from $1,000 to like $3,000 overnight, then it came down to $800 and then it went up to $10,000-$20,000, then it went to $50,000 and then it went to $75,000. Now, they're back down to $40,000-$50,000. So Mantle stuff is always going up and down."

Unusual Mantle items are the norm for Leland's, which seeks the rare and different. "The most unusual item I've sold?" Evans said when asked that question. "I've sold his retired number from Yankee Stadium, the one that hung in Yankee Stadium. I've sold giant life-size standups that were used in a television showroom to point to TVs that he was pushing at the time. It was like having a huge actual Mickey Mantle person in your house.

"I've sold the bat that he used in the 1964 World Series. I've had an incredible run of World Series bats that he used, and All-Star bats. I think I bought three of them in one two-month period, which is incredible because there's probably only six that exist in the world, and I bought three of them in like 60 days. It's incredible. These are the bats that were actually presented to him by Louisville Slugger for him to use in the World Series and All-Star games. I've got his '53 All-Star bat, his '56 All-Star bat, and I also have his, I believe, 1960 All-Star bat."

One reason there is so much Mantle memorabilia in the marketplace is because of Mantle's generosity, according to Evans. "He gave away a lot of stuff, because he wasn't really aware of the value of it and he was a generous guy. He gave away a lot of his possessions over the years. Like he gave away his bats and he gave away jerseys.

"The 1960 Mickey Mantle jersey that I sold for $111,000 last year actually came from the Yankees. There was a clothing store in New York City in Rockefeller Center that was doing a display in 1961 on the Yankees for a men's clothing store. They contacted the Yankees and asked them if they could have some uniforms. So they gave them a Mantle, Maris and a Berra and they hung them up in the store and they never gave them back and the Yankees never asked for them, either.

"The father willed them to his three sons. One of them got the Mantle and one of them got the Maris and they put them in the auction. The Berra son held onto his. The Maris sold for $66,000 and the Mantle sold for $110,000.

"We had a Rolex watch that was presented to Mantle for being in the 1964 World Series, and that originally came from his son and his son gave it to a friend of his. These are really high level pieces. You can really track down exactly where they're from."

Evans said he has several guys who concentrate on Mantle memorabilia. "There's guys I've dealt with for years who collect just Mickey Mantle things, and they have $100,000 collections devoted just to Mickey Mantle. And then there's people who will just buy Mantle stuff because they're sports collectors and Mantle is such an important icon in sports history. You have both.

"Any baseball collector will buy a Mickey Mantle item. It's like Wheaties; it's something that's right down the straight and narrow, real Americana. Mantle is like apple pie, anybody who is an American will like Mickey Mantle, if he's not a communist."

Evans said he believes Mantle items will always demand high prices. "You've got guys like Cap Anson or Lloyd Waner, and as time goes on, these names are going to be forgotten by a lot of people. Of course, the diehard purists will always know the importance of these players, but the masses will forget them to a certain extent.

"But a guy like Mantle is such a huge name and he represents and typifies an era so strongly that I believe he'll always be strong. Anyone who invests in Mantle memorabilia is getting a much safer bet than if they collected Mike King Kelly stuff, or Jose Canseco stuff, because I don't think they have that magical importance, that blue-chip type of player who'll always be considered one of the greatest."

Being a native New Yorker, Evans is a big Mantle fan. "I actually did a project with Mantle, and he promoted one of our auctions. We did a press conference with him and he signed and authenticated one of his uniforms. It was not the one that sold for $111,000, it was the one that sold for $71,500. It was the first uniform to sell for a lot of money before that whole thing started. This was a few years back.

"He was a doll," continued Evans. "He was just great. He was right there on time and he was a pleasure to deal with and the media loved him. He was totally unpretentious and a regular guy. We loved that, the press loved that; he was the perfect symbol for this company for that day. He was great, and I am a big Mickey Mantle fan because of the way he holds himself."

Evans, however, is not a fan of most of the new Mantle memorabilia items being produced. "Some of it is good and some of it is not. You have these Upper Deck authenticated bats selling for a ridiculous $1,750, and of course, he's signing balls all the time. There's horrible lithographs being produced I'm sure, at this very moment. I mean there's not that much great stuff. The stuff that's coming out now for the most part is garbage. But the older stuff is just so expensive it makes it harder for the collector."

While Mantle currently has an exclusive autograph contract with Upper Deck, Evans said that won't last. "He'll be back. That's not going to last forever. It's kind of sad, but that's just the way things have gotten. The hobby's become somewhat elite. But it's just like when I was a kid. I waited outside the stadium. If you're willing to bust your butt a little bit, you can get what you want."

It's the pursuit, not the value, which drives this Mantle card collector

By Rick Hines

Wayne Wyckoff admits he might not have the most unusual Mickey Mantle memorabilia collection, but he won't take a back seat to anyone when it comes to the number of Mantle items he owns. And it all started with a Berk Ross card.

"The only card I had from that era was from a kid named Jimmy Rafferty; he gave me a nearly complete collection of Berk Ross cards, one of which was a Mantle and it was like a perfect card. I've still got it today. That's what sort of started me in this.

"I had that one card, (and) probably had a lot of others, but when I went into the service I hid some of my better ones, like all the Berk Ross ones, up in my room. I had a banana box full of them, packed. You could hardly lift the box, and when I came back from the service I asked Mom what happened to them. She said she forgot what she did with them.

"But the best ones I kept, and that one was the Berk Ross Mickey Mantle. The rest of the Berk Ross cards I traded for a left-handed Mickey Mantle glove. So I have a left-handed glove, plus four different right-handed gloves." (Note: these are Rawlings Mantle models, not game used.)

One of Wyckoff's Rawlings gloves was advertised by Phillies cigars. "I'm probably one of the few people who has the letter that came from the Phillies Cigar Co. that congratulated the person. It says, 'I would like to thank you for your interest and patronage in our baseball special offer. I know that you will enjoy using the fine Rawlings baseball glove.' It was from Phillies Cigars, 9th Avenue and Columbia Avenue, Philadelphia 22, Pa. This was about 1953.

"And it was signed by Mickey Mantle on the bottom and then it had his name underneath that," said Wyckoff, from New Jersey. "It says, 'Have fun, Mickey Mantle.' Of course, that was not a real signature, it was a stamped signature. But how many people could have that letter?"

Of all his Mantle items, Wyckoff thinks a complete set of Bazooka cards, 1959-1968, is the rarest. "Most people don't know," he said, "in 1966 and 1967, if you look at the picture it's exactly the same; they both have a number seven on them, but they are different. In 1967, Mantle was on a panel with Leon Wagner and Gary Peters. Whereas in 1966 it was Mantle, Leon Wagner and another guy (Ed Kranepool).

"If you just cut out the picture of Mantle, you wouldn't know which set you had it from, but the letters don't line up when it says New York Yankees and Mickey Mantle on the '66s. So in order to be complete, it would be a 10-card set." The hardest Bazooka Mantle to get, in his opinion, is the last one, in 1968, he said.

Although Wyckoff has been collecting only about seven years, his collection is the envy of his collecting friends. "Everybody knows I'm not out for the best; I've got a few cards that almost look like they were bike motors. But if I say I've got them all, we're not arguing how nice they look, we're just saying I got it."

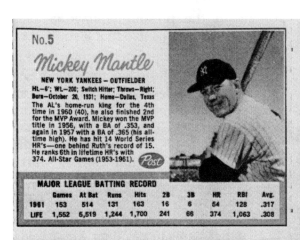

Four Post Cereal cards feature Mickey Mantle.

Wyckoff has a complete run of Mantle's Topps cards except the 1969 Super card, valued at $1,500 in the third edition of the "Sports Collectors Digest Standard Catalog of Baseball Cards." His collection also includes all of Mantle's Bowman, Post Cereal and Jell-O cards, including the one that was in *Life* magazine, and all of the Topps stamps. Other Mantle cards in Wyckoff's collection include the 1954 Dan-Dee Potato Chip card, 1954 Red Heart Dog Food, 1954 New York Journal-American and the card off the back of the 1969 Transogram box.

"The Dan-Dee that I have isn't nice because it was in the potato chips and most of them come stained. I don't have the Transogram statue, but I've got two Mantle Hartland statues. How I got two, I don't know, but I've got them. I don't have too many doubles; I've got maybe five things that I know that I've got two of."

Wyckoff's favorite Mantle item isn't high priced ($40) and will probably come as a surprise. "The one that I always say I like the best that people don't understand why — because it's probably one of the few cards that doesn't even show Mantle on it — is the Topps 1961 card No. 406. It says 'Mantle blasts 565 foot home run.' That's probably the one I like the best.

"There could have been longer balls hit, maybe, but none has ever been recorded as such, so that's probably

Mantle's 1954 Red Heart Dog Food card.

Mantle's 1961 Topps card, #406.

one of the reasons. I have a 1964 Topps Standup; I like that also."

Wyckoff has purchased most of his items, although he has received some in trade for electrical work (he is an electrician by trade). "I really have no other baseball items other than Mickey Mantle, because then people say how this or that card is worth $100 and they'll sell it to me for $10. But I tell them, 'Look, if it hasn't got Mantle on it, I don't want it.'"

Other items in his Mantle collection include Topps buttons from the 1950s, instructional books by Mantle, yearbooks, store-model bats, ballpoint pens shaped like bats, etc. "Another nice item I have is a bat rack from, I may be wrong about the year, but I think it was from 1954 or 1955.

"I've even got three different matchbook covers with him on the flap. I've got the Baseball Bucks, that was a $10 bill that Topps put out. I've even got one of the mock-ups of, I think, the 1957 Hires Root Beer card. It shows Mantle batting with the bat on his left shoulder, so it's like a cut-out. It was like what Hires Root Beer was going to have for 1956 or 1957. I think Bowman was going to take them over because that's when they went out of business.

"I've got all the records, too, that I know he was on. He was on, I don't know if many people know this, on Coral Records; he was on with Theresa Brewer. There's a blue one (label) and an orange one, too. The blue one, which most people probably have, says 'Sample Copy, Not For Sale.' This was a promo given out to the disc jockeys at the time. I've also got an orange copy that was actually used in the juke box. There can't be too many of the orange ones around.

"I've got two pictures, too, that most people don't have," continued Wyckoff. "One says 'Champion Whiz Kids Ball Team Winners 1947.' It shows Mantle in the picture without a uniform. As a matter of fact, he was only 16 years old when that was taken. And I have one in 1948 when they were the champions again. It was taken in Baxter Springs, Kan., and that year he had a uniform. He was born in '31, so that made him 17 years old then. This was before he ever got to Joplin or Independence."

Wyckoff plans to keep his collection intact until his grandson is ready for college. Then, he'll part with it. He estimates his collection is worth close to $100,000, but that's a guess.

"To tell you the truth, I never did it, even now, for money. I only did it for the challenge. When you ask me how much it's worth, that's only my opinion. Maybe it's worth less, maybe it could be worth a little more. Some of the cards, like I say, are not the best because we can argue all day long about this one's better, it's off-center, out of focus, a million-and-one things wrong with it."

Although he has never met Mantle personally, Wyckoff has interviewed him, sort of. "I've got a video in which Mantle answers a bunch of questions; I think Red Barber was asking him the questions. I wrote the questions down that Red Barber asked, and when every time Barber would begin to speak, I'd turn the volume down and I would read the question, trying to keep the same pace that Red Barber did.

"So when I turned up the sound — if I'd say, 'Hey Mickey, how did you first start out batting as a switch-hitter?' — then I would turn it up and he'd say how his father started him when he was 4 years old and he'd go on and talk about that a bit."

It's quality, not quantity, that counts to this Mantle memorabilia collector

By Rick Hines

A tour of this shrine will literally leave Mickey Mantle collectors weak-kneed and in awe.

New Jersey collector Alan Schackman owns one of the most unusual and complete Mantle memorabilia collections around. His infatuation with Mantle is obvious — most of his basement is devoted to a mini Mantle museum.

As a youngster who grew up in the shadows of Yankee Stadium during the 1950s, Schackman has always been a Yankee fan.

"At that time, Mickey Mantle was the Yankees, really," said Schackman. "I would assume he was almost every kid's hero, who was a Yankee fan in the '50s. If you were a pitcher, it would have been Whitey Ford, but any other player, it would have been Mickey Mantle, I assume."

Schackman watched his heroes on television and attended several games at Yankee Stadium with his father and grandfather. He saw Mantle play in person, but he never met him, except indirectly through the card collection he built as a kid.

"Every boy was a card collector," he said. "The old scenario, we used to flip the cards in the schoolyard, and we'd put them on our bicycles to make noise and everything. Of course, I had all the complete runs of all the sets when I was growing up, the Topps and so forth, in the '50s.

"And when I went to school, like everybody else, my mother threw them away or they got discarded. They were just little pieces of cardboard at that point. Nobody ever thought there'd be any value in saving them in the future."

So, from the late 1950s until the early 1980s, Schackman found other things to occupy his time. "It's a funny thing. I grew up basically as a stamp collector but I stopped collecting stamps and first day covers when I went to college because I couldn't afford to keep up with the hobby. And then in the late '70s I started getting back involved with that and I started collecting first day covers and stamps.

"I've since sold off my stamp collection because it really didn't mean much to me anymore. It wasn't like looking at my Mantle stuff, looking at it and glowing. The stamps just laid around and they were nothing. But in 1983, they came out with stamps of Babe Ruth, and there were so many different cachets coming out for that; that really just sort of rekindled my spirit in baseball.

"I was already collecting the 1939 issue, I had quite a few of those first day covers, and when the Babe Ruth issue came out I decided I wanted to get as many different cachets as I could for this issue, because that was the first issue I really got heavily involved in. I'd say there's probably over 1,000 different first day covers for that issue.

"What I did, I contacted several dealers to send me everything they had, and in doing so, I got a number of duplicates and I didn't know what to do with them. So I happened to go to a card show with a friend, and I think Bob Turley was there. Seeing Bob Turley and just the name rekindled my whole childhood again. And I took a few first day covers with me and got them autographed at the show.

"That was the first time I actually saw *SCD*. I didn't even know anything about it before that. I picked up a copy at a card show and I was reading through it. I started seeing ads, mail-in ads for different shows where you can mail in your items to get them autographed if you couldn't go there in person."

Schackman started doing that, basically for Yankees from the 1950s. Then he branched out into Hall of Famers and other players. "From that point on, I just started going to card shows and I started seeing pictures of Mickey Mantle around. It just lit up my whole youth. It was almost like a childhood," he said.

"So, I started buying pictures of Mickey Mantle, and at that point the cards were still fairly cheap, so I started buying cards. I guess one thing led to another and before I turned around I was going to shows. Every time I saw something with Mickey Mantle on it or was involved with Mickey Mantle, I started buying it.

"And I started getting to know some of the dealers and they would save things for me. Some of the bigger dealers today just automatically send me items on approval. If I need it, I keep it and I send them a check. If I don't need it I send it back and it goes into auction. Basically, that's how I got started."

But as you'll see as you read on, Schackman was and is after quality, not quantity. "Even with stamp collecting, I wanted quality material. I didn't want to collect garbage, and I knew of Mickey's popularity and I guess maybe somewhere down deep, maybe it just dawned on me that maybe this might be an item not only so much collectible, but something that might be worth something in the future to give to my son.

"So I really started getting involved with that, but also I started collecting photos and balls of other Yankees, of the '50s and '60s, and I got involved a little bit with Hall of Famers.

Perez-Steele cards are popular among autograph collectors.

"Every time somebody gets inducted into the Hall of Fame, of course, I'm getting all the new autographs for that. I get a ball, a picture, a Gateway. Some other companies come out with cachets of induction day and I'll send away for those. And little by little I spread into Perez-Steele cards, Hall of Fame postcards. It's really the autographs that got me going."

With so many unique Mantle memorabilia items, it would be difficult to choose a favorite. But Schackman has an answer.

"I have so many different and unusual items, it's hard to say," he began. "The thing I like the most is a ring that I wear occasionally, a Mickey Mantle ring. It was a limited edition of 20 rings that were made by, I think, Balfour; that's the company that makes the All-Star and World Series rings. Somebody told me they call it a retirement ring; I don't know if that's true or not.

"It's got a No. 7 made out of square diamonds on a blue background, and it's engraved Mickey Mantle," he said. "On the side it's beautifully engraved, showing a cutaway of Yankee Stadium and a picture of Mantle batting. It's got his World Series stats and his '56 stats. It's beautiful. I love it.

"In fact," continued Schackman, "I was wearing it once at a show and I was having some things autographed by Mickey and he looked at it and he looked up and he smiled. He asked me, 'Where'd you get it?' I told him I got it from a dealer. I guess that's my most prized thing, because I had seen one of those about four or five years ago; a friend of Mickey's was wearing one. In fact, he was sort of flaunting it in front of me. And I always wanted one.

"I told a few of the dealers that I know if they ever saw one to let me know. Early in '92, one of them popped up and I just grabbed it. Whenever I go to a card show or any sports type function, I always wear it. That would be my most prized possession, what I get the most enjoyment out of."

One-of-a-kind items have also found their way into Schackman's collection, including one of Mantle's expired driver's licenses and one of his American Express cards, both obtained from a dealer. There's a story behind the credit card.

"It was an old one of his that I guess he just cut in half and threw away. Somebody must have picked it out of the garbage and glued it back together. The autograph is intact on the back, where you sign your credit card. I'd say those are two of my most unusual items. I also have one of the Jell-O boxes with the Jell-O card; I've got the entire box with the Jell-O still in it."

Schackman estimates he probably has 99 percent of Mantle's baseball cards. "The only ones I really never got involved with are the recent ones with Score, who came out with autographed cards. I don't really collect cards, so I'm not going to go out and buy packs of cards to get a card like that. If I see one at a show, maybe I'll buy it, but I haven't seen any. Other than that I have basically almost everything."

Schackman even has the Red Heart dog food card, complete with the label from the can, and it's autographed. "I have it framed on my wall," he said. One of the few cards he doesn't have is Mantle's 1960 Post Cereal card.

What Schackman has the most of is autographed Mantle photos — more than 1,100 of them, all different.

"At least half of them are wire photos," Schackman said, "many of them just one of a kind. Some of them are so unusual, he's (Mantle) never even seen them. He gets a kick out of them when I go to a show and he'll autograph them for me. He'll stop and he'll look at them and read the captions on the back. He'll just reminisce about the photo also. In fact, he's asked me for copies of some of them, which I copied and mailed to him."

Imagine having more than 1,100 autographs of one athlete, your favorite ballplayer. If that player is Mickey Mantle, whose autograph tickets go for about $30 these days, we're talking big bucks. How does Schackman get his photographs signed?

"Some of the photos I bought autographed; most of them I got autographed myself, of course, not in person. Sometimes I sent them out to private signings. I have friends who would be doing private signings with Mickey through his son, and I would send sometimes 30 to 40 photos and get them autographed. One time I had about 300 I needed autographed, and in a matter of a year I got them all done, basically through a lot of private signings.

"It's funny, his most recent prices are $55 for an autograph. I was getting them done years ago as low as $10. It shows you the value of the autograph industry. I don't know what's going to happen now with Upper Deck, what's going to happen with them. I just read in your recent *SCD* where Score Board has DiMaggio and they're asking $185 for a photo, $210 for a flat item.

"And somebody had a private signing with Ted Williams recently; they're asking $100 for a photo to be autographed. I can just imagine what Upper Deck is going to ask for having a photo or flat item autographed by Mantle once they start doing it.

"It's got to get to a point where they're just going to price themselves out," continued Schackman. "Who's going to want to go out and spend $200 to get something autographed by Joe DiMaggio anymore? And look at all the dead Hall of Famers; their baseballs are still under $100."

Schackman displays his autographed photo collection in binders. "I have them broken down into different categories with the wire photos from rookie shots, action shots, single shots and multiple autographs, three or four players together. Those I enjoy. I enjoy getting a photo with four or five people in there who are still alive and the hunt to try and get them autographed.

"I had one photo that took me almost a year to get finished. It was a photo of the Yankees coming into Milwaukee. I think it was in '57 for the World Series, and they were getting off the airplane. They were standing on the rollaway staircase, there must have been about seven or eight of them. It took me almost a year to get all those players, either through the mail, mailing it directly to the player, or waiting to see them at card shows. I enjoy those the most."

Another of Schackman's prize items is a 1960 uniform of Mantle's. "I have the pants and shirt," he said. "What I did was I bought a mannequin. There's a new type of mannequin that's almost like the old pipe cleaners. They're made out of foam and wire inside where you can shape it and sculpture it into any shape you want — it's like a sports-type mannequin.

"But I have the uniform on that, and I have the arms bent and it's holding a bat. I've got a batting helmet on it, and it looks real nice when you're walking through the room seeing a mannequin standing there holding a bat."

Another unique piece of Mantle memorabilia Schack-

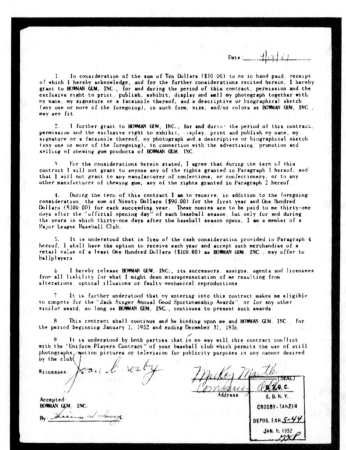

Mantle's 1951 Bowman baseball card contract.

man owns is Mantle's first Topps and Bowman contracts. "Yes, I have the original Topps contract that he signed in 1952, along with the check that Topps gave him for $50; of course, it's endorsed on the back. And I have the '51 Bowman contract that he signed also."

Schackman owns two Mantle game-used bats. "One is a regular bat and the other is his 1953 All-Star bat, game-used bat, from Cincinnati. That was his first All-Star game. I guess that's a significant bat, being his first All-Star game."

So, with all the rare and unusual Mantle items in Schackman's possession, what's left for him to collect?

"Actually, the only thing that I don't have now is, I guess, a glove, an actual game-used glove. I have a few mint model Rawlings gloves from the '50s, kids models. I have a left-handed glove and a right-handed glove, but they're just models, autographed models. But I don't have an actual game-used glove. Those are, I imagine, very scarce."

Another item Schackman has that would be the envy of most Yankee-Mantle collectors is a complete run of autographed team balls from 1951-1968, the length of Mantle's career.

"I had a friend over the other day and I was showing him the evolution of the autograph and we were looking at the balls and how his (Mantle's) autograph had changed through the years. Now, it's the same autograph that has been evolving since around '61 or '62.

"I have a complete run of all the Yankee yearbooks that he was in. Actually, I started in '50, which was the first Yankee yearbook," said Schackman. "I go from '50 through '68, and I also have his 1949 Independence Yankees yearbook. I'm sure there's not too many of those around. It pictures him as a switch-hitting shortstop for the Independence Yankees. He actually came up as a shortstop, but he always overthrew first base, and, of course, they had Rizzuto."

(12-face)

(12-back)

Mantle was given this watch after the 1964 World Series.

Schackman also owns Mantle's watch from the 1964 World Series. "The 1964 Yankees lost the World Series to St. Louis, and in lieu of getting a ring, I don't know if the whole team got it or what, but Mickey was given a Rolex watch which is inscribed on the back the '1964 World Series' and it has the Yankee emblem on it. I wear that occasionally when I wear the ring."

Does Schackman ever tire of his search for new Mantle items? "Not really," he said, "although I go to card shows and 99 percent of the time I never find anything there. I look, but I never find anything. Basically the dealers, or an auction, will pop up with something unusual or different. Even photos — every so often I'll go to a show and I'll find something.

"It's amazing to me that I can still find something once in a while. My memory is that I can't remember what I had for lunch two days ago, but I can go to a show and look through a dealer's photos, maybe 50 or 100 photos, and know if I have every one of them or not."

I can top that!

I knew I had to write after reading Bob Lemke's column about the huge store display for the 1962 Post cereal cards ("The Bleacher Bum," Feb. 18).

I agree, that is a "great" item. I have a "great" item myself. I may not have all the pictures of Mickey Mantle, but I think I have the biggest.

Enclosed is a photo of the Mick on a billboard in the Allentown, Pa., area. The billboard comes in 12 sections — six on the top, six on the bottom. In the photo, I'm holding the "T-2" section. Each section measures 5 feet by three-and-a-half feet, making the entire poster 10 feet high and 21 feet long. The billboard sections were given to me by Dave Hammes, opertions manager of Creative Displays in Allentown.

The billboard only appeared in two states that I know of — Pennsylvania and New York. It is one of my most prized possessions, and, like the cereal display, there is never going to be that many around. It's most likely one-of-a-kind.

Wouldn't the Post Cereal display and the billboard make a stunning display side by side? — *Joe Balitza, Palmerton, Pa., March 18, 1983, Sports Collectors Digest Reader Reaction*

Chapter 3

The legend lives on

Memories of "The Mick" live on

By Rich Marazzi

If the game of baseball ever had a nearly perfect fictitious character, it was probably Mickey Mantle. He is blonde, handsome and well-muscled. Combine this with his Oklahoma country boy innocence and his ability to hit a baseball to another planet, and the image is perfect America — like apple pie and Chevrolet. Maybe he was the real Roy Hobbs, certainly the Frank Merriwell of his day.

The greatest switch-hitter of all time, "The Mick" hit 536 home runs, including a record 18 in World Series competition. Ten times he homered from both sides in the same game. He won the Triple Crown in 1956 when he batted .353 with 52 four-baggers and 130 RBI. He won the A.L. MVP award three times (1956, 1957, 1962) and was selected for 20 All-Star games. Mantle played more games as a Yankee (2,401) than any other player, despite his injury-plagued career.

On top of this, he had lightning speed. Stretching a single into a double with his patented stand-up slide was a thing of beauty that brought fans to their collective feet. After he walloped a 565-foot moon shot off Senators' pitcher Chuck Stobbs in 1953, the blast was measured by Yankees' PR director Arthur Patterson. Thus came the birth of tape measure homers.

Mantle was part of 12 Yankee pennants and 7 world championships which overshadowed his then-record 1,170 strikeouts.

"The Mick"
MICKEY MANTLE

The greatest switch-hitter ever, Mickey Mantle.

Mickey was exciting to watch. His walk from the on-deck circle to the battor's box was always greeted by a loud crescendo of cheers, jeers, boos, you name it. Nobody ever had that charisma.

Whether you loved or hated him, he kidnapped your emotions. There have been others with more glamorous statistics, but few, if any, had the presence like Mantle. His baseball card prices today reflect the aftershock of his brilliant career. Mickey's lifetime .298 average doesn't tell the story.

In recent years much has been written about the other side of this baseball hero. He was not the model shy country boy that fans gawked at from the grandstand. The man definitely had impurities, he was no gem. Mickey swung just as hard after hours as he did in the batter's box.

In his 1985 publication titled "The Mick," he admits to not being a good family man. He confesses to heavy drinking, carousing and frolicking with his buddies after dark. He led a dangerous social life, like a highwire act in a windstorm.

Once driving while intoxicated with his wife Merlyn in the car, he crashed into a telephone pole. But the police covered for him and there weren't any drunken driving charges filed. Both he and his wife avoided serious injury. Spending time hunting and in gin mills often took priority over time spent at home with his wife and four sons. This is something he painfully regrets.

I had a chance to chat with Mickey a few weeks ago on a warm July night at Yankee Stadium. The ex-Yankee slugger talked about his childhood in Commerce, Okla.

"I had about 10 friends. We would choose up sides every day and play all day long. I really believe that might be the best thing to do for young kids. Sometimes I would hit 100 times a day. Experience is a great teacher.

"I was lucky I had a father that knew a lot about baseball. My dad was a great student of the game. He knew that someday there would be platooning in baseball. If I would hit both ways, I would have a lot better chance of playing. The day I joined the Yankees is when Casey Stengel started to platoon."

Born in 1931, Mickey was raised during the Great Depression, a period the Mantles struggled to survive. His dearly loved father, Mutt Mantle, was a farmer and later a lead miner. Mickey was named after Mickey Cochrane, the Hall of Fame catcher who was deeply admired by Mutt. But Mickey's first idol played in St. Louis.

"My first hero was Stan Musial. I grew up in northeastern Oklahoma about 200 miles from St. Louis. We didn't have TV so we listened to the radio all of the time. Harry Caray used to broadcast the games.

"When I saw Joe DiMaggio he became my idol. Then I saw Ted Williams hit. I think he's the greatest hitter that ever lived so he became my idol," said Mickey.

Mantle's body was packed together well as a young kid. A three-sport star in school, Mickey was playing long ball during his scholastic days. One of his hitting exhibitions brought him a sum of money that almost got him in trouble. He explained:

"I hit three home runs in Baxter Springs, Kan., playing in a Ban Johnson League. The fans took up a collection and gave me $58. I took the money because in those days it was a lot of money. My dad only made $50 a week working in the mines.

"The coach, from Picher, Okla., called the coach at Commerce. He said if I kept that money that would make me a professional and they wouldn't let me play football my senior year." The money was returned.

Three legends — Joe DiMaggio, Mickey Mantle and Ted Williams

Not being able to play football would have been a crushing blow to Mickey since the pigskin sport was his favorite. He modestly boasted, "I wasn't a headbutter, but if I got around I could out-run everybody."

Shortly after high school Mantle was signed to a Yankee contract as a shortstop by scout Tom Greenwade for the remainder of the summer and a $1,000 bonus.

Mickey's first stop was with Independence in the Class D Kansas, Oklahoma and Missouri League, where he played under Harry Craft, a man he highly respected. One of his teammates was the colorful Lou Skizas, who Mantle calls "A pre-fifties hippie from the streets and alleys of Chicago who had a girl under his arm before and after every game."

Mantle batted .313 at Independence, but made 47 errors at shortstop. The next year (1950) he played in Joplin, where he was reunited with Craft and hit .383 with 26 homers. At the end of the season he joined the Yankees at Sportsman's Park in St. Louis during the club's final two-week swing as a non-roster player, but did not see any action. Because of his erratic arm he eventually switched to the outfield.

In 1951, the Yankees and Giants switched spring training camps with the Yankees going to Phoenix, Ariz., and the Giants to St. Petersburg, Fla. Mantle was an amalgam of

Ruth and Cobb, hitting home runs and batting .402. It proved to be his ticket to the big leagues.

The Yankees' scheduled opener in Washington was rained out, so the team returned to New York to open against the Red Sox. The Yankee lineup read: Jackie Jensen (LF), Phil Rizzuto (SS), Mantle (RF), DiMaggio (CF), Yogi Berra (C), Johnny Mize (1B), Gil McDougald (3B), Jerry Coleman (2B) and Vic Raschi (P). Before the game, Berra walked up to Mantle and said, "Hey kid, are you nervous?"

Mickey looked at him and said, "No."

Yogi joked, "Well, how come you're wearing your jockstrap on the outside of your uniform?"

Mantle managed to scratch out a few hits, but went 0-for-April as far as home runs were concerned. The glitter and tinsel of the majors was no longer fun. Going to the park became a hassle as fans jeered and taunted him. His mastery of kicking water coolers and smashing bats grabbed more headlines than his play on the field. Still today, Mickey has never outgrown his short fuse temper for losing.

"It was a bad fault that I had. I never did really get over it. I still can't stand to lose. If I'm playing golf and make a bad shot, I'll throw a golf club. The other day I hit a caddy in the back with a sand wedge. It's a bad habit. But, I'd rather see a guy who gets mad when he doesn't do good than one who doesn't care."

In mid-July of his rookie year, Mantle was sent to Kansas City, a Triple A affiliate of the Yankees. He was dejected and his confidence cracked like a broken bat, but his father influenced him to stay. In the next few weeks he went on a tear, hitting .361 with 11 home runs and 50 RBI. It was back to New York. When he returned he was like an IBM stock to the Yankees; their future was guaranteed.

Mutt Mantle came to New York for the World Series between the Yankees and the Giants. What should have been a joyful time for both father and son turned into a tragedy. In the sixth inning of Game Two, Mantle, playing right field, converged on a

Courtesy B&E Collectibles

Mantle admits he had a short fuse as a youngster.

68

high pop fly in right-center field between him and DiMaggio. Mickey heard "DiMag" yell "I got it," and held up, catching his spikes on the rubber cover of a drain hole burried in the grass. Ironically, it was Willie Mays, his city rival, who hit the ball. Mantle was removed from the game and his leg was wrapped.

The next day, Mickey entered the Lenox Hill Hospital accompanied by his dad, who collapsed when his injured son leaned on him on a curb. Both ended up as hospital roommates. Mickey's knee was operated on for torn ligaments while his father was diagnosed as having Hodgkin's disease, a cancer that strikes the body's lymph nodes. Mutt lost his battle with the disease at age 39, a heartbreaking loss for Mickey.

Mantle's World Series mishap was the beginning of a career marred by injuries and infirmities. He lamented, "It did hinder my career a lot. I think I could have hit 600 home runs."

Generally speaking, World Series time triggered Mickey's juices. He was really the first "Mr. October" with his 18 round-trippers. When asked about those famous subway series between the Yanks and Dodgers during the 1950s, he smiled and said, "I loved it. City against city right here in town. I used to love the bus rides from downtown. The Yankees would leave Yankee Stadium and pick up Billy Martin and me and go over to Brooklyn. If we beat them, the Brooklyn fans would throw tomatoes at us while we were in the bus leaving the park."

One has to wonder what Mickey would have done had he played in cozy Ebbets Field instead of the gaping chasms of death valley in Yankee Stadium.

"If I played in Ebbet's Field or maybe Detroit, I would have hit over 700 home runs. When I played, Yankee Stadium was 461-feet to dead center, 457 to left center, and 407 to right center."

Since Mickey was not a pull hitter he figures that he lost at least 10 home runs a year at Yankee Stadium. Multiply that times his 18 years and that's another 180 that could have been added to his lifetime total of 536.

World Series time also had its moments for Mickey. Take the 1960 autumnal classic when the Yankees lost to the Pirates. The Bronx Bombers scored 55 runs compared to 27 for the Bucs. New York batted .338 while Pittsburgh had a club average of .256.

Maris and Mantle hit 115 home runs in 1961.

MICKEY MANTLE

Had he played in Detroit, Mantle might have hit 700 home runs.

Mickey simply says, "With the exception of my dad dying, it was the biggest disappointment in my life."

The 1961 season was an epic year for the Yankees and baseball. Roger Maris set a new home run mark with 61 and Mantle trailed with 54. The team hit a major league record 240 home runs. Some baseball savants say that this was the greatest team ever assembled. Was this the greatest team Mantle ever played on?

"That's pretty hard to say because the first team I played on in 1951 won five straight World Series; that's not too shabby. The pitching staff with Allie Reynolds, Eddie Lopat, Vic Raschi and Whitey Ford was one of the best. I believe the 1961 team was the best offensive and defensive team I played on."

Tales of Mantle and Maris feuding were media garbage. During the '61 season, Mantle shared an apartment with Maris and Bob Cerv in Queens, N.Y., close to Kennedy airport. They were close friends for many years. Before Roger lost his battle with cancer, Mickey was a faithful caller.

In today's age of megabucks contracts and player agents, Mantle would have commanded an astronomical salary. But back in the '50s, the owners called the shots. Mickey's contract squabbles with Yankee General Manager George Weiss almost seems like a fairy tale today. In '56 when Mantle won the Triple Crown he made $32,500. He hoped to double his salary the following year.

Weiss balked, but co-owner Del Webb came through with $65,000. Weiss went as far as threatening to send Mickey to Cleveland for Herb Score and Rocky Colavito. He even pulled out a detective's report that outlined some of Mantle's and roommate Billy Martin's escapades.

Weiss was tough for Mickey to deal with. In 1957, Mickey won his second straight MVP award and was offered a $5,000 cut in salary, but settled for a small raise. Between '58 and '59 he was raised $2,000 and was cut $10,000 prior to the '60 season.

Such absurd management tactics were common during the pre-union days. It's no wonder that Marvin Miller and the players' union gained the strength they did.

Can you imagine Mantle negotiating with George Steinbrenner and his liberal check book? Would Mickey have liked to play for George?

"Sure — first of all I'd be making about 2-3 million dollars a year. I'm a tough loser and he hates to lose, too," stated Mantle.

During the mid-60s, the Yankee dynasty suddenly collapsed with a dramatic thud. Mickey reasoned, "Everybody got old at the same time. It was like a balloon busting. Also, when other teams were paying the big bonuses, Dan Topping and Del Webb (Yankee owners) didn't come out with the $50,000 bonuses, so the minor league system deteriorated."

In the late-1960s, teams pitched around Mantle. Watching Mickey walk to first base became a boring side show. Opposing pitchers weren't too worried about pitching to names like Charley Smith, Steve Whitaker and Bobby Cox.

On March 1, 1969, Mickey announced his retirement. Five years later he was inducted into the Baseball Hall of Fame with his buddy Whitey Ford.

Like his playing career, his post playing days have been a mix of success and failures in the business world. His son Billy was diagnosed with Hodgkin's disease nine years ago. The disease which has plagued the Mantle family is fortunately in remission at this writing.

Bowie Kuhn's ridiculous banning of Mickey from baseball because of his association with the Claridge Hotel in Atlantic City where he does PR work was lifted by current commissioner Peter Ueberroth. Mickey also does public relations assignments for the

Reserve Life Insurance Co. in Dallas and is a commentator for Yankee games on cable television.

The argument still rages on as to who was the greatest center fielder in New York during the 1950s. Was it Mickey or the Duke? Mickey shared his thoughts:

"I never felt a personal rivalry while it was going on. Mays has some great statistics. He played many years without getting hurt. The bottom line is what you have to look at and he had it. As for me, Willie and 'The Duke,' Willie was the greatest." But he added, "There were four or five years through there when I was better than he was."

True — maybe better than anyone who ever played the game. — *Rich Marazzi, Batting the Breeze, Feb. 13, 1987*

Talkin' baseball — Willie, Mickey and the Duke.

Starring "Mick" and "Slick"
Yank fantasy camp fulfills middle-agers' dreams

By Kevin Huard

"I have been an avid Yankee fan since I knew how to say baseball and a serious collector of baseball cards and Yankee memorabilia for the past 10 years. When I read about the Mickey Mantle/Whitey Ford Fantasy Baseball Camp and found out that I could spend a week with Mickey, my childhood hero, and Whitey and many other of my heroes from the 1950s and '60s, I knew I had to go.

"The players have been great and the stories from Skowron, Bauer and Slaughter have been priceless. Getting three hits off Ron Guidry and one each off Catfish Hunter and Whitey Ford was a big thrill. I couldn't wait every morning to put on the Yankee pinstripes and get out on the field. Watching the fans from the field, instead of watching the players from the stands, is a picture your mind will never forget." — *Barry Gordon, age 44*

If you are a Yankee fan between the ages of 25 and 80, maybe somewhat out of shape, and game to live out dreams of your childhood, the Mickey Mantle/Whitey Ford baseball Fantasy Camp could be a momentary fountain of youth for you.

In November of last year, I had the pleasure of being invited to the camp by Camp Administrator Wanda Greer. From the moment my plane touched down in Florida, until the time I departed, it was like 1961 all over again.

I had the opportunity to watch grown men (they're called campers) forget their workday pressures and live out their dream by playing ball and socializing with their heroes.

The memories are guaranteed to last a lifetime.

Imagine, if you will, sitting in the dugout listening to Ralph Houk and Hank Bauer discussing game strategy; Mickey Mantle telling jokes to Johnny Blanchard and Moose Skowron — that's just a little flavor of what the camp is like.

The fantasy campers come in all shapes and sizes. They come from all walks of life. And they're not all thirty-something Wall Street stockbrokers. There are firefighters, pharmacists, detectives, merchants, insurance salesmen, doctors, construction workers, truck drivers, even a famous musician and composer (Marvin Hamlisch).

One 60-year-old retired store owner, Al Abrams, was attending his 44th baseball fantasy camp. The average age of the campers was 45. The oldest camper was 71 years young.

In many instances, registration in the camp is a special birthday, anniversary or holiday gift from a wife or other loved one.

Physically, campers came in varying degrees of fitness. Most campers visited the trainer's room at least one time for strains, sore muscles, pulled ligaments or other assorted aches and pains.

The combined efforts of Wanda Greer, her husband Mike, Whitey and Mickey, the coaches, trainers, cameramen, equipment people and groundskeepers make for a professionally-run camp that provides memories that last a lifetime.

From a personal standpoint, it was great to get together again with my friend, Mickey Mantle Jr. Mickey Jr. was a participant in the camp and exhibited his slugging skills by hitting a home run in one of his at bats — shades of his famous dad.

The most enjoyable part of the camp for me was talking with some of the former Yankee greats. I had the opportunity to interview Mickey Mantle.

SCD: Do you think there are people who might be out there selling forged Mickey Mantle autographs?

Mantle: I don't know. They say that there are people who are doing Roger (Maris), Joe (DiMaggio), Ted Williams and myself. If I see one that I don't think is me, I'll say so. I've seen a few like that. But most of them are mine, I think.

SCD: Your signature has changed a little bit over the years.

Mantle: It's changed a heck of a lot since my first years. It hasn't changed much since collecting has become big. Ever since I've been signing things at card shows, it's been about the same.

SCD: You've done a couple of Willie, Mickey and the Duke shows together with Willie Mays and Duke Snider.

Mantle: We did one together down in Atlanta that turned out great.

SCD: Frank Robinson had some words of praise about the 1961 Yankee team you played on. It was perhaps one of the greatest teams of all time.

Mantle: We had a heck of an infield. It was one of the best infields ever put together. Bobby Richardson, Tony Kubek, Clete Boyer. (Moose) Skowron was on that team, too. Moose hit 28 home runs. The catchers hit about 60 home runs. Elston (Howard), Yogi (Berra) and Johnny (Blanchard) hit about 60 home runs together.

SCD: Your restaurant in New York is popular with fans.

Mantle: I enjoy it. When I'm in New York I go there almost every day. It's doing real good. People have a good time there.

SCD: There are a lot of collectibles and memorabilia items on display there.

Mantle: I've got a lot of stuff that is my own there. Somebody gave me a painting of me and Roger together. It's in the back booth on the right-hand side. We call it the Roger Maris booth. It's got the painting of me and him and he gave me a baseball just before he died with his picture on one side.

He signed it to me. It says, "To Mickey, the greatest of them all." It's encased. We had a charity auction at the restaurant and there were some balls that we auctioned off with (Don) Mattingly's picture on one side and mine on the other.

SCD: You mentioned that you never really collected baseball cards of yourself, but you used to bring home cards for your kids.

Mantle: They (Topps) used to send us boxes of gum cards and my boys would take the gum out and throw the cards away. — *Kevin Huard, Feb. 2, 1990*

Classic Mantle photo Ray Gallo's "claim to fame"

By Tom Mortenson

When Rhode Island portrait photographer Ray Gallo got a call from the William Esty Advertising Co. of Oxford, N.Y., in September of 1956, he was delighted...

"They wanted to know if I'd be interested in photographing Mickey Mantle for them," recalls Gallo.

"I was shocked. I couldn't understand why they had singled me out to do 'The Mick.'

Ray Gallo's claim to fame is a classic Mantle photo.

74

Just imagine, here I was getting the chance to photograph my hero, the idol of all baseball," he says.

Gallo remembers vividly the night he went to Boston's Fenway Park to take the photograph.

"It was Ralph Terry's debut — he was getting his brains beat out. I remember Casey Stengel was at the top of the dugout, screaming his lungs out. He was saying some words that couldn't be printed in a family magazine," remembers Gallo.

After the game, Sy Mann of the Esty Co. introduced Gallo to his subject, the 25-year-old Mickey Mantle. It was the year that Mantle was tearing up the American League, finishing with a .353 average, 130 RBI and 52 homers (several of them tape measure shots).

He went on to win the triple crown that year.

Yet, despite all the fame, adoration, and media attention heaped on the young

MICKEY MANTLE

The "Mighty Mick" of '56

The "Mighty Mick" of 1956, his Triple Crown year.

Mantle, Ray Gallo knew that the center fielder was a relatively shy, humble subject, someone not always easily accessible for photographers.

Once introduced, Mantle asked Gallo how he wanted him to pose. Gallo responded by telling him to relax. "Just be Mickey Mantle, the ballplayer," Gallo said.

Today, Gallo recalls, "He was in the dugout, and I tried to get him to relax. I directed him to cross his legs.

"I used a 2 1/4 Graflex Speed Graphic press camera. I was getting it focused and (Mantle) asked me, 'What will this picture be used for?' I told him it was going on the cover of The Christian Science Monitor. Well, he breaks out with this grin and I snapped the shutter," says Gallo about his unique shot.

"I only took one exposure...I knew I had it," he beams.

Gallo sent the print to the Esty Co. and received numerous compliments.

"People who saw the photograph thought that it was the best Mantle photo they had ever seen, including The Mick himself," tells Gallo. "He has a print of it in his office in Dallas."

Noted collector Barry Halper also owns a print, according to Gallo.

For 25 years, Gallo himself had an original black-and-white print hanging in his studio. "One day a few years ago someone came in and said, 'that print belongs in the Hall,'" Gallo said. He then contacted Hall of Fame director Howard Talbot Jr. to inquire if they were interested. They were. A 24" x 28" black-and-white print was handpainted in color by Yvette Andreoni and donated to the Hall of Fame in 1982.

Since photographing Mantle in 1956, the 65-year-old Gallo has gone on to produce several award-winning pieces. He has photographed other celebrities, including Presidents Reagan and Kennedy, Robert Kennedy and Eleanor (Mrs. Lou) Gehrig, as well as other ballplayers. These include Joe DiMaggio, Ted Williams, "Pudge" Fisk, Rocky Colavito and Bud Harrelson.

But the Mantle photo is the one that stands out in Ray's mind.

"It's my claim to fame," he says. — *Tom Mortenson, Nov. 29, 1991*

Mickey's Place showcases rare memorabilia

By Dave Moriah

The exterior of Mickey's Place in Cooperstown, N.Y.

So, your cousin Freddy thinks he's pretty hot stuff at Mickey Mantle trivia, does he? He's got all the key numbers down on the guy who wore #7 (and #6 early in his career) — 52 homers, 130 RBI and a .353 average in the Triple Crown year of 1956, 536 lifetime homers, 18 in the World Series, etc. etc. etc. You've never been able to stump him. Until now.

Next time you see Freddy, ask him this one. What was the Mick's selective service number? That's right, the one on his draft card. When Freddy starts whimpering and begging for the answer, you can tell him with absolute certainty it is #34-60-31-165.

Mickey's Place is a mini Hall of Fame.

You don't believe me? You can check out the actual dog-eared draft card behind a glass case in a most extraordinary display of unusual, vintage memorabilia in Cooperstown, N.Y. No, it's not in the official National Baseball Hall of Fame Museum. It's across the street in a store called "Mickey's Place."

Actually, to call Mickey's Place merely a store is to do it a disservice. The sign out front announces it as a "Baseball & Sports Emporium," which is not a bad crack at summing up the history-rich environment inside. Yes, there are current baseball cards, 8-by-10-inch autographed photos and similar staples of the card shop world.

But as you go deeper into the spacious display area, which covers two large floors, you are transported into a collector's paradise. You are surrounded by vintage uniforms, weather-beaten gloves used by Hall of Famers, a Most Valuable Players trophy from the 1950s, and a mind-boggling array of Mickey Mantle memorabilia, almost all of which is autographed.

You pinch yourself to be sure you haven't stumbled onto a remote wing of the Baseball Hall of Fame by mistake. No, it can't be the Hall for one key reason — many of these items have price tags on them! (Note: The Hall of Fame has a strict policy of neither purchasing nor selling any true memorabilia. It does have a gift shop and catalog business featuring mass produced items.)

Mickey's Place is undeniably the "clean-up hitter" in the rich lineup of baseball-related businesses on Cooperstown's Main Street. Although Mantle has no direct connection to the enterprise, the friendship between the Yankee legend and Mickey's

Place co-owner Tom Catal is what sets the store apart in Cooperstown's crowded marketplace.

Mickey's Place specializes in memorabilia of New York baseball teams in general, and Mantle items are one of a kind and intensely personal, like the aforementioned draft card or his genuine Texas cowboy hat. Both of them were given to Catal directly by Mantle.

"One day I was over at Mickey's house in Dallas and he emptied out his wallet for me," Catal reported. He added, "I've got a couple of other cowboy hats of his, just like that one, at home."

The story of how Catal, a former government bond broker in New York City, came to be a buddy of the great Mickey Mantle is a simple one. It's also every show promoter's wildest fantasy.

"I was the promoter at the first card show Mickey ever did," Catal said. "It was back in 1979 at Hofstra University on Long Island. At the end of it Mickey turned to me and said, 'Tommy, I had a really good time. If you'd ever like me back, just call my agent.'

"So, I called him in again. At the second show he asked me to go out with him for a drink. I said I couldn't leave right then, so he asked for my home phone number and said he'd call me the next time he came to New York.

"I went home and thought, sure, Mickey Mantle is going to call me at home! But in a couple of weeks he did. We went out one night and pretty soon he'd look me up when he came to New York and I'd visit him when I was in Dallas."

By the way, the fee Catal paid Mantle for that appearance was a whopping $2,500!

Mickey's Place, a baseball and sports emporium.

"That was a lot of money at the time," remembered Catal. "Believe it or not, the way we set up was a $3 admission charge and everyone got a free autograph. I managed to lose a few hundred dollars on the whole deal."

All in all, the few hundred dollars turned out to be a good investment. His access to Mantle has yielded an astounding number of autographs on a dazzling array of items, though Catal refused to sell anything of a personal nature which Mantle gave him as an act of friendship.

"Some of my favorite items are not for sale. There's a game-used glove, Mickey's Texas license plate, a signed program from a baseball tour to Japan." And of course, the draft card.

Whether for sale or not, all of it is on display at the store. And if Mantle memorabilia is the main course, make sure you save room for the dessert bar! There's plenty of it.

Mickey's Place also sports many other rare, and frequently expensive, memorabilia from baseball's past. Befitting its location in Cooperstown, Catal specializes in autographs and artifacts of Hall of Famers.

"I like letters, or anything that really reveals the game and the times," Catal explained as he exhibited several framed examples.

There are two which date back almost 50 years and offer proof, as if we need it, that there was a far simpler and more personal era of player-fan relations.

A signed letter on vintage St. Louis Brown stationery is from Hall of Famer Rogers Hornsby, thanking a fan for his recent letter of support for the hapless Browns team he was managing. In the other, Joe DiMaggio wrote on Yankees stationery apologizing to a youngster for his delay in responding to an autograph request!

Three autographed Babe Ruth items are also on display and for sale. The most poignant and historically interesting was a photo of the Babe at home plate during his farewell day at Yankee Stadium, signed in his familiar script during the last days of his life. It was available at $2,395.

Rivaling Mantle's draft card in the category of "Bizarre personal sundries of the rich & famous" was the social security card of Hall of Fame pitcher Charles A. "Chief" Bender. Surely you would impress your cousin Freddy with the knowledge that Chief Bender's social security number was 182-03-5918.

Catal bought the Bender card at a Leland's auction for "about $350." Many of the rare and expensive items in the store came through Leland's and Sotheby's recent auctions.

Other material comes in off the street. "There seems to be a lot of older, quality baseball articles around Cooperstown. Sometimes people just walk in with it after cleaning out their attics or barns," Catal said.

Celebrities come in off the street as well. Catal's favorite was actor Charlie Sheen, who recently received hobby notoriety by purchasing the controversial Bill Buckner error ball. Sheen spent about $9,000 at Mickey's Place, buying a 1923 World Series press pin and several other collectibles.

"He was in with his father, Martin Sheen, and one thing led to another and suddenly we were out in the middle of Main Street on a quiet winter day playing football in the street!"

Joe Jackson's nephew was in town in 1992 for the induction ceremonies and stopped in the store. He showed off his uncle's 1917 World Series ring and told Catal a touching story.

A display of vintage memorabilia at Mickey's Place.

"He said that Shoeless Joe said to him on his deathbed, 'Wear that ring proudly. I never threw a game.'"

New in 1993 at Mickey's Place is an upstairs display area entitled "Subway Series." Dedicated to the great New York teams of the 1950s, it is filled with mementos of Mickey, Willie and the Duke. To set the right ambience, there is a continual showing of films like the "Babe Ruth Story" and "Pride of the Yankees."

A visit by anyone who remembers Ebbets Field, the Polo Grounds, or "old" Yankee Stadium is sure to trigger a rush of memories (and perhaps an irresistible urge to reach for the checkbook!)

Mickey's Place is open year round. In the summertime, expect to elbow your way through the crowds; from October through April you can have the place to yourself. It's a pace that suits the former Wall Street bond broker.

"The pace is very concentrated for four or five months, which is just long enough for me. I'd go crazy standing in a store all year long," Catal said. "Then the winter comes and we can take it easy, buy some stuff and work on the store."

The "we" of Mickey's Place includes Catal, business partner Vin Russo, store manager Andrew Vilacky and several part-timers for the busy summer season. Their formula seems to be working. Though reluctant to reveal gross revenues for 1992, Catal doesn't hesitate to say, "It was a very good year."

Cooperstown cash registers have been singing the past few years, seemingly immune to the well-publicized slump in memorabilia sales around the nation. It's a marketplace which is booming but volatile, with storefronts changing like free agents in the off season.

Mickey's Place has survived more than three years in such a climate, and has become a star attraction for those who value older, more unusual items. Your cousin Freddy would love it! — *Dave Moriah, Aug. 27, 1993*

Chuck Stobbs
Senator lefty served up Mantle's 565-foot clout

By Fluffy Saccucci

On April 17, 1953, at Washington's Griffith Stadium, Mickey Mantle stepped to the plate batting right-handed in the fifth inning with a man on, two out and the Yanks leading 2-1.

With one mighty swing he blasted a 1-0 fastball from Senators' lefty Chuck Stobbs completely out of the ballpark. It was a prodigious drive to left that was later measured out to be a major league record 565 feet!

Stobbs, in recalling that monster shot by Mantle, very calmly said, "I threw the ball, he hit it, and then it went for a home run," but he quickly added that the ball traveled as far as it did because the wind was blowing out a gale that day.

Stobbs went on to say that the titanic homer didn't make much difference to him until people started making comments and gestures about it soon afterwards.

Left-hander Chuck Stobbs compiled a 107-130 record during his 15-year major league career, pitching for the Red Sox, White Sox, Senators, Cardinals and Twins. He is best remembered for giving up Mickey Mantle's 565-foot home run at Washington's Griffith Stadium in 1953.

Chuck Stobbs served up Mantle's 565-footer.

"When I came out to the ballpark the next day, the team's game sponsor, National Bohemian beer, had put a ball up on their sign in left field near where Mantle's ball went out of the park and then all of a sudden I thought, 'Did it really go that far?'" he asked.

Stobbs said that he'd rather be noted for some other things than the long blast and added, "But at least I'm noted for something, I guess, whether good, bad or indifferent."

Of the 183 homers he allowed over his major league career, Stobbs couldn't recall giving up many tape-measure shots, but figured there must have been a few and added, "None stick out significantly in my mind as much as Mantle's. "

In deference to Stobbs, however, he did enjoy some success pitching versus Mantle. "One of the best years I ever had against Mantle I think he went 2-for-25 or -26 against me," recalled Stobbs. "That particular season he had two singles up the middle and nobody ever said anything about that!"

An accomplished major leaguer over his 15-year career between 1947 and 1961 with the Red Sox, White Sox, Senators, Cardinals and Twins, Stobbs chalked up some fairly impressive numbers. They included a 107-130 won-lost record in 459 game appearances, 897 strikeouts and an ERA of 4.29.

Stobbs considered 1956 his best year, when he compiled a 15-15 record for the Senators. "Because that's the most games I ever won in a season, and when you win 15 for a last-place club I think you did pretty well," he explained.

The Shot That Shook the Records

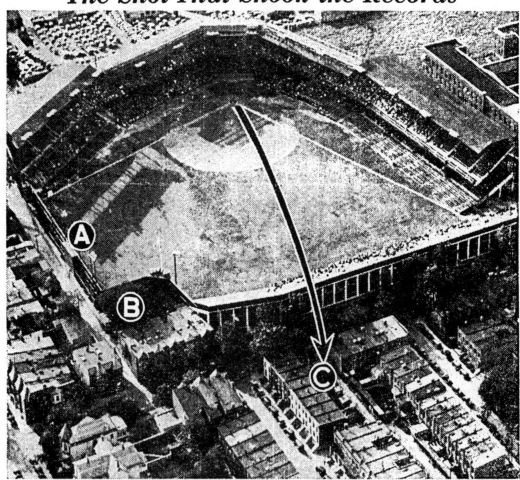

—Photo by United Press and N. Y. Daily News

THE TRAJECTORY of Mickey Mantle's tremendous homer at Griffith Stadium, April 17. The ball traveled 565 feet before landing in a yard (C) beyond the left field wall. Herculean drives in the past by Jimmie Foxx and Joe DiMaggio in the same direction landed high up in the bleachers. Other colossal clouts were hit by Larry Doby (A) and Babe Ruth (B).

Where it started at and where it ended up...

On the flip side, Stobbs considered 1957 his worst year when he went 8-20 with the Senators.

"That was my worst season because I came off such a good year in '56. I'd been successful before, but all of a sudden I asked myself if I was ever going to win or if I was even in the right profession, and I ended up with doubts," he said.

The most memorable game for Stobbs came when he started on Opening Day 1954 at Griffith Stadium.

"Then-President Dwight D. Eisenhower threw out the first ball and in that game I went 8 2/3 innings and we (the Senators) ended up beating the Yankees 5-3 in 10 innings on a Mickey Vernon two-run homer," recalled Stobbs.

Stobbs told *SCD* the two toughest hitters he ever faced were George Kell and Joe DeMaestri.

"Kell was a super hitter who really hit the ball well, and DeMaestri was a tough hitter and I don't know if I ever got him out," remembered Stobbs.

Between Sept. 5, 1956, and June 21, 1957, Stobbs suffered through some adversity. In that stretch he lost 16 straight games.

Stobbs said that during that negative streak he pitched well in a few of the games and still didn't win, and added that later on in the streak he developed a mental block whereby he ended up having no confidence whatsoever.

"And certainly if you have no confidence in what you do, you're certainly not going to do it well," stated Stobbs.

Stobbs' favorite park to pitch in was Yankee Stadium and that was because of the publicity that one received pitching in New York.

"If you pitched well in New York, everybody knew about it because at that time everything that went on came out of New York, and if you beat the Yankees everybody knew about it," reflected Stobbs...

...Collectors and fans alike might like to know that if they are interested in checking out the bat that Mickey Mantle used to swat that record 565-foot home run and the ball that Stobbs served up for it, both souvenirs are on display at the Baseball Hall of Fame in Cooperstown, N.Y. — *Fluffy Saccucci, July 9, 1993*

The hardest shot Mickey Mantle ever hit

By Kevin Huard

Mickey Mantle made the term "tape measure home run" popular on April 17, 1953. Batting right-handed against Washington Senators pitcher Chuck Stobbs at Griffith Stadium, Mantle chrushed a fastball some 565 feet from home plate. The ball and the bat he used are now displayed at the Baseball Hall of Fame in Cooperstown, N.Y.

The ball that Mickey believes was the hardest one he ever hit was offered to him on the evening of May 22, 1963, at Yankee Stadium. The Yankees were playing the Kansas City A's. With the game

A's pitcher Bill Fischer.

tied at seven runs apiece going into the bottom of the ninth inning, A's manager Ed Lopat signaled for his best reliever, Bill Fischer.

Fischer had a 6-0 record at the time and was regarded by many as the best control pitcher in either league. His Major League record of 84.1 consecutive innings without giving up a walk was testimony to his excellent control.

Fischer retired the Yankees easily in the ninth and 10th innings. When the 11th inning began, the first batter he faced was Mickey Mantle. Mantle had not had a hit in the game at that time, although he had been on base three times with walks. With a bat borrowed from reserve first baseman Dale Long, Mantle quietly approached the plate.

Bill Fischer worked the count to 2-2 with curves and breaking stuff. On the second strike Mantle swung so hard and was fooled so badly on a curve that he almost went down. He stepped out of the box, regained his composure and stepped back in.

A's catcher Haywood Sullivan called for the next pitch to be a fastball. Fischer nodded his approval, wound up and fired a blazing fastball toward homeplate. Mantle was thinking fastball and wasn't about to be fooled this time. Then came the lightning.

Mantle swung with all his herculean power and sent the pitch rocketing skyward toward the light tower high above the right field roof. Observers in the press box estimated that the ball came within three feet of leaving the stadium.

They all agreed that the ball was still on the rise when it hit the steel facade. This was the second time Mantle nearly sent a ball soaring out of Yankee Stadium. The first one came on May 30, 1955, against the Senators' Pedro Ramos.

The Ramos home run hit the facade, but was a descending fly ball. The Fischer home run was a line shot still rising.

Recently Mickey had this to say about the mammoth (Fischer) blast: "If a ball could be hit 700 feet, this was the one. It definitely was the hardest ball I ever hit."

Mathematicians and physicists conservatively agree that the ball would have traveled a minimum of 625 feet if not impeded by the facade.

This is what observers had to say about the tremendous home run:

Yogi Berra: "That's it!"

(Umpire) Lou Dimuro: "I have never seen a ball hit as hard, or a man that swings as fast."

Jim Bouton: "How can you hit a ball that far?"

Bill Kunkel: "That son of a gun, zooooommmmmm."

Joe Pepitone: (shaking his head in amazement, then a slight grin) "I hit one like that when I was 15 and worked out here (Yankee Stadium)."

Whitey Ford: "I hit 'em that hard, only they don't go that far."

Bobby Richardson: "That would take four of my best shots."

Ralph Houk: "How would you like to have that chopped up in singles for the year? Seeing that was worth all agony I went through. If he had hit toward the bullpen it would have been out."

Tom Tresh: "I didn't think anybody could hit a ball that hard. You can't estimate how far that ball would have gone."

Hector Lopez: "That's the hardest ball I've seen hit in a long, long, long time."

Frank Crosetti: "That's the hardest I've ever seen anyone hit a ball. Foxx, Ruth, anybody. I don't believe a man can hit a ball any harder. It went out like it was shot out of a cannon."

Ralph Terry: (when asked if all Oklahomans hit like that) "There's only one man."

Norm Siebern: "He ought to have a league of his own. He's too much for everybody else."

Bill Fischer: "He gets $100,000 a year, I get $10,000. He has to be making it for some reason."

Credits: Sports Cavalcade, by Lou Sahadi, January 1964; The National Baseball Hall of Fame; *TV Guide*, January 1982.
— *Kevin Huard, Nov. 29, 1991*

Popular Hall of Famer talks about the hobby

By Kevin Huard

It could be argued that Mickey Mantle may not have been the greatest all-around player to ever play the game of baseball. Although he certainly did his share, he didn't hit the most home runs, drive in the most runs, or hit for the highest lifetime average. He isn't a miracle worker and he doesn't walk on water.

But just try convincing that to baseball-crazed fans who spent their youth in the '50s and '60s, especially New York Yankee fans. There's an aura that comes over them when discussing the Mick.

Mantle, who led the New York Yankees to 12 pennants during his 18-year career, is easily the single-most popular baseball player in the past 40

**Baseball's most popular player
in the last 40 years...**

years, and he's probably more popular today, nearly a quarter century after his retirement, than he was then. Collectors know of his popularity. His baseball cards and memorabilia are some of the most expensive and most sought-after in the hobby.

Born and raised in Oklahoma, the "Commerce Comet," who was named after Mickey Cochrane by his father, flashed onto the major league baseball scene in 1951, during Joe DiMaggio's final season. Although Mantle slumped during his rookie season and was sent back to the minor leagues for a time, he gave fans an indication of what was to come with 13 home runs, 65 runs batted in and a .267 batting average.

A possessor of blinding speed before an assortment of leg injuries slowed him, Mantle was just as likely to drag bunt for a base hit as slam one over the wall. He, in a nutshell, could do it all with a bat in his hands.

Twice during his career Mantle blasted more than 50 home runs in a season, including 1956 when he won the Triple Crown. During that glorious summer 35 years ago, the Mick belted 52 home runs, drove in 130 and hit .353. His RBI count that season was the only career best among those figures. He hit 54 homers in 1961 and he batted .865 in 1957.

In 1961, Mantle and Roger Maris set the baseball world on its collective ear, combining for 115 home runs, still a record by teammates in a season. Maris, of course, set the single-season record with 61, while Mantle finished with the aforementioned 54. He missed several games down the stretch due to an illness.

The greatest switch-hitter in baseball history, Mantle, a three-time Most Valuable Player, announced his retirement just before the 1969 season. He finished with 536 home runs (eighth all-time), 1,734 walks (fifth all-time) and 1,110 strikeouts (eighth all-time). In 12 World Series, Mantle slugged 1.8 home runs and drove in 40, both records.

Mantle's career was culminated in 1974 when he was voted into the Baseball Hall of Fame during his first year of eligibility.

Recently, from the Harbor Club (near Atlanta, Ga.), he took time to reflect upon his baseball career and his thoughts about the sports collecting hobby for the following *SCD* exclusive interview with Kevin Huard.

SCD: Did you save any important memorabilia from your career?

Mantle: I've got a 500 home run ball, three MVP trophies, the Triple Crown, the Hickock Belt, the, Silver Bat. I've got a tape measure that they gave me when I hit the 565-foot home run in Washington. Somebody gave me a tape measure. I've got a lot of baseballs, like the one I hit when I went past (Jimmie) Foxx.

SCD: Isn't one of your proudest pieces of memorabilia something you got from Roger Maris?

Mantle: Yes, it's in the (Mickey Mantle's in New York City) restaurant. Roger gave me a baseball just before he died with his picture on one side. He signed it for me. It says, "To Mickey, the greatest of them all."

I have some stuff in the restaurant. There's a painting of Billy (Martin) and me. We have a Roger Maris booth and a Billy Martin booth.

SCD: *SCD* readers and fans could see some of the items you kept from your career next time they're in New York City if they stop by Mickey Mantle's Restaurant across from Central Park.

Mantle is proud that he wore pinstripes longer than any other Yankee.

Mantle: When they retired my number at the (Yankee) Stadium, they gave me a uniform, and I have it.

SCD: You mentioned that you never really collected baseball cards yourself, but you would sometimes bring them home for your boys.

Mantle: They (Topps) used to send us boxes of gum cards and my boys would take the gum out and throw the cards away.

SCD: What are you most proud of in terms of your career, and why?

Mantle: Well, over 18 years, there's so many things. A lot of people don't realize it, but I played more games as a Yankee than anybody else.

SCD: That's right, that's still a record.

Mantle: I played in about 2,401 games as a Yankee I think. I'm proud of my 18 World Series home runs. I was proud to be on the same team in 1961 when Roger hit 61 homers. I think that was the best baseball team ever.

I was proud at the end of my career when the players told me I was a great teammate and stuff like that, proud of going into the Hall of Fame my first try.

When my number was retired with the Yankees, number three, four and five were the only ones retired at that time. Those numbers belonged to Ruth, Gehrig and DiMaggio.

SCD: On your autograph, it seems like almost every time you sign, whether it's a photo or a ball, you never see a smudged Mickey Mantle autograph. Is there a reason why you take a lot of time to sign?

Mantle: Well, if a kid's paying $30 for me to sign something for him, I feel like he's got a right to get a good one.

I see some kids come through the lines that don't look like they can afford it anyway. And not just because of that. I just feel that I should do as good as I can.

I don't like to pick up a ball when there's five autographs on it and I can't tell who signed it. I like to see who else is on the ball. Sometimes you can't even see who's on the ball.

SCD: Certainly the Mantle autograph is probably one of the most legible in the hobby, and in this day and age a lot of players sign autographs real quick to get through the line. And the autographs of course change over 20-30 years, but yours probably got better over the years when you first played. You obviously take your time to give somebody a signature.

Mantle: Well, actually, it really p— me off when it doesn't come out good. If I sign an autograph and it doesn't look good, it makes me mad.

I just got through signing copies of my book, "My Favorite Summer." We had 1,956 hardback books, and we just sold Score 1,656 books. It's a leatherbound, and I had to sign it in gold on the cover.

We're just sending them back to Score Board now, so it will probably be a couple of weeks before they're out. But you talk about hard to sign, that might be the hardest thing I've ever gotten into. That gold stuff is hard to write with anyway, and then on leather.

SCD: How about signing caps in silver pen?

Mantle: This was worse. The ones that I didn't think came out very good — I took out and we're going to get some more.

SCD: People have seen you do that. Sometimes when collectors have gone through the autograph line with a picture and you didn't think your autograph came out that good, you send the kid up to get another photo.

"There he is, son...the greatest."

Mantle: I'll do that several times if it doesn't look very good. Because I do try, and sometimes it just doesn't come out.

SCD: Your signature has changed somewhat over the years.

Mantle: It's changed a heck of a lot since my first years. It hasn't changed much since collecting has become big. Ever since I've been signing things at shows it's been about the same.

SCD: How does it make you feel, at a show, when fans say 'We think you're the greatest?' Do you ever get sick of hearing that?

Mantle: That's half the fun of doing the show, to have guys compliment you. I've had a lot of people ask me that question, "Don't you get tired of doing this," and the answer is no, because it's flattering as hell. I haven't played for 22-23 years. For people to still remember you and come up and have tears in their eyes and say that I was their boyhood idol and everything, it's pretty flattering. And then they bring their kids with them, and say, 'There he is, son. That's the greatest ballplayer that ever lived.'

SCD: And they really mean it too?

Mantle: Oh yeah, a lot of guys have tears in their eyes, and it makes you get goosebumps sometimes.

SCD: About Roger Maris' asterisk, you have some pretty strong feelings about that. They've finally removed that asterisk from Roger's home run total of 61.

Mantle: Well, there never should have been an asterisk anyway. I know they did remove it. I don't think there ever was one to tell you the truth. Who was that that said there should be an asterisk? Ford Frick?

They don't have it now and they never should have. As far I'm concerned that's probably the achievement in professional sports that I've ever seen. People have been trying to do it ever since Ruth did it, and nobody ever had.

SCD: People that know anything about Mickey Mantle realize that he was in the home run race right up until the last week and a half of the '61 season. Unfortunately, you had that virus and had that shot in the leg that turned bad. Otherwise, if you had stayed healthy, you might have pushed Roger beyond 61. You may have hit 61 yourself.

Mantle: But it didn't happen. I was on Bob Costas' show recently. He had it figured out where Roger was at bat 590 times or something. Anyway, percentage-wise, I had more home runs in times at bat or something than he did.

I don't know how they figured that out, but they figured out that if I had been up as much as Roger I would have hit as many according to the percentage, one out of every 10 or 11 or something like that.

SCD: In 1956, when you hit 52 home runs, you had a tremendous home run per at bat ratio. You were walked so many times that you really didn't get that many at bats. You lost about 140 at bats because of walks. If you take 140 at bats and if you hit a home run even once every 15 times, that's another eight, or 10 homers.

Mantle: Of course I imagine that Ruth walked some too, you know.

SCD: A lot of big home run hitters walk 100 or more times a year. What does it mean to you to be a member of the exclusive 500 home run club?

Mantle: It means a lot. I've got about 80 or 90 of those 500 home run bats that everybody's (signed) on. I signed them. They are the last bats I signed. I've got about — well my kids have them — I think about 80 of them.

SCD: Is there any reason you don't sign bats anymore?

Mantle: It's just that when I go to a card show, it takes like an hour and a half longer to sign bats. You know what I mean? It takes me three hours to sign 700 autographs, and if I'm not going to sign bats in a card show for kids that are paying money to get them signed, then I'm not going to sign.

Hey, I don't sign for my own kids, my mom or anybody. It comes down to the thing that I don't want to sign them at card shows, and if I'm not going to sign them for kids who are paying money to get them signed, then I'm not going to sign them for anybody.

SCD: Mickey Mantle does not sign bats for anybody. Even ballplayers who have played with him can't get a bat signed by Mickey Mantle?

Mantle: I'll tell you, it's really embarrassing. Every once in a while, you'll see somebody coming up with a bat, or you'll get a bat in the mail.

Peter Jennings, he has a bat, and he called the restaurant to get it signed and I just told him I can't sign it. It's harder than hell to turn somebody down once in while, but you've got to.

You can't just sign one every once-in-a-while. If I'm going to sign one, I'm going to sign one for everybody.

SCD: Any opinion about today's ballplayers? Could they play in the '50s or '60s? Do you respect some of them?

The talent today is too watered down, says Mantle.

89

Is the talent too watered down?

Mantle: I'm not one of the oldtimers that doesn't think they're as good today as we used to be. The only thing I believe is that it's too watered down. There are too many teams. If you cut it back to eight teams in both leagues like it used to be when I played, it would be as good or better than ever.

Kids nowadays are bigger and stronger; they can run faster. All 10 pitchers on a team can throw 85-90 miles an hour. But there are so many teams, and they're fixing to add on again. There's a lot of guys playing that couldn't play in those days. But if they had just eight teams in both leagues, I think it would be as good as ever.

SCD: Now with the expansion of two more teams it will be watered down even more. Several teams have problems with their pitching staffs. They can't get two or three real first-rate pitchers like it was in the '50s.

You had a couple of all-stars in your early years with the Yankees in Eddie Lopat and Vic Raschi, along with Whitey Ford and Allie Reynolds.

Mantle: The one thing that's different than when I came up in '51 with that Yankee team was that, once you got past — like if we were playing the St. Louis Browns and we knocked out their starter, say Ned Garner — well, we could probably have a field day because they didn't have anybody in the bullpen to bring in. Nowadays, if you knock out the starter, they've got two or three guys in the bullpen that can throw as hard as the starter, or just as good.

SCD: Starters today are expected to go only five or six innings.

Mantle: I think all they do is just shoot for six innings. They feel like they've had a good day if they go six.

SCD: Then there's a million-dollar reliever that is going to come in.

Mantle: A long reliever and a short reliever.

SCD: You drew the correlation that you made something like $1.3 million over your 18-year career. It sounds like a lot of money, but it really isn't when you compare it to today when ballplayers like Roger Clemens are making $5 million a year.

Mantle: Clemens gets more for one game than I made all year. He gets $100,000 a game.

SCD: You have no grudges against the ballplayers making that kind of money?

Mantle: Heck no. When I played the television revenue wasn't what it is now. (George) Steinbrenner signed a contract not too long ago for 10 years, for $500 million. I think the players should participate in that. They're the ones that are doing the work.

SCD: You don't think it's going to dry up sooner or later?

Mantle: I can't see it keeping on like it is. (Bobby) Bonilla's wanting $6 million a year.

SCD: Do you know of anybody that is worth $5 million a year?

Mantle: No, not to play ball. But I still don't begrudge the players. Somebody asked me the other day what's the difference between now and when I played. I said, "Well, when I played we were dumb — now the owners are."

When you give a guy a five-year contract for $5 million a year, not everybody — like Clemens, he pitches his a– off — but there's so many guys that sign five-year contracts that haven't even played 20 or 30 games a year. I mean it takes a lot of incentive away from you. I think you should get paid for what you do.

SCD: That's why you guys had to perform because you were only paid on accomplishments of the previous year. You usually got just a one-year deal. If you did well like you did in '56, you'd sign for X amount of dollars in '57.

Didn't you have a little problem with the administration of the Yankees in '57 because your power totals were down a little bit although your average went up about 12 or 15 points? Didn't they want to cut your salary?

Mantle: I was the Most Valuable Player in '56, and then in '57 too. The first contract I got in 1958 was for a cut because they said I didn't do as good as I did in '56.

SCD: What eventually happened?

Mantle: I finally held out and got a $10,000 raise. I was the Most Valuable Player two years in a row.

SCD: What do you like to do when you have some free time these days?

Mantle: About all I can do for exercise anymore is play golf. And I like to fish. I like to go down to the Harbor Club (Lake Oconee in Georgia) if I have a week off and play golf and fish. The people down there are kind of used to me now.

It's like you kind of blend in and I really like that. It's only an hour out of Atlanta. It's easy to get to and easy to get back. We stay pretty busy, so whenever I get a couple of weeks off, or a week off even, I go fishing and play golf. It's really relaxing, and you loosen up down there.

SCD: You can be yourself down there and people aren't always bugging you for autographs? You can have dinner at a restaurant or walk into a grocery market and be basically accepted as just another member of the community?

Mantle: Right. Everybody is just kind of friendly.

SCD: We understand that you may be cutting down a little bit on the card shows next year. You do about 12 shows a year, taking you to different parts of the country. Does the traveling to card shows get to you after a while?

Mantle: The travel is just about the worst thing about the card shows. We usually get there on a Friday and do mail-in orders. Then we do the card show on Saturday and Sunday. That's not really that bad — about three hours a day. But we do a lot of other stuff, too.

It's not just card shows that makes us travel. We went to New York to do a commercial for a new watch that I have out. It's a limited edition of 536 watches — one for each home run I hit. It's an 18 karat gold watch. They gave me watch number seven.

It comes with a letter of authenticity that says on July 7, 1951, I hit my seventh home run. I signed the letters of authenticity. I've been on Regis Philbin's and Dick Cavett's shows plugging the watches. Those are some of the things I do.

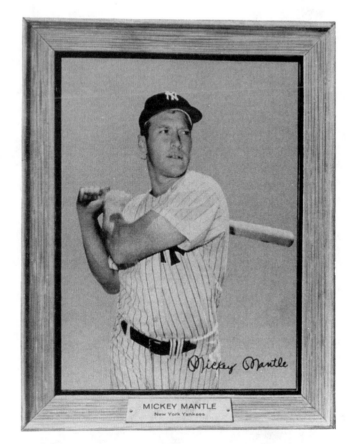

Mantle golfs and fishes for relaxation.

Whitey (Ford) and I have the fantasy camp down in Ft. Lauderdale (Fla.) every year. It's the last week in October, the first week in November. It's for two weeks. So it's not just the card shows; we do a whole lot of different things.

We also have a golf tournament — the Mickey Mantle Golf Tournament represents the Harbor Club. We're also thinking about having a fishing tournament. Then I have a Mickey Mantle tournament in Joplin, Mo., for the benefit of Oak Hills Hospital.

The golf tournament at Lake Oconee is for the Starlight Foundation. That's for seriously ill children. We try to make as much money as we can for the Starlight Foundation every year.

SCD: We understand it was quite successful last year. You had a number of former baseball and football players there?

Mantle: Yes. Jimmy Orr brought in a good bunch. We had Johnny Unitas, Earl Morrall, Tom Matte and Charlie Johnson for the tournament. We had a great bunch there last year. The last day got blown out because a fertilizer plant blew up and we had to evacuate the county, so we lost one day last year.

SCD: How would you like to be remembered as a ballplayer and as a person?

Mantle: I'd like to be remembered best as being a good teammate. I'd like that on my headstone. I'd like for it to say, "The best teammate we ever had, the Yankees."

SCD: In talking to Johnny Blanchard, Hank Bauer and Ralph Houk, they say as great a player as you were, no matter how well you were doing, it was more important for you to see the team succeed than yourself. They said, as long as you were contributing to the team, you were happy.

Mantle: I think that's true. — *Kevin Huard, Nov. 29, 1991*

Chapter 4

It's showtime!

Autograph session with Mickey Mantle

By Steve Schultz

Being a Yankee fan and Mickey Mantle fan all of my 37 years, I was overjoyed after seeing an ad announcing that Mickey Mantle was going to appear at the 1978 Detroit Camper Show.

I started gathering items I hoped my hero would sign.

Mickey was going to appear for three days: Friday night, Saturday afternoon and Sunday afternoon.

I decided I would try Friday night.

Arriving from Ann Arbor around 6:15 p.m., I had time to find the Timber Shores Resort Booth where Mickey was scheduled to be.

As 7:00 p.m. approached my anticipation was sky high.

Mickey arrived at 7:05 p.m. and started signing pictures that Timber Shores Resort had for him to sign. I began to wonder if he would sign the items I had with me. I observed at this time he was very friendly, especially with the smaller children. I went up to him and asked if he would sign a copy of his book "Whitey and Mickey" and a baseball my Dad and I got in the 1950s which Mickey hit into the Tiger Stadium stands during batting practice.

He signed without any problem. I then thanked him and while he was autographing pictures for a number of fans, I took a couple of pictures.

When there was a lull in signing I decided it was time to see if Mickey would sign my other articles. I know he doesn't like to sign a lot; it took over a year for him to sign and send to me a Hall of Fame Plaque. I went to him and asked if he would sign my other articles and Mickey said, "You already have three autographs."

And I said, "No, only two." I then brought out the following items which I thought were unique: a June 9, 1969, Mickey Mantle Day program; a 1974 Yankee Press Book; Mickey Mantle Day program, Sept. 18, 1965; Old-Timers Day program, Aug. 3, 1974 (Mickey was inducted into the Hall of Fame that year); 1974 National Baseball Hall of Fame and Museum Book; and a 45 rpm record of "I love Mickey" by Mickey Mantle and Teresa Brewer. He must have thought my items were unique as he signed them all and we had a nice little talk.

We talked about his "I Love Mickey" Record and he indicated to me not many people had a copy, not even him. I told him I was a Yankee fan and especially a Mickey Mantle fan all of my life, which was hard living in Michigan, and he agreed it must be difficult. He was very courteous while he was signing and we were talking. Lastly he signed two photographs which he was giving to everybody — one for me and one for my collecting friend and Yankee hater in Hollywood, Fla.

I feel very lucky he signed all of my items. Mickey did refuse to sign any baseball cards a few fans had brought for him to sign, at least on Friday night when I was there.

Two things really impressed me. One was that the younger children of 8-10 did not know who Mickey Mantle is. Many fathers wanted to take their children to see him, but the kids' response was "Mickey Who?"

Second, at least on Friday night, there were not very many fans on hand to see this superstar.

Putting it in perspective, though, a person would have to be at least 20 years old now to remember Mickey as a player since the last game he played was in 1968. A superstar of the past, but almost a forgotten man now.

Feb. 10, 1978, was a very significant day for me as I finally met my hero — Mickey Charles Mantle. — *Steve Schultz, March 31, 1978*

Over 4,000 attended West Coast convention

By Bob Keisser

Move over, Mickey Mantle. You've got company at the top of the inflationary baseball card heap.

Without question, the hottest card in the hobby recently has been the 1952 Topps Mickey Mantle, old number 311. And that fact was borne out at the 11th annual West Coast Convention.

But Mickey has some competition, in the form of the rare 1954 Bowman issue Ted Williams.

Two years ago, the expensive Mantle could have been had for around $75.

Lately, he's been going for upwards of $1,000. The card was sold by Garden Grove, Calif. collector/dealer Tony Galovich for $1,400 and just after that, at the New Jersey Show, the card went for $1,750.

Equally stunning, though, was the price a gem-mint Williams brought in a walk-in auction at the West Coast Convention. The Williams card had been hovering around $150, but when it showed up for the auction, it sold for a whopping $435.

Earlier in the convention, a dealer had sold the card in excellent shape for a reported $300. The same dealer was seen frowning by the time the three-day show came to an end.

The '52 Topps Mantle, '54 Bowman Williams and '53 Topps Willie Mays were the cards in biggest demand at the show, with the Williams the rarest and the Mays the most prolific. It seemed as if every other dealer had a Mays for sale, ranging in price from $150 (good shape) to $250 (excellent). A good-plus Mays went for $219 in the last day auction. — *Bob Keisser, Dec. 31, 1979*

Mickey Mantle Show
Southfield, Mich.
Oct. 10-11, 1981

Mickey Mantle will appear Oct. 11 at the Southfield Pavillion — his first appearance at a Midwest card show.

Mantle will appear on Sunday from 11-3 p.m. and sign 1,200 autographs. Autograph tickets are being sold at a series of pre-Mantle shows in the Detroit area, and will not be available through the mail. The cost is only $5 for the autograph color picture, and admission to the show. The color picture is a limited-edition, numbered exclusive issue.

The show will be held in Southfield, Mich., a suburb of Detroit. — *advertisement, Sept. 25, 1981*

They say that Mickey Mantle gets $10,000 just to show up at autograph shows. Now you know why they charge so much for autographs... — *Irwin Cohen, On the Baseball Beat, May 22, 1987*

Willie, Mick & Duke appear in Georgia

By Bill Ballew

Baseball card show history was made over the July 4th weekend as Willie Mays, Mickey Mantle and Duke Snider headlined the Cracker Classic Baseball Card Show in Marietta, Ga., near Atlanta.

The two-day show, held in the Cobb County Civic Center, featured the three baseball legends together for the first time at a card show. Nearly 9,000 people attended the July 2-3 show, promoted by Baseball Buddies Card Shop in Marietta.

The Cracker Classic featured 96 tables and more than 50 dealers from throughout the United States, including national dealers Alan Rosen and Dick DeCourcy. Merchandise for sale had a heavy emphasis on older baseball cards with numerous uniforms and new cards also available.

"We attracted a lot of people who had never been to a card show," said Chip Nelson of Baseball Buddies. "Mantle, Mays and Snider were many of the older collectors' heroes. Hopefully we've raised interest and drawn more people into the hobby."

Planning and arranging for Mantle, Mays and Snider to be at the same show at the same time was no small feat. In fact, the show took nearly a year to put together.

"Duke and I have the same agent, Greer Johnson, and Baseball Buddies got in touch with her. Then they worked it out with Carl Kiesler about Willie," said Mantle. "Anyway, they got us all three together and we're all real pleased with it.

"I was afraid that it might be too close to the Fourth of July and that everybody might be going out fishing or to the lake," added Mantle. "But evidently they did pretty good."

According to Morris Nix, promoter of the show and owner of Baseball Buddies, another show is in the planning stages for next year.

"I believe this was one of the largest, if not the largest, regional card shows in the country this year," said Nix. "We learned a lot this year so next year will be even better.

"People have asked me what it's like to promote a show," Nix continued. "I tell them it's like a blind date. You get real excited but you don't know whether it will turn out to be Christie Brinkley or the Wicked Witch of the West." — *Bill Ballew, Aug. 5, 1988*

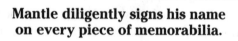

**Mantle diligently signs his name
on every piece of memorabilia.**

Sports Collectors Digest Profiles Mickey Mantle

Recently in New York, "The Mick" gave autograph fans their money's worth with a signature and more.

By Pete Dobrovitz

It looked like a line to the cashier at a garage sale; they hold clocks, beer steins, posters, antique pictures and plates. Even to the casual observer, the turnout to have Mickey Mantle put his signature on any one of these items was truly amazing. But no one continues to be more amazed than The Mick himself.

Sure his book ("The Mick") is still selling well in paperback. Sure, he's popping up every now and then as a color commentator on SportsChannel's Yankee broadcasts. But, that still doesn't explain why hundreds of people were willing to pay out $15 for a Mickey Mantle autograph. It doesn't even matter that it was his third Upstate New York appearance in less than six months!

As Mickey Mantle leaned forward in his chair, he offered his own observations on the cause of "Mantle Magic" that knows no limits.

"When I first came up to play in '51, DiMaggio was just getting out of baseball. And that was like his era. The guys that are in control right now are the people, the fathers, that grew up with me. You know what I mean? I'm 50, 56 now. So that most of the people that are around 40 years old now are guys that grew up about the same time that I was playing ball. It might be my era; I don't know! Willie Mays, Duke Snider and myself, Hank Aaron, guys like that — we're more popular now than we've ever been," he says.

Scanning the crowd, you can see no one "demographic," though — no one age group. There were young guys who weren't even around when Mantle retired. But they've heard tales of the Legend. They've witnessed the card prices skyrocket. There are balding and silver-haired men with Yankee jackets or T-shirts. Mick's just the latest member of personal Pantheon; Ruth, Gehrig, Joe D and now The Mick. But, look closely and you will see the Baby Boomers.

Mantle sees them, too. "I sit here whenever I'm doing a card show and a guy will come by. You know, you can tell he's like a president of a company or something. And, he'll have his kid with him and he'll say, 'There he is, son.'

"Almost everyone of them will say, 'I've waited 30 years for this.' They'll shake hands. It really makes you feel good. I played for like 20 years; retired in '68 and to have people still remember you and feel like that about you, it's really great. I have a lot of people say, 'Don't you get tired of it?' Hell, no! I don't get tired of it. It's flattering to me."

On this day, Mantle will sign 800 autographs in three hours. (It would actually take three hours, 29 minutes to get through it all.) Promoter Allan George declines comment on Mantle's fee at the request of Mick's booking agent.

There will be no bat signings. Not an arthritis problem; just an acknowledgment by Mantle that his signature for $15 on a bat will automatically blossom into an item worth 10 times that fee! There will be no personalizations.

It's just simple math. 800 signings in three hours works out to one "Mickey Mantle" every 13.5 seconds! Still, Mantle shakes hands, makes polite conversation.

All the time he's signing, he's smiling. With so many reports of superstars who never even look up or sign with a scowl, Mantle offers a much different philosophy. "I feel like we should take a little time. We take pictures and stuff. I don't try to sign it and just tell them to get on out. When someone says, 'He's the greatest player that ever lived,' I am, as I said, flattered."

But could he ever have imagined in those early years, that his first card would sell for $6,000+, with others right behind? "No, no way. The only thing I can figure is that if Ted Williams was here, I'd line up and pay $10 for his autograph!" Believe it or not, the man whose cards can command hundreds of dollars a piece owns none of his own! "If I had about 20 or 30 of them, they wouldn't be worth nothing."

Mantle says he never really paid much attention to his portraits on cardboard. He really has no favorite card; no favorite pose. But he is quite adamant about one thing. "I hate signing bubble gum cards! I mean, I like signing 8-by-10 pictures, baseballs or something like that. But those baseball cards are really hard to sign! You've only got three hours to sign, and there's no place to write on them!"

Mantle's signature itself has become one of the most easily recognizable logos in the hobby. The first loop that forms the "M" in Mickey almost looks like a "B" stretched out for a nap. Or a dog ear that runs into a capital "N." The second loop on the "M" that forms Mantle looks slightly different. More like a "P." One thing's certain. It's no scribble. And Mantle wouldn't have it any other way.

"I try to write so they can read it. I figure, if somebody's going to pay $3 to get in here (actually it was $3.50), $10 for an autograph (actually it was $15), you've got to try to give them something they can read."

The strangest thing he was ever asked to autograph? Mantle grins, hesitates, "Well, ah...," he chuckles. I tell him this is a family publication. "Well, the strangest things? Whenever you're in a show, they've all got baseballs, or pictures or something like that."

How often does he see something truly unique? A really special item? "Every show... out of 900 items to sign, there'll be 40 or 50 that I haven't seen." Any he wished he could own himself? "Oh yeah. Pictures of me and Ted Williams. Me and Joe D. Me and Musial." (Growing up in the Midwest, Musial was one of Mantle's first boyhood idols.)

"There's a lot of things that I've seen that I'd like to have down in my restaurant in New York. Last night I signed about 400 pictures for a guy named Ed Keats up around Albany. He had me and Willie and Duke and Joe D. All in one picture. And all the other three had signed it. And, I kept one of them! (He laughs out loud.) I think he knows I kept it!"

Mantle's days after baseball are now filled with a wide variety of activities. Show appearances are just a small part of Mantle Inc. "I'm with Reserve Life Insurance Co. of Dallas, Texas. I'm vice president in charge of public relations. I've been with them since 1972. I do 15 games with the Yankees on SportsChannel.

"I do maybe 15 or 20 public appearances like this here a year. And I'm with a new arthritic drug called, ah...well, I don't think I'm supposed to say anything about it right now."

Mantle did go on to explain that the medication, in pill form, will be produced by the Ciba-Geigy Pharmaceutical Co. He'll do commercial endorsements. The product will not be sold over the counter, however. It's prescription only. Mantle, no stranger to arthritic pain in his knee joints, gives the drug unsolicited praise already.

"It helps my knees. I got to where I couldn't hardly play golf at all. I can't tell you to get it; you need to see your physician. It's let me play golf again."

It makes you realize just how far we've come. Two decades ago, it was common for orthopedic surgeons to open up knee injuries and just start yanking out cartilage. Knee joints were cleaned out of tissues that worked as shock absorbers. Joints scraped bone against bone.

One can only imagine what The Mick would have achieved in this era of arthroscopy, and advanced treatment techniques for minor pulls and muscle tears. We tend to remember Mantle as a great player, hobbled with career-shortening injuries. We forget that he began as a real speedster, once timed around the basepaths in 13 seconds flat. Casey had to check the stopwatch with an encore performance.

One can only imagine the kind of salary he'd command today. After winning the Triple Crown in 1956, Mantle hoped to hold out for a new contract at $35,000. That's little over half the minimum paid to big leaguers today. Still, George Weiss felt he was only worth $32,500. So Mickey settled. He wouldn't crack $100,000 until 1963.

We only talked for a little while. It was time for Mickey to get on with his signing. At this card show, 774 people would pay the admission and jam the aisles. Promoter Allan George gave away another 1,000 free admissions to several local youth groups, police athletic organizations and scout troops.

"Sometimes, it's just good to get new people into the hobby," he noted. Before the show, George had expressed some concern that the hobby may have hit a mid-season slump. After all, the Madison Square Garden show and the National had just concluded. And as mentioned earlier, Mantle had been in town just four months ago. He didn't need to worry. It was another Mantle SRO.

Fans seemed to really enjoy themselves and dealers were, by and large, ecstatic. One, who had reported a dismal day with Joe D, now termed this his "second best show ever." Still another said it was her career best.

Dealers came from as far away as Michigan and Florida to share in the Mickeymania, and they weren't disappointed. Wandering the aisles in hot pursuit of '52 Bowmans (rapidly disappearing with all other '50s material), I couldn't help but notice so many new faces. Kids with dads in tow...

...Back to the most pleasant part of this show — its unassuming star. The time I spent talking with Mantle was really something special. No tantrums about camera, or lighting. No hesitation to answer any questions.

When you see it work in person, you realize a good part of the "Mantle Magic" is that living inside the Legend is a little kid from Oklahoma with a glove, looking for some buddies to play Pitch and Catch, Annie Over or Major League. He's still a fan himself — Musial and Williams are still around. I had waited nearly 30 years to meet him. It was worth the wait. — *Pete Dobrovitz, Sept. 9, 1988*

Mickey Mantle was, of course, difficult by mail, unless you knew his "alternate" address — a bank in Dallas that employed him in a public relations capacity at the time.

At the work locale, he signed with reasonable speed and verified authenticity. Very few people knew of this alternate address, however.

The person who told me about it, collector Bill Mendel, of (then) Downers Grove, swore me to secrecy, and insisted that I not use it in one of my columns. (Now you know how I can call myself Constant Writer; this was 1974, remember.) — *Dave Miedema, Up Autograph Alley, June 9, 1989*

Willie, Mickey and the Duke
The first blockbuster show of the '90s

By Jim Kelly

"Isn't he the greatest? Look at him. He's still my hero." Those could've been the words of any fan, in awe of his idol. But it was Tom Catal, partner in Big League Promotions, who was impressed by the former New York Yankee who hit 536 home runs.

Mickey Mantle was one of four guests (all center fielders) who kicked off the new decade with a big show in Las Vegas East, Atlantic City. The Say Hey Kid, Willie Mays, Dodger great Duke Snider and youngster Keith Miller of the New York Mets were the guests of Big League Promotions Inc. to kick off the new year with the first major card show of 1990.

And while the show was not without its problems, Big League took every opportunity to please the fans/customers for "Baseball '90" at Trump Plaza.

Shows in Atlantic City tend to cater to spectacular. This is where Mike Tyson turns opponents into notches on his boxing gloves. This was the city that gave birth to the 500 HR show, a theme which shows no sign of slowing down. So it shouldn't have been any surprise that baseball fans camped out at 4 a.m. on Saturday to wait the arrival of New York Yankee great Mickey Mantle.

"I can't understand it," Mantle would tell me later, when asked about his continuous and, might I add, growing popularity.

I arrived late Friday night Jan. 5 just in time to miss all the ruckus. The traditional preview prior to a full two-day event was blemished by a slight error which got the show off to a rough start.

Promoter Fred Davies, given the obligatory "no problem" by Trump Plaza officials, was met by angry dealers who were forced to wait hours before being able to set up their tables. One dealer was stalled six hours. However, Davies and his crew worked diligently to smooth out the opening night bumps, Friday night having been a promoter's nightmare.

After all, still to come was the musically most famous center field of "Willie, Mickey and the Duke" immortalized in song by Terry Cash.

His lyrics certainly do "Talk Baseball."

Big League Promotions Inc. (Davies, Catal and for this show Jack Farscht) seemed to cover all the bases from a promotional aspect. New York radio/TV announcer Spencer Rose was at the microphone to make announcements. Finally a pro on hand at a show, instead of someone screeching into a microphone like it was amateur night.

One of Spencer's announcements was for free — that's right, FREE autographs of Keith Miller, New York Mets center fielder. The food service was adequate (separate room close by) and the autograph lines were run smoothly.

A nice touch was the Big League crew wearing special shirts for the show, announcing "Baseball '90, A new decade" with facsimile autographs. The shirts added to the professionalism of the crew, which was outstanding.

Saturday's portion of the show went "according to plans," said Davies, having ironed out the wrinkles by now. The only disappointment on this day may have been to the public when Spencer Rose made the announcement at 9:13, "There are no Mickey Mantle autograph tickets available for today."

Just 13 minutes into the show, the Mick was sold out. It seems as though he's appeared everywhere — twice — but this man is the exception to the card show rule. He's a legend.

And not surprising, most of the sales activity was tied to Mantle material. Dealer Scott Goodman, dressed in tux and outfitted with National-type material, sold a Mickey Mantle game-used bat for $3,000.

"I'm a BIG Mantle collector," said 36-year-old John Taube, who purchased the bat. "It's a K55 from the 1965-71 period. It's nice...I have other mementos, more game-used bats and Mantle memorabilia." The price is believed to be the highest paid for a Mantle bat.

One dealer had the famed 500 HR poster (blank) for sale for $20. These were the ones given out by promoters of the Tropworld show for autograph purposes. Completely signed and framed, this item is now in the $1,000 range.

Saturday's activities ran smoothly and Davies and crew gave me free rein to roam Trump Plaza with a pen in hand. First stop, Keith Miller, who I knew wouldn't be quite as busy as Willie, Mickey and the Duke. The good looking New York Met was, however, kept busy by virtue of a "free" opportunity to the public. Does he mind signing until his wrist caves in?

"It doesn't bother me, really," said Miller, laughing. But what's not a laughing matter anymore is the fans' perception of the people they pay to watch play — and get autographs from.

"Oh yeah, I sign all my mail," said Miller when asked about the barrage at home. That's nice to hear, especially amid reports of some players just dumping piles of unopened mail into the garbage. "Shows provide a chance for people to get autographs who wouldn't ordinarily have a chance to see the players," said Miller.

And for the game itself. Any scoops? "Right now, Andy Van Slyke is the best all-around center fielder in the game," says Miller.

Duke Snider, always a congenial guest, signed and smiled without incident for the next several hours, as did Willie Mays. Now there's news.

Apparently Willie is doing his best to change his card show image, tarnished by several incidents of grumbling and rudeness. Mays posed for pictures, smiled and was even cordial at times. On to my hero.

Mickey Mantle, who will be 59 this year, is still the main attraction. Co-promoter Tom Catal, who has worked with Mickey over the years, says "I love 'im. He's still the greatest."

It's odd. Aaron has 755 home runs, the most of any major league player, but it's the man listed number seven on the list that everyone seems to flock to.

"I can't explain it," said Mickey.

Dressed in a jogging outfit complete with fresh Nike sneakers, #7 went through the day-long process of putting his signature on everything placed in front of him. Baseballs, 8x10s, posters, books, whatever memento of the Mick you wanted signed. Well, almost everything. "No bats" was obvious, but one customer was miffed when Mickey refused to sign a replica uniform. Why not?

"Because I don't want to," drawled Mickey as those nearby cracked a smile. Hey, he's the Mick.

"There's a time factor involved," said number seven. "You have to have two people stretch out the material so it doesn't bunch up. And while they're holding it, I've got to sign it. It takes too much time and it costs these guys (pointing to Catal) money. It hurts the promoter."

Nice to hear a guest actually is concerned about the outcome of a show. And what about those bats? Mick is talking to me while signing, so he takes advantage of the opportunity to change subjects.

"Hmmm. First time I've ever seen that. Three signatures on the sweet spot."

But Mick, what about limitations? "There's no limit on baseballs, pictures." Will there ever be a limit a la Joe DiMaggio? "No, I don't believe there will."

Greer Johnson, who handles Mickey's promotional activities, asks politely if we could "do this some other time." I agree, especially since customers are paying $30 each for Mickey to put his right-handed signature on their favorite piece of memorabilia.

"Later" would never come, since Mick was just as busy the following day for the same reasons. Understandable. Everyone's tugging at Mick.

Sunday's portion of the show was similar to Saturday's in almost every respect. Almost to the minute, Spencer Ross repeated the Mantle autograph story — Sorry, sold out. This spurred some activity for those with baseballs and pictures already signed by the Mick. Generally, sales were OK among dealers I questioned during and after the show.

Collector/dealer Len Lustik purchased a pair of Babe Ruth autographed balls for an undisclosed sum. Other customers trying to sell goods brought 500 HR baseballs and posters which were partially signed to peddle.

* * *

It's late in the afternoon Sunday. Willie, Mickey and the Duke have taken care of show business. Trump Plaza guests for the card show (estimated at up to 8,000) begin to filter out. Time for a last few minute deals, or better yet, pack up early to avoid the rush home.

"Ladies and Gentlemen," announces Spencer Ross, "the Giants have just lost in overtime." It's the last bit of excitement for the weekend now that the new year and new decade have been ushered in with the first big baseball card show.

I stop by the table laden with promotional material for other shows. I have a choice of 11 "spectacular events." But #7 isn't scheduled for any of them. He's still the hero, the idol of thousands. Even if he won't sign bats. "Ya gotta love 'im," says Catal. We do, Tommy. We do.

"Has Everyone Gone Batty?"

I cringed at even mentioning the word, probably the most often used word of 1989. While Jack Nicholson and Michael Keaton brought Batman to big screen the on last year, "Bat" is anything but "in" this year. You couldn't walk down a department store aisle without something shaped like, or monickered with, a Batman. Even the cereal aisle is full of Batman Cereal.

But the real Batmen shiver when they hear that three-letter word: bat. The 11 members of the 500 Home Run Club seem, for the most part, to be in agreement about those wooden clubs. They won't sign them, or they want a premium price (because we all know how much more difficult on the fingers it is to sign them).

Why? What could be the reason? What's the big objection to these real Batmen refusing to put their names on a piece of wooden posterity?

"Cause I don't want to," said this former player in his Oklahoma drawl.

"Maybe they're holding out because it's the last thing they have," offered show promoter Fred Davies. But is it really money? Card show grapevine has Mickey Mantle turning down an offer from one person for $100,000 — to sign one hundred bats!

Here's the latest scoop on the Bat 11:

Aaron — "I want what Mantle is getting" is the cry from this corner. Limited show schedule; may sign bats in private for $50 each.

Mays — won't sign through the line but will for the promoter; about $30 each.

F. Robinson — will sign through the line at regular price; although he was heard in Rochester, N.Y., to have said, "Thanks, you just made my day," when someone brought several sticks through the line.

Killebrew — still signing through the lines at regular prices; don't tell him what the other guys are doing.

R. Jackson — his price has risen slightly in the past year (whose hasn't?) but so far still signing wood.

Mantle — Good luck. He's said to have turned down close friend Whitey Ford. Another Joe D. To borrow a line from the lion in the Wizard of Oz: "Not nobody, not nohow."

Schmidt — Howard Hughes was easier to find; but reports say when you see him, "no problem."

T. Williams — I apologize. I may have started this one. I had the Splendid Splinter sign 50 bats at the AC Show last year. Right afterwards he said, "No more bats." You can still get them for about $60.

McCovey — Beginning to grumble. A promoter recently told me he's limiting the number of bats. He's next.

Banks — He'll be 59 on the last day of January and wouldn't it be a nice present to us if Ernie stayed the same and continued signing bats. Didn't he always say, "Hey, let's sign two."

Mathews — He's with Killebrew. And "Thank you."

Seems like those completely signed 500 HR bats from last year's show were a real bargain. It would cost about $300 in autographs, plus the bat and then you'd only get 10! Mickey "Not for my mother" Mantle will simply not sign.

If the three other members were alive today, they'd sign boldly, proudly. — *Jim Kelly, Feb. 2, 1990*

Mickey Mantle autographs

Show persona: Like Ted Williams, as one of the Big Three (Joe DiMaggio is the third), almost has to go the assembly line route at show appearances to allow everyone who wants an autograph to get one.

By mail access: Don't waste the stamps.

Signing taboos: Mantle balks at signing bats, uniforms, and most other items (other than baseballs) for regular folks. Mantle has also had a changing policy on signing Perez-Steele items, either signing, not signing, or else signing at an inflated rate, depending on his mood. He currently signs them at normal rate.

Forgery concerns: Mantle fakes occur more than any other living 500 Home Run Club member, but dealing with solid, reputable autograph dealers will eliminate most of your worries.

Equipment availability: Mantle's bats, like Ted Williams' bats, are truly rare and very costly in authentic form. An interesting trend in the last year is that I have had at least two dozen people at shows around the country tell me they had Mantle bats, only to learn, after inspection or description, that their items were invariably "MM5" Louisville store models. — *Dave Miedema, Up Autograph Alley, May 18, 1990*

Mickey and Willie star signers at Long Island show

By Robert Obojski

"What's your most prized memento from your baseball career?" a fan asked Mickey Mantle as he was signing autographs at the National Pastime's Fourth Long Island Classic Baseball Card, Collectibles and Memorabilia show staged on Sept. 14-15 (Saturday and Sunday) at Hofstra University's Fitness Center in Uniondale, N.Y.

Answered Mantle without a second's hesitation: "It's the ring I'm wearing on my left hand right now...the Hall of Fame induction ring I received at Cooperstown in 1974.

Sure, my World Series rings are important, but the Hall of Fame ring was given to me for career achievements, and not for a single year's performance."

Mantle was in an outgoing mood at the Long Island Classic show as he appeared on both Saturday and Sunday. He limits himself to 700 autographs per session, and also took time to sign some 800 mail order items, making the total 2,200.

Commented Harvey Brandwein, who operates the National Pastime with his partner Steve Hisler: "Mickey could have easily signed more than 3,000 times because the demand was so great, but he always sticks to his pre-arranged limit."

The $38 fee for Mickey's signature apparently is no deterrent for the big name hunters. (Mantle does not sign bats.)

Despite the fact that the lines leading to his table were long, Mantle chatted with the fans, posed for pictures and even personalized items whenever he felt he had a few extra moments.

When signing a group photo that included Ken Boyer, the late St. Louis Cardinals third baseman and manager, Mickey commented:

"Kenny Boyer was a great fielding third baseman, a real power hitter, and one of the most competitive players I ever saw. I can't understand why he's not in the Hall of Fame."

SCD spoke to one serious collector who specializes in New York big league baseball memorabilia, and who had Mantle sign 10 different items, including a 1951 New York Yankees World Series program. The program cover already had the signatures of Joe DiMaggio, Duke Snider and Willie Mays, and with the addition of Mantle, four of the greatest center fielders in New York history have inscribed the program, giving it very special value.

This particular collector also had Mantle sign headline newspaper stories on two or three of Mickey's longest "tape-measure" homers, and a summer 1961 *Time* magazine with Mantle portrayed on the front cover. Said the memorabilia buff, "Material like this is interesting in itself, but with the addition of the autographs the stuff is worth a lot more."

Total attendance for the two-day show came to approximately 4,200; 2,000 fans turned out on Saturday and 2,200 on Sunday.

Observed Harvey Brandwein: "the big attractions on Sunday were Mickey Mantle and Willie Mays. We were more than satisfied with the attendance for the weekend."

Some 134 dealers manned nearly 200 tables at the Hofstra University Fitness Center (fancy term for gymnasium).

Mays was kept busy by the autograph seekers as he signed 1,110 times (at $22 a crack), including mail orders. — *Robert Obojski, Oct. 18, 1991*

Mantle star signer at New York show

By Robert Obojski

"What was your reaction after you learned that one of your old Yankee uniforms sold for $111,100 at auction this past January?" Mickey Mantle was asked when he was appearing at the "Madison Avenue 33" baseball card, collectibles and memorabilia show staged on Feb. 1-2 (Saturday and Sunday) at New York City's Armenian Church Ballroom and sponsored by the National Pastime.

"That's really unbelievable," said Mantle. "I never made more than $100,000 playing for the Yankees, and now someone pays more than that for my 'sweats.' I wish I had saved my underwear from that uniform...then it would have been worth even more," quipped Mantle.

(The Mantle uniform that drew the huge figure was from the 1960 season and was auctioned by Leland's at New York City on Jan. 15. Knockdown price was $101,000, with a 10 percent buyer's fee being tacked on.)

Mantle admitted at the same time, however, that the value of the dollar has changed significantly over the past 30-plus years.

Mickey, who was present for both days of the show, signed his full quota of 1,400 autographs, or 700 for each session — at $38 per signature. (Mantle does not sign bats at card shows.)

Commented Harvey Brandwein, who operates the National Pastime with his partner Steve Hisler: "Mantle could have signed hundreds of additional autographs because of the great demand, but he always sets a per-session limit."

The three Griffeys (Ken Sr., Ken Jr., and Craig) manned autograph tables on Saturday, while Barry Bonds and Carlton Fisk were on hand on Sunday.

Paid admissions for the two-day affair eclipsed the 5,000 mark.

"That's the best attendance we've ever had for a two-day show in New York City," observed Hisler. "The fact that we featured big-name autograph guests, including Mickey Mantle, had a great deal to do with the giant turnout."

More than 5,500 autographs were signed, including mail orders. All 110-plus dealer tables were sold out long before the start of the event.

The strong attendance at Madison Avenue 33 was particularly impressive since the New York Yankees FanFest was staged on the same weekend at the Javits Convention Center in Manhattan. Most members of the '92 version of the Yankees showed up to sign autographs, plus a number of stars from yesteryear, including Whitey Ford, Hector Lopez, Johnny Blanchard, and Clete Boyer.

Mantle takes signing seriously

Mickey Mantle never signs an autograph in a slap-dash manner — he always takes the time to write his signature boldly and clearly, and always adheres to a collector's request as to where the autograph should be affixed on a particular memorabilia specimen. Though he usually can't take time to personalize an autograph he'll almost always add tidbits of information — if requested — like his major league home run total (536) record World Series home run total (18), MVP years (1956, 1957, 1962), Triple Crown year (1956), etc.

"I realize that a small percentage of guys who get invited to card shows don't much care what their signature looks like," Mantle told *SCD*, "but I'm here to please the fans, and the least I can do is to make the autograph look presentable."

Moreover, he never refuses a request to have his photo taken, and is generally more than happy to exchange a few words with fans who pass through his autograph line.

It's hard to believe that Mickey Mantle, the former "Boy Wonder" of baseball, is now 60 years old, and that he broke in with the Yankees as a 19 year old more than 40 years ago, in 1951. Despite the weight of all those calendar years, Mickey still exudes a certain type of boyish charm.

During his first few seasons with the Yankees, Mantle was acknowledged as being the fastest man in the game — and no one could reach first base from home plate quicker than he could. Yankee Manager Casey Stengel was astounded at Mantle's sheer speed and in this respect invited champion college trackmen from all across the U.S.A. to race Mickey back in the early 1950s.

"Did you ever lose any of those races to the college stars?" he was asked. Replied Mantle:

"I can't recall that I ever lost any special races. They (the college boys) all dressed in regulation baseball uniforms, with spikes, and Casey kept bragging that I couldn't be beat...and so I couldn't make a liar out of him. In fact, he almost drove me nuts with all those 'track meets' at Yankee Stadium, but he did all this to promote baseball in New York."

An old-time Yankee fan in attendance at the show said he witnessed many of those races, and recalled that Mantle was beaten once, in 1951, and that was by former Olympic champ Jesse Owens. Said the fan:

"Owens was 38 at the time, but he was still in great shape and gave exhibitions well into his forties. Owens managed to nose out Mantle in a 45-yard dash by a whisker." — *Robert Obojski, March 13, 1992*

Greer Johnson interviewed
Booking agent for Mickey Mantle and other celebrities

By Kevin Huard

Undoubtedly you've seen ads for card shows in *SCD* or other hobby publications promoting appearances by Mickey Mantle, Whitey Ford or other celebrities. In those ads you may have noticed a line of type that proclaimed "Mickey Mantle's appearance arranged by Greer Johnson Enterprises."

Or maybe you've noticed an attractive lady at a card show attending to the business arrangements of Mickey Mantle or another celebrity. That person is Greer Johnson.

A former grade school teacher, Greer left the teaching profession six years ago to embark on a totally new career as a celebrity representative. She has quickly gained the reputation as a successful, tough-but-fair businesswoman who looks out for the interests of her clients.

Recently Greer discussed what it's like to represent a living legend and other sports celebrities.

SCD: How did you get involved in the hobby as a representative of Mickey Mantle?

Johnson: Well it goes back about six years ago and I had met Mickey in Atlantic City when he was doing public relations for the Claridge Hotel. I had been up there with friends on junkets who would go up and gamble at the hotel on weekends. I knew Mickey as a friend.

At the time, I was teaching school. I taught school for 12 years before I got out of it, and I just happened to mention to Mickey one day, I said, "I'm tired of teaching, I've got to find something else to do. I'm ready for a career change. I'm burned out in teaching."

So he asked me, "Have you ever thought about being an agent for celebrities?" I grew up in the south. I had no idea what he was talking about. I had not had marketing or any college classes, or any formal education in marketing or anything of that nature.

I said, "What is it?" And he explained what you do and I thought about it for about two days. I gave it some thought. At the time, not being married, no children, not any type of a relationship, I was free to do whatever I wanted to do.

I went to my superintendant at the school and said, "What do you think? I've got this opportunity to change my career and get into a whole different career direction," and she said, "if you don't try it, you're crazy."

So I quit my job teaching in North Carolina, and moved to Atlanta and started my own company. I've been doing it now for over five years, close to six years. Of course I started with Mickey, and if it hadn't been for Mickey I'd still be teaching school probably.

Greer Johnson books all of Mickey's card show appearances.

I owe everything to him. He has been great. Of course I started with him with his shows, and just small things really. I started with real small appearances, and really just watching a lot of how he did things, how other people were doing the types of jobs that I'm doing now and just learning. By being there and watching and listening I learned as I went.

SCD: Do people waiting in line for autographs get to see the real Mickey Mantle?

Johnson: It's important to me for people to understand Mickey, because I see Mickey differently than other people. I understand why he says the things he says, and does the things that he does. Most people read it so opposite of what is really going on with Mickey when he gets upset.

 He's not upset with the person coming through the line if something gets messed up, if he messes up. He gets frustrated because he wants everybody in that line to be happy. And if he messes up a picture — and he has done this — he will tell the promoter, "Go get another picture and bring it back and let me sign again." And he will buy the picture. He will refund the guy his money or whatever.

Greer Johnson gave up a teaching profession to become Mantle's agent.

He's a perfectionist, and I'm a perfectionist. I think that's why we work so good with each other. He expects a lot of me and I expect a lot of him.

I'd like to tell a story that I think will show a side of Mickey that most people don't know. We were in California doing a card show, and a fellow came up and he had two little boys with him and it looked like they had come right off of the farm.

They had their overalls on. They didn't look clean. They didn't look like they had a whole lot of money. And so they were standing in front of him. Mickey was signing. I think they had two baseballs, one for each of the sons.

It seemed pretty apparent that they didn't have the money or couldn't afford the balls, much less to get them signed, plus the admission fees. And while Mickey is signing, he's figuring up in his head what this fella has spent on these autographs.

So as the guy walks off, Mickey looks at me and he says, "That fella can't afford the fees for these autographs." So he pulls out a $50 bill from his own pocket and he gives it to me.

He said, "Greer, take this money back and give it to this guy. He can't afford these autographs, and give the guys their money back."

It just so happened that there was another table there from an insurance company that Mickey was affiliated with, and they were selling policies. Well, the guy had gone over there and I guess he was going to buy an insurance policy.

So I went over and I gave the guy the $50 and I said, "Mickey would like to give this back to you." The guy didn't say anything, he stuck the money in his pocket. The promoter came over and he said, "What are you doing?"

And Mickey said, "Well, I told Greer to take the $50 back over to the guy. He couldn't afford the autographs." The promoter just went into hysterics.

He said, "That guy happens to be one of the most wealthy landlords in Orange County." But that just shows you a side of Mickey that most people don't know. He's got such a big heart.

SCD: He's always retained his country boy image, or treats people now like he did 40 years ago.

Johnson: And sometimes when he acts mad, he's not mad, he's embarrassed. If someone comes up to him and they say something that puts him on the spot or embarrasses him, he will act like he's mad, but actually he's not. That's his reaction. That's the way he covers up for it.

But he is modest, and he is very sensitive. He worries a lot more than he would ever lead you to believe.

SCD: He's really concerned about his fans?

Johnson: Absolutely. If it weren't for the readers, I mean most of the readers of *SCD* have given us the opportunity to do the things we do. And if it weren't for them, we wouldn't have a business. There would be no Greer Johnson Enterprises if it weren't for the people.

And that's something that Mickey and I understand. I mean we know that if it weren't for them, we wouldn't have a job. Thank God people care that much about Mickey.

SCD: You read *SCD*?

Johnson: Oh, I call it my bible. The *SCD* is my bible.

SCD: You're concerned about keeping the hobby on a certain level. You're always willing to cooperate if there's questionable merchandise out there?

Johnson: I do not want to see anybody unhappy with Mickey. With anything that we've done, we try really hard to make people happy. Sometimes you can't make everybody happy, but we do the best we can.

I think that a lot of my success comes from teaching school. I picked up a lot of skills in teaching school, public relations and business.

SCD: This is a big year for Mickey. It's the 30th anniversary of that great Yankee team and this year Mickey turned 60. It's also the 40th anniversary of Mickey's rookie season with the Yankees.

Johnson: He's got the heart and the attitude of a youngster.

SCD: Because he is so famous, is it difficult sometimes for Mickey to be seen in public? Can he ever get any privacy?

Johnson: Well, it's tough. And it goes back to if it weren't for those people wanting the autographs, then we wouldn't have a job. But on the other hand, it's a catch-22.

You do want some privacy. You do want to be able to go out to a nice restaurant and have a meal and be able to carry on a conversation with friends. And a lot of times that is difficult when people are asking for autographs.

You need people to care about you and you feel an obligation to them. Mickey really wants to be treated just like anybody else. He doesn't like people to make a big fuss for him.

He wants to be able to go and eat just like everybody else — or go into a grocery store. He likes to be able to do things like that. And for him, in a lot of places, it is tough.

SCD: Greer, you're tough, you're independent, you're successful, you're confident. You're certainly good for Mickey Mantle.

Johnson: When I was nine years old, my mother died. I was the eldest of two brothers and a sister. I spent most of my childhood bringing up my family.

I started working when I was 13. I worked at a dry cleaners. I continued to work from then on until today. I've always worked, all through high school, college.

With my mother being sick for so long and my father having three young children to take care of, finances were tight, so everybody had to pull their own weight.

SCD: Did you enjoy teaching?

Johnson: I loved teaching. I loved the kids. I taught in North Carolina. Then I moved to Reedsville, N.C., and taught. And I started getting more into city school systems.

SCD: Do you have fun going to all the card shows?

Johnson: Yes, I do. You get to see the same people a lot and you remember people. You might not remember their names, because there are so many, but you do know them. It's fun.

SCD: What do you think of the people that come in line, people that you see at shows that have this deep respect for Mickey? Does that show through sometimes?

Johnson: Oh absolutely. It thrills me to see the thrill that they're getting to see Mickey. And after we do a show, when we're in the car going back or whatever, we'll talk about people that came through the line and about their responses and how they reacted to Mickey.

I've seen people that I truly — all kidding aside — thought we were going to have to get paramedics for. In Atlanta, we were doing a card show, and a woman came up and she was shaking. She was almost hysterical after meeting Mickey.

I asked her, "Are you OK?" And she was just trembling all over and crying. Sometimes it's a little harder for me to understand how men have this fixation about Mickey. It's a thrill for me to see what these people get from that. Card shows are something that we want to continue doing.

When you see these people coming through, and you see their faces and the thrill that they're getting out of meeting him, it would be really tragic to take that away. Just seeing him on TV is one thing, or passing in the airport, that's something else.

With the way that the business and industry has gone, sometimes people question whether it is a true Mickey Mantle autograph. I think these shows offer an opportunity for people to say, "this is the ball I saw him sign."

SCD: For the $35 or $40 that a collector pays for a Mickey Mantle autograph, the person has approximately five-six seconds of Mickey's undivided attention. Do you think that is more important to most people than just the autograph itself?

Johnson: I've had a lot of people say that they come to the show and pay their money — not necessarily for the autograph — but to actually meet Mickey and shake his hand. Just anybody that comes through the line will ask to shake his hand, and of course, take pictures, too.

SCD: After 1961, Mickey became, not just a Yankee, but a baseball legend. Fans wanted Mickey to do well, even if they favored an opposing team.

Johnson: We are constantly getting people coming up to us and they'll say, "You know, I was a Red Sox fan, but I loved you Mickey," or, "I was a Dodger fan, but I loved you Mickey."

And the way their faces light up, and to see the guys that are 45-50 come through the line is enjoyable. They'll bring their little kids with them, and they'll say, "Hey son, this is the greatest baseball player ever, this is Mickey Mantle," and those little kids are looking up at him and the fathers are just glowing.

I find it ironic that the guys that are standing there now telling their kids that this is Mickey Mantle, and saying what a great guy he is, what a great baseball player he was, are the ones that were at the ballpark with their fathers watching Mickey play.

And I think Mickey represents, too, a lot of bonding with fathers and sons. Fathers took their kids to the ballpark to watch Mickey play, and there's that special time, father-son relationship. And now at these card shows, I see the same thing happening but just at a different level.

SCD: Does Mickey ever carry cards on him that he gives out to people that ask for an autograph when they see him in person?

Johnson: Yes. We use those a lot in restaurants, airports or walking down the streets of New York. We just give them one of these cards and it just means so much to them. It makes Mickey happy because he's been able to please someone.

Sometimes when people come up to Mickey and he acts like he's imposed upon a little bit, or at card shows when he gets aggravated, and somebody will give him something to sign and they'll say, "use a silver pen!" First of all, Mickey knows whatever item you give him, he already knows what should be used.

He's done this for how many years. He knows exactly what kind of pen to use. He knows exactly where to put it. When somebody says "use the silver one," he knows it should be a Sharpie. And if it doesn't turn out right, he acts like he's aggravated.

What it is, he's dissappointed because he wants to give every person in that line the very best autograph that he can give them, and if it gets messed up, he puts the blame on himself.

SCD: Back to Greer Johnson Enterprises. Who else do you represent?

Johnson: Of course, Mickey is my exclusive, and he keeps me extremely busy. I've worked with Whitey Ford, Yogi Berra, Moose Skowron, Hank Bauer, Johnny Blanchard, Tommy Tresh and Harmon Killebrew. I'm now working with Jimmy Orr and Gary Carter.

SCD: Are you starting to work with some of the newer ballplayers?

Johnson: Yes. There's a local player that we're about to begin working with. I'm doing some expanding and taking on some new people and trying to spend more time with other players as well, but it's just difficult because Mickey does require a lot of time.

SCD: In terms of Mickey Mantle, how many card shows do you anticipate him doing next year?

Johnson: Well, we try to keep the amount down. There's such a large demand across the United States. I try to keep it down and I try to do them across the United States and not just one area. It just goes back to supply and demand. I don't want to overexpose Mickey in any one area.

SCD: Some people might believe that with the number of shows Mickey's going to do, his autograph is going to go down in value. He does private signings sometimes. Is there a concern about flooding the market? Some ballplayers do two shows a week or so.

Johnson: Well, I feel like two a month is too much. I try to keep it down to one a month. But then something will happen and we'll miss a month. Then you have people that keep wanting you to come back every year.

SCD: What's the future hold for you?

Johnson: I love what I'm doing. I absolutely love it, I really do enjoy it. I enjoy working with Mickey, and we've gotten to a place now that Mickey trusts what I'm doing, he trusts my judgment.

What I would like to see with Mickey and Greer Johnson Enterprises is to get Mickey in some corporate work. I would like some major endorsements, corporate outings, tournaments, golf tournaments, that sort of thing. — *Kevin Huard, Nov. 29, 1991*

Chapter 5
The price is right
Off The Top Of My Head

By Tom Gregg

MONEY Magazine's
most valuable baseball cards:

1. American Tobacco Honus Wagner, issued 1909, $12,500.
2. Goudey Napoleon Lajoie, issued 1934, $6,500.
3. American Tobacco Eddie Plank, issued 1919, $5,000.
4. Topps Jim Konstanty Standup, issued 1951, $2,500.
5. Topps Mickey Mantle, issued 1952, $1,700.
6. Bowman Ted Williams, issued 1954, $1,075.
7. American Tobacco Sherry Magee, issued 1919, $950.
8. Topps Willie Mays, issued 1953, $700.
9. Topps Henry Aaron, issued 1954, $300.
10. Topps Roger Maris Yankees variation, issued 1967, $300.

The $30,000 Mantle card.

This list "includes most of the heavy hitters," *MONEY* says. Thanks to much similar sensationalistic news coverage (invariably mentioning the Wagner and Mantle cards), the general public now thinks that any 10-year-old card in any condition ought to be worth at least a few bills. Which means you can offend people, but good, merely by offering them a fair, full Beckett price for stuff they've dredged up from the attic. — *Tom Gregg, Dec. 31, 1980*

Wirt's Words

By Wirt Gammon
Debits and Credits

Credit to *Sports Illustrated* for taking notice of baseball card collectors and the prices of some rarer cards. It traces the surge in Mantle 1952s from $1,200 over a year ago to $3,250 in July and then — after more such cards surfaced — down to $1,765. It noted that other superstar cards had experienced similar trends, and now the market has bottomed out and is on the upswing. *SI* notes that attention is suddenly paid to rookie cards, with Bob Horner last year (prices at $2.50 now) and George Brett's card, which is now $7 though it was only 75 cents four months ago. — *Wirt Gammon, Jan. 20, 1981*

'52 Topps set continues to increase; so does Mantle!

For this issue of the *Price Guide*, which updates card values from 1948 to 1970, we have once again added more than two dozen new entries to our individual listings. Many of them are "rookie cards," including the first appearances of popular players like Bill Skowron, Jimmy Piersall, Whitey Herzog, Felipe Alou, Willie Davis, Bert Campaneris and others.

Interest in rookie cards seems to be continuing and our price guide reflects that — especially for future Hall of Famers. The rookie cards of Nolan Ryan, Willie McCovey, Gaylord Perry, Jim Palmer and Johnny Bench are all accompanied by plus signs this issue.

You'll also notice lots of plus signs behind the cards of Mickey Mantle, who is consistently popular with collectors of all ages. His big card — the legendary 1952 Topps Mantle — is creeping upward again, according to our panel of card pricing experts. We're now listing the value at $1,100 for an Ex-Mt example, an increase of $100.

Speaking of '52 Topps cards, we've raised slightly the value of commons in that set to better reflect the actual state of the market, and we've jumped the complete set price to $7,800 in Ex-Mt. Some members of our price panel suggested we raise it even higher.

Collectors and dealers are already speculating on what might happen to the famous 1963 Pete Rose rookie card, as the Reds' new player/manager prepares for his final assault on Ty Cobb's career hit record. This is the card that brought the widest range of recommendations from our price panel — from a low of $125 in Ex-Mt to a high of $400. The *Price Guide* currently lists the Rose rookie at $285, and, for now at least, that's where we left it. — *Dec. 7, 1984*

Call it Mantlemania!

Without even the slightest doubt, the most popular pre-1980 baseball cards are those of former New York Yankee great Mickey Mantle. The Oklahoma hayseed who became the pride of the country's largest city was the hero of most children of the post-World War II baby boom.

Mantle claims he would have hit 1,000 lifetime home runs had he been able to play his career free of injuries. Stories of Mantle taping his body from the ankles to the waist so that be could perform on the playing field are not exaggerated. Even today, young fans who never experienced the prodigiousness of a Mantle home run want a baseball card of "The Mick" for their collections.

Entire ads featuring nothing but Mantle memorabilia have appeared recently in *SCD*. At card shows, display cases of just Mantle cards adorn dealers' tables. Prices of Mantle cards continue to skyrocket in the various price guides. "Mantlemania" is at its peak.

I attended the Chicago Labor Day weekend show and spoke with several respected dealers about the Mantle craze. They confirmed my thoughts by stating that Mantle cards are some of the most overpriced items in the hobby. Quality Mantle cards in strict Nr Mt to Mt condition are not overpriced, but anything below Nr Mt usually is. This was true in Chicago where I saw Mantles from the 1960s in VG-EX and Ex conditions with selling prices in excess of $100.

Card #200 in the 1963 Topps set is Mickey Mantle. Card #201 is Cecil Butler, a nondescript pitcher who played in 11 major league games. If a count could be made, most advanced collectors wouldn't be surprised to learn that more Mantle cards exist today than Butler cards. The point I'm trying to make is that Mantle cards in Ex or lesser conditions are not rare or scarce. They are in abundance and, in most cases, are overpriced. Shop wisely!
— *Dan Albaugh, Price Guide Report, Sept. 25, 1987*

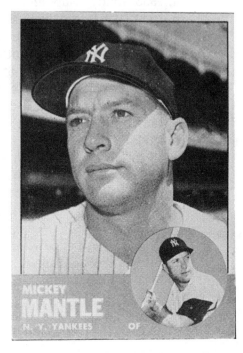

Mantle's 1963 Topps card, #200.

SCD's Top 20 Most Valuable Baseball Cards

Although most of us who collect baseball cards do so because we truly love baseball and the hobby, we also recognize the hobby's huge investment potential. Apparently so does everyone else.

With the hobby's tremendous growth over the past few years, more and more "mainstream" newspapers and magazines have been doing news and feature stories about baseball cards and their increasing values. Because of our close involvement in the hobby, many of these newspapers and magazines often contact *SCD* for interviews and other information.

Despite our best attempts to convey the nostalgic and "fun" aspects of the hobby, their questions — and articles — invariably emphasize the financial side of baseball cards.

Perhaps the most frequent request is for a listing of the most valuable

The classic 1951 Mantle Bowman.

baseball cards — which we, of course, are more than happy to provide. After providing this list to various other publications over the past few weeks, we thought our own readers might like to see it, too.

1. 1909 T206 Honus Wagner..$95,000
2. 1932 U.S. Caramel Charles (Lindy) Lindstrom.....................$18,000
3. 1909 T206 Joe Doyle (rare variation) $15,000
4. 1933 Goudey Napoleon Lajoie...$15,000
5. 1909 T206 Eddie Plank $9,000
6. 1909 T206 Sherry Magie $8,000
7. 1952 Topps Mickey Mantle..$6,500
8. 1951 Topps Current All-Stars Stanky.................................$5,500
9. 1951 Topps Current All-Stars Konstanty.............................$5,500
10. 1951 Topps Current All-Stars Roberts...............................$5,500
11. 1951 Bowman Mickey Mantle...$4,800
12. 1911 T3 Ty Cobb $3,500
13. 1933 Goudey Babe Ruth #181..$3,300
14. 1933 Goudey Babe Ruth #53..$3,100
15. 1933 Goudey Babe Ruth #149...$3,100
16. 1933 Goudey Babe Ruth #144...$2,800
17. 1912 T207 Irving Lewis...$2,800
18. 1912 T207 Louis Lowdermilk..$2,800
19. 1912 T207 Ward Miller..$2,800
20. 1911 T205 Ty Cobb $2,500

Mantle painting brings an amazing $121,000!
Topps auction nets $1.6 million!

By Steve Ellingboe

Last week's auction of treasures from the Topps Co. archives dramatically demonstrated two things: First, that baseball memorabilia has definitely moved into the big leagues of the investment world, and second, that Mickey Mantle is its undisputed king.

The auction, conducted by Guernsey's at New York's Hunter-College Aug. 19-20, brought record-high prices that astonished most hobbyists and left many of the 400 registered bidders shaking their heads in wonderment.

When Topps first announced its plans for the blockbuster auction, no one ever doubted the unique memorabilia would command some lofty prices. But once the bidding began, it quickly became obvious that the prices realized would far exceed even the greatest expectations.

According to Guernsey's, the sale grossed over $1.6 million, about three times the pre-auction estimate. Topps said it is donating "a significant" portion of its earnings to three different charities.

The auction catalog was filled with one-of-a-kind items never before made available to the public — original artwork, uncut production sheets, color photographs, signed player contracts and other pieces of baseball card history. But clearly the star of the show — and the object of all the media attention — was the original painting used to create the 1953 Topps Mickey Mantle card.

The card itself — and there are thousands of them around — sells for about $2,000 in Near Mint condition, so it's only reasonable to assume that the original painting — of which there is only one — would fetch a price many times that. It did.

The Mantle artwork — a relatively tiny 3 x 4 (only slightly larger than the actual card) — was among a group of six paintings from the 1953 set that proved to be the highlight of the two-day sale. The auction was already into its seventh hour, and running about 90 minutes behind schedule, when the six prized paintings were finally brought to the floor and placed, one at a time, before an anxious audience of collectors, dealers and investors.

The fireworks began immediately. Bidding on the Mantle artwork started at $20,000 and quickly escalated in $10,000 increments, until, within seconds, the price had jumped to over $50,000 and was climbing rapidly. Although several bidders were involved in the early going, only two remained past the $70,000 mark.

The crowd sat in stunned anticipation as the bidding war continued, one-on-one, between the two remaining bidders, seated on opposite ends of the room. The hushed gallery watched in silence, their **heads** turning from side to side, like spectators at a tennis match, looking to see which contestant would drop first.

The bidding war continued. Eighty thousand...then $90,000. Both bidders seemed determined and confident. The crowd stirred with nervous excitement as the bidding reached the $100,000 plateau. Then $110,000. Heads turned one final time, waiting for the kill shot. And when the $110,000 bid went unanswered, it was over. The entire process took less than 120 seconds.

The winning bidder flashed a broad victory smile as be calmly accepted a congratulatory handshake from his business partner and then, with a quick wave of his arm, proudly acknowledged the energetic applause from the appreciative auction gallery, now fully aware that they had just witnessed, perhaps, the single most dramatic moment in the young history of the hobby.

With the 10 percent buyer's fee added to each lot, the total price of the Mantle painting was a staggering $121,000, certainly among the highest prices ever paid for a piece of sports memorabilia.

The winning bid came from an unlikely source: the Marriott Hotel chain, which also purchased the 1953 Willie Mays artwork for an equally impressive $88,000. After the hectic bidding was over, Matt Jones, Director of Bar Operations for Marriott, told *SCD* that the hotel chain plans to use the two paintings for promotional purposes, displaying them, on a rotating basis, in the 10 "Champions" sports lounges that Marriott operates across the country.

From its aggressive bidding, it was obvious the Marriott group was prepared to pay whatever it would take to own the Mantle painting, but Jones declined to reveal just how high he would have gone.

"We did set a limit," he said, "but I'd rather not say what it was," adding that the $110,000 winning bid was "higher than we had expected it would be."

Jones' partner, Marriott Marketing Director Roger Conner, was delighted with the purchases.

"Mantle, Mays and Marriott," he mused aloud, as if reading an imaginary newspaper headline, "I love the alliteration."

"This is the most fun I've had in New York on a weekday," said the beaming Conner, apparently too caught up in the excitement of the moment to realize it was actually Saturday. "This is true baseball Americana."

Marriott's jubilant Roger Conner and Matt Jones.

Conner confided to *SCD* that Marriott had actually hoped to buy all six of the paintings, but "the bidding got too pricey. We wanted to keep them together," he said, "but it just went too high."

Conner said Marriott will probably display the Mantle and Mays paintings in its various sports bars "for the next year or so," and then sell them at auction with the proceeds going to charity.

The "losing" bidder on the Mantle painting, John Rue of The Rarities Group, a diversified collectibles wholesaler from Marlboro, Mass., did not go home empty-handed. Although Rue was shut out on the Mantle and Mays paintings, he was the successful bidder on three others, buying the Whitey Ford artwork for $35,200, the Bob Feller piece for $33,000, and the Roy Campanella for $16,500 (all prices include the 10 percent buyer's fee). Rue also was the winning bidder on a Mickey Mantle jersey, which went for $33,000.

The Rarities Group, primarily a coin wholesaler, is now actively branching out into other collectible areas, said Rue, the firm's chief purchasing officer.

John Rue (left) came up short on the winning bid, which Matt Jones flashed.

"We have been quietly buying quality baseball memorabilia and putting it away for future resale," Rue said. "Plus, we recently acquired what we believe is the best-known example of the number one Superman comic."

The Rarities Group is not at all shy about spending big money for quality collectibles. Last month, the firm was involved in purchasing the "King of Siam proof set," perhaps the most famous item in the numismatic hobby, for a price "in excess of $2 million."

Rue told *SCD* that his limit on the Mantle painting was $100,000, and he "reluctantly" dropped out when the bidding reached $110,000, acknowledging the difficulty of bidding against a corporate giant like the Marriott chain.

The sixth of the prized paintings, artwork used to create the 1953 Topps Jackie Robinson card, went to an unidentified private collector for $71,000.

Everything in the auction associated with Mickey Mantle brought prices many times their pre-sale estimate, as the former Yankee outfielder firmly established his position as the popular figure in the hobby today.

A run of original Topps contracts, cancelled checks, letters and other documents bearing Mantle's signature went for prices ranging from $1,000 to over $17,000 per lot.

A lot of contracts and cancelled checks signed by Yogi Berra, meanwhile, sold for $3,300, while Willie Mays' first contract with Topps went for $3,000, and a handwritten letter from Hank Aaron to Topps President Sy Berger brought a bid of $1,700. Dozens of other contracts went for between $50 and $2,000, depending, of course, on the player involved.

This display includes the original artwork for the 1953 Topps Mantle card.

The auction also included hundreds of uncut production sheets, which brought prices ranging from $200 to $3,000; original color transparencies of photos used to create various baseball cards, which sold for as much as $250 each; and dozens of "flexi-chromes," colorized black-and-white photos used in the card-making process in the early '60s, which sold for as much as $3,000. — *By Steve Ellingboe, Sept. 8, 1989*

Champions' bar founder has ultimate Mantle collection

By Joshua Evans

Beginning late this month the 1953 Topps Mickey Mantle and Willie Mays artwork recently auctioned off at the Topps auction will be on tour at several Marriott Corp. sports bars.

According to John Haveron, of Marriott's public relations department, the artwork, which garnered combined bids of $209,000, will be displayed in eight sports bars called Champions, each housed in Marriott Hotels.

The two 3 1/4-by-4 1/2 -inch paintings will be displayed along with the Champions old decor and sports memorabilia.

In addition to stops at Marriott Hotels in New York and San Francisco, the tour will stop for three days at the original Champions bar in Georgetown (Washington, D.C.). The paintings will end up at the Marriott's corporate headquarters in Bethesda, Md.

The paintings will be framed together, along with examples of the cards created from the paintings.

Although the 1953 Topps Mickey Mantle card displayed with the artwork will be in EX condition at best, to one collector it is worth more than money — the card is the original which Champions founder Michael O'Harro got out of a wax pack in 1953.

"I nearly refused to go on vacation with my parents to San Diego until I got that last card I needed to complete the set — Mickey Mantle," O'Harro said.

"This was my first year collecting and I just could not find it. We must have stopped at every five-and-dime and grocery store along the way buying packs of baseball cards.

"Finally, on Aug. 22, 1953, I bought a whole box and in the very last pack there it was.

"I bought another '53 Mantle years later to go with my set, but I will keep that one forever. It's very special to me."

Marriott will produce a limited-edition poster of the two paintings to coincide with the tour. They are negotiating with Mantle and Mays to have them appear with their paintings at each stop.

Negotiations are also in progress with Lloyds of London to insure the paintings for $1,000,000.

Marriott's ultimate plan is to auction off the artwork in the summer of 1990. The proceeds will go to a charity which benefits children. — *Joshua Evans, Balls in the Attic, Sept. 22, 1989*

Leland's auction brings out heavy hitters, Mantle jersey breaks $100,000 barrier

By Gary Dunaier

If the bidding at Leland's latest auction in New York City is any indication, Mickey Mantle is better than Babe Ruth.

The New York Yankees home pinstripe worn by the Sultan of Swat during the 1926 World Series against the St. Louis Cardinals was one of nearly 300 pieces offered by the New York auction house as part of its "Heavy Hitters" live auction on Jan. 15, 1992.

It was the first Babe Ruth jersey ever to be put up for public auction, and it sold for $82,500. That's not exactly chump change, but it played second fiddle to the final price of Mickey Mantle's 1960 New York Yankees home jersey — $111,100.

A lot of ones in that figure, quite appropriate for something from the ballplayer who is number one in today's collecting market. It surpasses the $71,500 paid for Mantle's 1967 road top at Leland's previous live auction in July 1991.

Leland's Inc. held its "Heavy Hitters" auction in New York.

The Mantle jersey was originally displayed for promotional purposes in the window of Whitehouse and Hardy, a clothing store located in New York's Rockefeller Center. They obtained it through a contact inside the ballclub, but the Yankees never asked for its return.

Until the auction, the jersey remained in the store owner's family. Joshua Evans, chairman of Leland's, said that the consignors were ecstatic and "in tears" when they learned how much the jersey finally went for.

The big surprise was that the Ruth jersey sold for "only" $82,500. There's a lot of history in that shirt, but it must be admitted that it doesn't have the visual appeal that the Mantle shirt has. In Ruth's day, Yankee jerseys didn't have numbers on the back, nor did the intertwined "NY" logo appear on the front.

Also, the tail was trimmed, and if you hold the jersey to the light, you can make out the name of a semi-pro team which used it after the Yankees were finished with it (a common practice in the late 1920s). Evans commented on how that may have been a factor in the bidding: "When you're talking about this kind of money, people want perfection. It just wasn't a great Ruth jersey. But it was the buy of the sale, no question of it." — *Gary Dunaier, Feb. 14, 1992*

How the Mantle jersey went for $111,100

By Gary Dunaier

At 8:08 p.m. New York time on Wednesday, Jan. 15, 1992, Mickey Mantle memorabilia history was made when the Mick's 1960 New York Yankees home jersey sold for a

122

record $111,100 at Leland's "Heavy Hitters" auction at the Southgate Tower Hotel in New York City.

Here's the scene: The Mantle jersey, along with Roger Maris' 1960 jersey (which was to be auctioned off immediately after the Mantle), are removed from a locked display case and brought to the front of the hall.

There's a sense of excitement in the room — the same room where, at Leland's previous live auction six months earlier, Mickey Mantle's 1967 road jersey sold for a then-record $71,500. And so, here is the call from auctioneer Claudia Florian as the bidding on Lot 43A is about to begin.

"Number 43A, doesn't need much introduction, for the 1960 home jersey of Mickey Mantle. This pinstripe is the first ever to be offered at public sale, the 100 percent is original and doesn't have any restorations.

"So, for number 43A, let's start here at $25,000 for this, let's start on this one at 25,000. 25,000. 26,000. 27,000 here. 28,000. 29,000 here.

"30,000. At 30,000. At 3250 here. 3250 with me, at 3250. 32 — 35,000. 3750. 40,000, it's at 40,000. 4250 here. At 4250. 4250 here. 42,500, rather, I should say, at 42,500, it's still here at 42,500.

(At this point a floor bidder enters a bid of $65,000.)

"65,000? (The floor bidder confirms his bid.) I'll acccept that. (Laughs.) That's my kind of bidder! A serious bidder at 65,000. It's your bid sir, now, left side at 65,000. Is there any advance on $65,000? 65,000.

Auctioneer Claudia Florian seeks bids on Mantle and Maris jerseys.

This is Mantle's 1960 Spalding home jersey.

"70,000 is next. 70,000 I have. It's at 70,000 here, right side, now, at 70,000. Any bid of 75, please? 70,000 here, is there any bid of 75? 75 now, left side, at 75,000.

"80,000. New bidder, now, in at $80,000. A new bidder in at $80,000. New bidder. Any bid at 85, please? I have 80,000, will someone say 85? I have $80,000 now. 85, now, 85 in a new place, there. 85. Will someone say 90, please? I have 85,000, extreme right, at $85,000, and 90.

"At $90,000 now. Center of the room now, at 90. Will you go to 95, sir? I have $90,000, I have — will you say 95? (At this point a floor bidder enters a bid of $101,000.)

"I'll take that. I'll take 101. You can conduct your own auction, I don't mind. I'll take $101,000. 101.

"The next increment can be 105, if someone wishes. I like round numbers. At 101, I have at the moment.

"$101,000. $101,000. Are you all done now? Don't know when you'll have another opportunity like this one, it's at $101,000.

"No bidding on the phone, then? $101,000, I like the sound of that. All done and selling, then at $101,000. (The hammer falls to much applause.)

"Could I have your paddle number, sir? 131. A lucky number, thank you."

(Author's note: The final price of the jersey, with the addition of a 10 percent buyer's premium, was $111,100.) — *Gary Dunaier, Feb. 14, 1992*

Chapter 6

The ultimate checklist

Mickey Mantle card checklist

1951

Set	No.	(NR MT)	(EX)	(VG)
1951 Bowman	253	8,000.00	4,000.00	2,500.00

This 324-card set features color art reproductions of actual photographs. The cards are 2 1/16-by-3 1/8 inches. The player's name is inside a black box on the card's front. The high-numbered cards in the series (from 253-324, including Mantle's) are considered the scarcest cards in the issue. The complete set is valued at $21,000 in Near Mint condition, and includes rookie cards for Willie Mays and Mickey Mantle. Commons numbered 1-36 are $20; commons from 37-252 are $14; commons from 253-324 are $60.

1952

1952 Berk Ross	—	1,200.00	600.00	360.00

Titled "The Hit Parade of Champions," the 1952 Berk Ross set features 72 unnumbered cards, issued individually, rather than as two-card panels in 1951. Cards are 2-by-3 inches. Phil Rizzuto is in the set twice, and backs for Ewell Blackwell and Nelson Fox are transposed. The fronts feature tinted color photographs, while the backs include biographical and statistical information from 1951. The complete set is valued at $4,500 in Near Mint condition. Commons are $12.

1952 Bowman	101	2,000.00	1,000.00	600.00

This 252-card set features facsimile autographs and color art reproductions of actual photographs on the fronts. The cards are 2 1/16-by-3 1/8 inches. Common players from 1-216 are valued at $18 in Near Mint condition; commons from 217-252 are $30. The complete set is valued at $9,000 in Near Mint condition.

1952 Tip Top Bread	—	1,500.00	750.00	450.00

This unnumbered set of bread-end labels includes 48 different labels, including two of Phil Rizzuto. The player's name, team and photo appear inside a star on the front, with the word "Tip Top" printed above. The labels are 2 1/2-by-2 3/4 inches. Commons are valued at $65 in Near Mint condition, while the complete set is valued at $5,500.

1952 Topps	311	30,000.00	15,000.00	8,000.00

This 407-card set was the largest of its day. The 2 5/8-by-3 3/4-inch cards feature hand-colored black-and-white photos on the fronts. Innovations in the set were the first-time use of color team logos as part of the card's design, plus statistics for the previous year and career were included on the back. The first 80 cards include backs printed entirely in black, which command a $10-$15 premium, or black and red. Cards 311-407, including Mantle's, were printed in limited supplies and are extremely rare. The complete set is valued at $70,000 in Near Mint condition. Commons from 1-80 are $50; commons 81-250 are $25; commons 251-280 are $40; commons 281-300 are $40; commons 301-310 are $40; commons 311-407 are $175.

1953

1953 Bowman color (with Berra, Bauer)

	44	400.00	200.00	125.00
1953 Bowman color	59	2,200.00	1,100.00	650.00

This is the first set of current major league players to use actual color photographs and is one of the most popular issues of the post-war era. Card fronts are blank. Backs contain the player's career and previous year's statistics. High-numbered cards (#113-160) are the scarcest in the set; numbers 113-128 are exceptionally difficult to find. Commons numbered 1-112 are valued at $30 in Near Mint; commons 113-160 are $40. The complete set is valued at $12,000 in Near Mint condition.

1953-54 Briggs Meats	—	2,200.00	1,100.00	660.00

This 38-card colored set was issued over a two-year span and features 26 players from the Washington Senators and 12 from the New York City area teams. The 2 1/4-by-3 1/2-inch cards, printed on waxed cardboard, were issued in two-card panels on hot dog packages sold in the Washington, D.C., area. The backs are blank. The style for the Senators' card differs from that of the New York players. Commons are valued at $100 in Near Mint condition; the complete set is valued at $8,000.

1953 Stahl-Meyer Franks	—	2,000.00	1,000.00	600.00

These nine cards, issued in packages of hot dogs by a New York area meat company, feature three players each from the Brooklyn Dodgers, New York Giants and New York Yankees. The unnumbered, white-bordered cards are 3 1/4-by-4 1/2 inches and feature color photos, the player's name and facsimile autograph on the front. Biographical and statistical information is included on half of the card back, which also includes a ticket offer promotion. The card corners are cut diagonally, although some cards with square corners (apparently cut from sheets) have been seen. Commons are valued at $125 in Near Mint condition; the complete set is valued at $4,500.

1953 Topps	82	3,000.00	1,500.00	900.00

This set was originally intended to be 280 cards, but six numbers (253, 261, 267, 268, 271 and 275) were not issued. The 2 5/8-by-3 3/4-inch cards feature painted player pictures and a color team logo on the front. The backs contain the first baseball trivia questions. Card numbers 221-280 are scarce high numbers. Commons numbered 1-220 are valued at $16 in Near Mint condition; commons 221-280 are $50-$90. The complete set is valued at $14,000.

1954

1954 Bowman	65	900.00	450.00	75.00

This full-color 224-card set includes a scarce Ted Williams card (#66) which, because it was pulled from the set, is valued at $4,250 in Near Mint condition. Williams' replacement, Jimmy Piersall, also exists as #66, and as #210. The complete set is valued at $4,500 in Near Mint condition, without the Williams scarcity. Cards are 2 1/2-by-3 3/4 inches. Approximately 40 other variations exist in the set, most of which involve statistical errors on card backs which were subsequently corrected. Both varieties appear to have been printed in equal amounts, so neither one has a premium value. Commons numbered 1-112 are $8 in Near Mint condition; commons 113-224 are $10.

1954 Dan-Dee Potato Chips	—	1,500.00	750.00	450.00

Issued in bags of potato chips, the cards in this 29-card set are commonly found with grease stains, despite their waxed surface. The unnumbered cards are 2 1/2-by-3 5/8 inches. The set consists mainly of Cleveland Indians and Pittsburgh Pirates. Photos of the Yankees players were also used for Briggs Meats and Stahl-Meyer Franks sets. Commons in Near Mint condition are valued at $60; the complete set is at $4,500.

1954 *N.Y. Journal-American*	—	450.00	225.00	135.00

This unnumbered 59-card set features players from the Brooklyn Dodgers, New York Yankees and New York Giants. The 2-by-4-inch black-and-white cards were issued at newsstands with the now-extinct newspaper. Fronts have promotional copy, the player's name and photo, and a contest serial number. The backs have team schedules. Common players are valued at $10 in Near Mint condition; the complete set is valued at $2,250.

1954 Red Heart Dog Food	—	450.00	225.00	135.00

This 33-card set was issued in three color-coded series by the Red Heart Dog Food Co. The fronts feature hand-colored photos on either a green, red or blue background. The 11 red-backed cards are scarcer than the others. Backs of the 2 5/8-by-3 3/4-inch cards have biographical and statistical information and a Red Heart ad. Each 11-card series was available via a mail-in offer. Commons are valued at $25 in Near Mint condition; the complete set is valued at $2,500.

1954 *Sports Illustrated*	—	400.00 to 500.00
		for the magazine with the cards inside
		- (black-and-white, issued Aug. 23, 1954)

This was *Sports Illustrated's* second issue ever. Inside it featured New York Yankees stars, including Mickey Mantle, on 1954 black-and-white and colored Topps cards. This magazine, which shows a horde of golf bags on the greens at the Masters, is as rare and as valuable as *SI's* first issue, which is dated Aug. 16, 1954, and featured Eddie Mathews on the cover.

1954 Stahl-Meyer Franks	—	2,500.00	1,250.00	750.00

This unnumbered 12-card set retained the 3 1/4-by-4 1/2-inch size from the previous year, but added three cards, including Willie Mays. The front's format is the same, but the backs are designed on a vertical format and include an ad for a "Johnny Stahl-Meyer Baseball Kit." Commons are $125 in Near Mint condition; the complete set is valued at $6,250.

1955

1955 Bowman	202	500.00	250.00	150.00

This popular 320-card set has player photographs placed inside a television set design. The cards are 2 1/2-by-3 3/4 inches. The high-numbered cards (#s 225-320) are the scarcest in the set and include 31 umpire cards. Common cards numbered 1-224 are valued at $9 in Near Mint condition; commons 225-320 are $25. The complete set is valued at $5,000 in Near Mint condition.

1955 Stahl-Meyer Franks	—	2,500.00	1,250.00	750.00

Four players from each of the New York City area teams are represented in this 12-card set. The 3 1/4-by-4 1/2-inch unnumbered cards again have full-color photos bordered in yellow with diagonal borders. The backs have a new promotion featuring a drawing of Mickey Mantle and an ad selling pennants and caps. The vertical format on the card backs again has statistical information.

Commons are valued at $125 in Near Mint condition; the complete set is valued at $5,000.

1956

1956 Topps	135	1,000.00	500.00	300.00

This 340-card set uses a portrait and action picture on the card fronts. Innovations in the set include team cards and two unnumbered checklist cards, plus cards for the two league presidents, William Harridge and Warren Giles. Cards were 2 5/8-by-3 3/4 inches. Three-panel cartoons are featured on the backs. Card backs for numbers 1-180

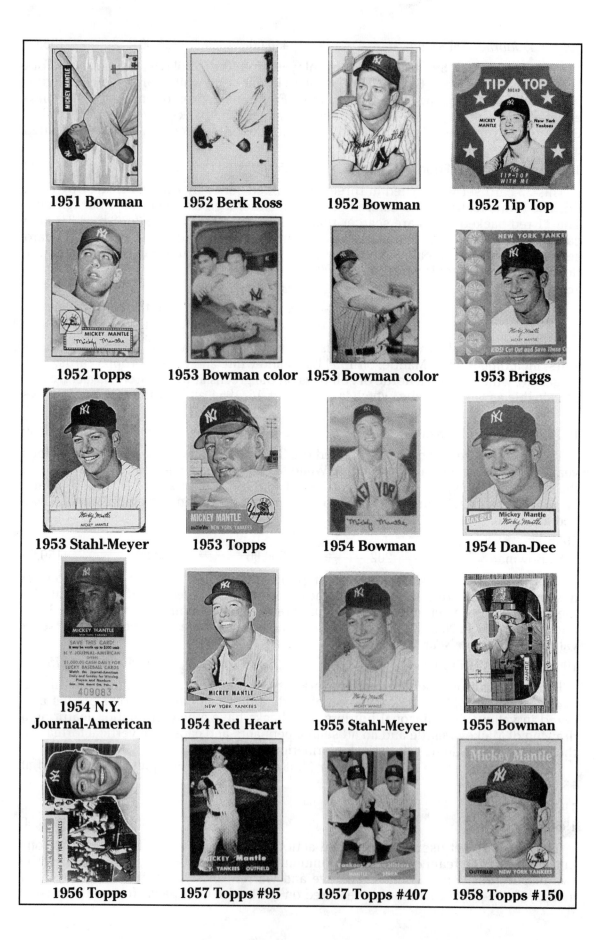

1951 Bowman   **1952 Berk Ross**   **1952 Bowman**   **1952 Tip Top**

1952 Topps   **1953 Bowman color**   **1953 Bowman color**   **1953 Briggs**

1953 Stahl-Meyer   **1953 Topps**   **1954 Bowman**   **1954 Dan-Dee**

1954 N.Y. Journal-American   **1954 Red Heart**   **1955 Stahl-Meyer**   **1955 Bowman**

1956 Topps   **1957 Topps #95**   **1957 Topps #407**   **1958 Topps #150**

can be found with either white or grey cardboard. Some dealers charge a premium for grey backs (1-100) and white backs (101-180). Commons numbered 1-100 are valued at $7 in Near Mint condition; commons 101-180 are $9; commons 181-260 are $15; commons 261-340 are $9. The complete set is valued at $7,500 in Near Mint condition.

1957

1957 Topps	95	900.00	450.00	275.00
1957 Topps (Yankee Power Hitters/Berra)				
	407	400.00	200.00	125.00

Topps reduced the size of these cards to today's standard 2 1/2-by-3 1/2 inches. The 407-card set also used real color photographs instead of the hand-colored black-and-whites of previous years. Innovations in the set included complete player statistics on the back and cards featuring more than one player on them. Card numbers 265-352 are considered scarce. Four unnumbered checklist cards were also created. They are quite expensive and are not included in the set's $7,500 value in Near Mint condition. Commons numbered 1-264 are valued at $7; commons 265-352 are $18; commons 353-407 are $7.

1958

1958 Topps	150	550.00	275.00	165.00
1958 Topps (World Series Batting Foes/Aaron)				
	418	150.00	75.00	45.00
1958 Topps (All-Star)	487	100.00	50.00	30.00

This 494-card set includes one card, #145, which was not issued after Ed Bouchee was suspended from baseball. Cards are 2 1/2-by-3 1/2 inches. The number of multiple-player cards increased in this set, and for the first time, checklists were incorporated into the numbered series, as the backs of the team cards. Another major innovation is the inclusion of 20 "All-Star" cards.

Common cards numbered 1-110 are valued at $7; commons 111-440 are $5; commons 441-495 are $4. The complete set is valued at $5,000 in Near Mint condition.

1959

1959 Bazooka	—	2,000.00	1,000.00	600.00

This set of 23 unnumbered cards was issued on boxes of Bazooka one-cent bubble gum. The individually-wrapped pieces of Bazooka bubble gum were produced by Topps Chewing Gum. The cards are 2 13/16-by-4 15/16 and are blank-backed. Mantle was one of nine cards issued first which are therefore more plentiful. Commons are valued at $125 in Near Mint condition; the complete set is valued at $8,500. Complete boxes would command 75 percent over the cards' prices.

1959 Home Run Derby	—	1,200.00	600.00	400.00

This 20-card unnumbered set was produced by American Motors to publicize the Home Run Derby television program. The cards measure approximately 3 1/4-by-5 1/4 and feature black-and-white player photos on black-backed white stock. The player name and team are printed beneath the photo. This set was reprinted (and marked as such) in 1988 by Card Collectors' Co. of New York. Common players are valued at $100 in Near Mint condition; the complete set is valued at $4,000.

1959 Topps	10	450.00	225.00	135.00
1959 Topps (Mantle Hits 42nd Homer For Crown)				
	461	35.00	17.50	10.50
1959 Topps (All-Star)	564	300.00	150.00	90.00

These cards, which include a facsimile autograph on the front, have a round photograph with a solid-color background and white border. The 572 cards in the set made it the largest ever at that point. Card numbers below 507 have red and green printing with the card number in white in a green box. Cards 507 and above have printing in black and red and the card number is in a black box. Card numbers 199-286 can be found with either white or grey stock, which is less common. Common cards numbered 1-110 are valued at $5 in Near Mint condition; commons 111-506 are $3; commons 507-572 are $15. The complete set is valued at $5,000.

1959 Yoo Hoo Soft Drink (b&w) —   undetermined

This unnumbered set of six features only New York Yankees.

1960

1960 Bazooka (single)	31	300.00	150.00	90.00
(panel with Mantle/Hobbie/McMillan)				
	31-32-33	450.00	225.00	135.00

Three-card full-color panels were found on the bottoms of Bazooka bubble gum boxes. The blank-backed set has 36 cards, each numbered at the bottom. The single cards are 1 13/16-by-2 3/4 inches; the panels are 2 3/4-by-5 1/2 inches. Common panels are valued at $75; common single players are $5. The complete singles set is valued at $1,200; the common panel set is at $1,750.

1960 Nu-Card (Mickey Mantle Hits Longest Homer)				
	22	12.00	6.00	3.50
1960 Nu-Card (Mantle Hits Longest Homer At Stadium)				
	50	12.00	6.00	3.50

These 3 1/4-by-5 3/8-inch cards are printed in a mock newspaper format, with a headline, picture and story describing one of baseball's greatest events. The cards, numbered in the upper left corner, are printed in red and black and offer a quiz question and answer on the back. Certain cards, however, can be found entirely in black; they command a premium. The 72-card set is valued at $225 in Near Mint condition; common players are at $1.25.

1960 Post Cereal	—	1,500.00	750.00	450.00

These 7-by-8 3/4-inch cards were found individually on the backs of Grape-Nuts cereal boxes; they covered the entire box. Seven baseball and two football players were in the set, which is valued at $4,500 in Near Mint condition; common cards are $350. Each card, blank-backed, has a full-color photo on a color background with a wood frame design on the front. The player's name, team and facsimile autograph are on the front, also. A panel on the side of the box contains biographical information.

1960 Topps (Rival All-Stars/K. Boyer)				
	160	50.00	25.00	15.00
1960 Topps	350	375.00	175.00	110.00
1960 Topps (All-Star)	563	250.00	125.00	75.00

These 3 1/2-by-2 1/2 cards use a horizontal format with a color portrait and a black-and-white action photograph on the front. The backs have statistic lines for just the previous year and lifetime totals, plus a career summary and a cartoon. Common cards numbered 1-440 are valued at $3 in Near Mint condition; commons 441-506 are $4; commons 507-572 are $10. The complete set is valued at $4,000.

1961

1961 Bazooka (single)	2	300.00	150.00	90.00
(panel with Mahaffey/Mantle/Santo)				
	1-2-3	450.00	225.00	135.00

The characteristics of this 36-card set are identical to the 1960 Bazooka cards. Common single players are valued at $5 in Near Mint condition; common panels are $60. The complete singles set is valued at $800; the complete panel set is $1,500.

1961 Nu-Card (Mickey Mantle Hits Longest Homer)

422	10.00	5.00	3.00

1961 Nu-Card (Mantle Hits Longest Homer At Stadium)

450	9.00	4.50	2.75

These cards are similar to the 1960 cards, except they are 2 1/2-by-3 1/2 inches. The 80 cards in the set are numbered on the fronts and backs, from 401-480. These cards also have just a black-and-white photo and headline on the front; the back has a story in place of the quiz found on the 1960 cards. It appears the set may have been counterfeited; although it is not known when this was done, the counterfeits can be detected by the unusual blurring and fuzziness. The complete set is valued at $125 in Near Mint condition; common players are at 50 cents.

1961 Post	4	100.00	50.00	30.00

There are 200 cards in this set, but with variations there are more than 350 cards. This popular set was the cereal company's first attempt at a large-scale set. Cards were issued individually and in various panel sizes on the thick cardboard stock of cereal boxes, as well as on a thinner stock, in team sheets issued directly by Post via a mail-in offer. Individual cards, numbered in the upper left corner, are 3 1/2-by-2 1/2 inches. They have full-color portrait photos of the player, along with biographical information and 1960 and career statistics. Card backs are blank. The complete set, without variations, is valued at $1,750 in Near Mint condition. Common players are $2.

1961 Topps (A.L. Home Run Leaders)	44	30.00	15.00	9.00
* (with Colavito, Lemon, Maris)				
1961 Topps	300	400.00	200.00	125.00
1961 Topps (Mantle Blasts 565-ft. Home Run)				
	406	40.00	20.00	12.00
1961 Topps (MVP)	475	125.00	62.00	37.00
1961 Topps (All-Star)	578	400.00	200.00	120.00

Topps returned to a vertical format for this 587-card set, which is numbered through 589. However, only 587 cards were printed; no cards were printed for numbers 426, 587 and 588, while two were printed for 463 (a Braves team card or Jack Fisher). Actually, the Braves team card is checklisted as number 426. Innovations in the set include numbered checklists, cards for statistical leaders and 10 "Baseball Thrills" cards. High-number cards 523-589 are scarcer than others. Common cards numbered 1-370 are valued at $2 in Near Mint condition; commons 371-522 are $4; commons 523-589 are $25. The complete set is $5,500.

1961 Topps Dice Game	—	2,500.00	1,250.00	750.00

This obscure test issue, which may have never actually been issued, has 18 unnumbered black-and-white cards, each 2 1/2-by-3 1/2 inches. There are no identifying marks, such as copyrights or trademarks, to indicate the set was produced by Topps. The card backs contain various baseball plays which occur when a certain pitch is called and a specific number of the dice is rolled. A common player is valued at $100 in Near Mint condition; the complete set is at $7,500.

1962

1962 Bazooka (single)	—	200.00	100.00	60.00
(panel with Mahaffey/Mantle/Stuart)				
	—	500.00	250.00	150.00

These paneled cards are similar to those issued in 1961, except this year they are not numbered and the set has increased to 45 cards. Panels containing Bob Allison/Ed Mathews/Vada Pinson, Johnny Romano/Ernie Banks/Norm Siebern and Don Zimmer/ Harmon Killebrew/Gene Woodling were issued in shorter supplies and command

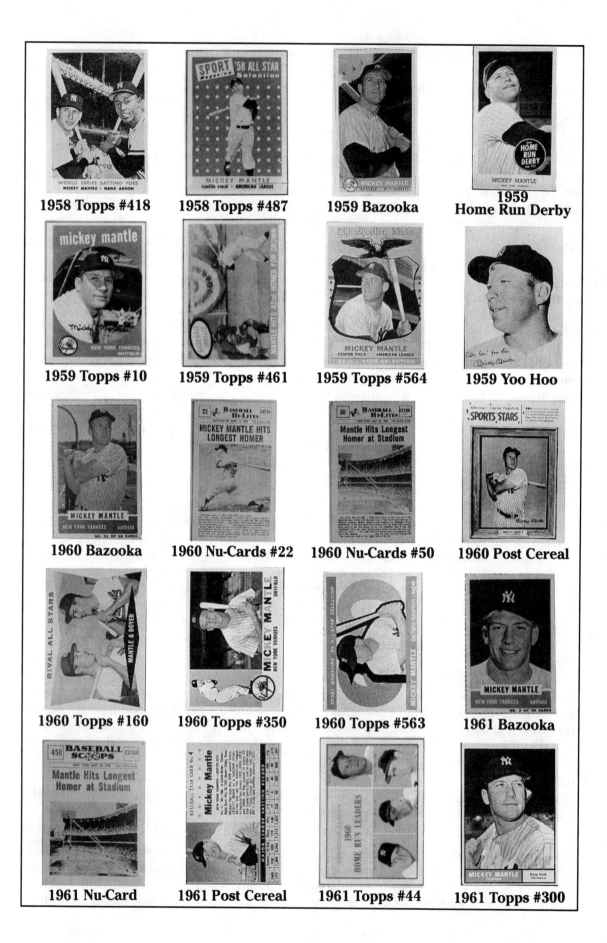

1958 Topps #418

1958 Topps #487

1959 Bazooka

1959
Home Run Derby

1959 Topps #10

1959 Topps #461

1959 Topps #564

1959 Yoo Hoo

1960 Bazooka

1960 Nu-Cards #22

1960 Nu-Cards #50

1960 Post Cereal

1960 Topps #160

1960 Topps #350

1960 Topps #563

1961 Bazooka

1961 Nu-Card

1961 Post Cereal

1961 Topps #44

1961 Topps #300

higher prices. Common panels are valued at $30 in Near Mint condition; common singles are $8. The complete panel set is $3,500; the complete singles set is $1,800.

1962 Exhibit Statistic Backs	—	90.00	45.00	27.00

These unnumbered, black-and-white, 3 3/8-by-5 3/8-inch, cards were issued by the Exhibit Supply Co. of Chicago, Ill. They feature statistics on the back, in black or red. Red backs are three times greater in value. The 32-card set is valued at $425 in Near Mint condition; commons are $3.

1962 Jell-O	5	700.00	350.00	210.00

These are virtually identical to the 1962 Post Cereal cards. This 197-card set was issued only in the Midwest. The Jell-O cards are easy to distinguish from the Post cards of that year by the absence of the red oval Post logo and red or blue border around the stat box. Cards which have been neatly trimmed from the Jell-O box should measure 3 1/2-by-2 1/2 inches. Common players are valued at $5 in Near Mint condition; the complete set is $4,500.

1962 Post (from box)	5	80.00	40.00	24.00

There are 200 cards in this set, which features the Post logo on the card fronts and players' names in script lettering. Cards, which are blank-backed, were issued in panels of five to seven cards on cereal boxes. American Leaguers are cards 1-100; National Leaguers are 101-200. With variations, there are 210 cards. The complete set is $1,500 in Near Mint, without variations; common players are $1.50.

1962 Post (from ad)	—	90.00	45.00	27.00

The cards of Mickey Mantle and Roger Maris were reproduced in a special two-card panel for a *Life* magazine insert. The stock for this insert is slightly thinner, with white margins.

1962 Post Canadian (script name large)				
	5	200.00	100.00	60.00
— (script name small)	5	125.00	62.00	37.00

This 200-card Canadian set is scarce due to much more limited distribution in Canada. Whitey Ford has two cards — one for the Dodgers and a corrected one for the Yankees, which is scarcer. The blank-backed cards were printed on the backs of cereal boxes and contain full-color photos. The biographies and statistics are in French and English. The Post logo is in the upper left corner. The complete set is $2,500 in Near Mint condition; common players are $3.

1962 Topps (Manager's Dream/with Mays)				
	18	100.00	50.00	30.00
1962 Topps (A.L. Home Run Leaders)				
	53	40.00	20.00	12.00
* (with Gentile, Maris, Killebrew)				
1962 Topps	200	450.00	225.00	135.00
1962 Topps (The Switch Hitter Connects)				
	318	50.00	25.00	15.00
1962 Topps (All-Star)	471	125.00	67.00	37.00

This 598-card set features photographs set against a woodgrain background. The lower right-hand corner appears as if it is curling away. This set contains the first multi-player rookie cards. Cards in the second series (#s 110-196) have two distinct print variations — early prints have a very noticeable green tint; subsequent runs have been corrected to clear photos. The complete set, without variations, is valued at $5,000 in Near Mint condition. Common players numbered 1-370 are $2; commons 371-522 are $4; commons 523-598 are $12.

1963

1963 Bazooka (single)	—	300.00	150.00	90.00
(panel with Mantle/Rodgers/Banks)				
	—	400.00	200.00	120.00

This numbered 36-card set of 12 panels is smaller in size than the previous year's issue. The 1963 cards are 1 9/16-by-2 1/2; panels are 2 1/2-by-4 11/16. The player's name, team and position are situated in a white oval space at the bottom of the blank-backed card. Common panels are $30 in Near Mint condition; common single players are $5. A complete panel set is $1,500; a complete singles set is $800. Five 1963 Bazooka All-Time Greats cards were also included in each box of bubble gum.

1963 Exhibit Statistic Backs	—	150.00	75.00	45.00

This unnumbered 64-card set, produced by the Exhibit Supply Co., features black-and-white photographs on thick cardboard. Career statistics on the back are printed in black. The cards are 3 3/8-by-5 3/8. Commons are valued at $3 in Near Mint condition; the complete set is $525.

1963 Jell-O	15	250.00	125.00	75.00

These cards are virtually identical to the 1963 Post cards except they are smaller, at 3 3/8-by-2 1/2 inches. The Jell-O cards have a red line which separates the 1962 statistics from the lifetime statistics. This line begins and ends closer to the statistics, compared to the red line on the Post cards, which extends almost all the way to the borders. The 200-card set is valued at $3,000 in Near Mint condition; commons are $2. Many cards in the set are scarce; they were printed as the backs of less popular brands and sizes of gelatin.

1963 Post Cereal	15	325.00	162.00	97.00

Numerous color variations appear in this 200-card set, due to the different cereal boxes on which the cards were printed. These cards are slightly narrower than the 1963 Jell-O cards, by about 1/4 of an inch, at 3 1/2-by-2 1/2 inches. The blank-backed cards have a color photograph, player biography and statistics on the numbered fronts. No Post logo appears on the cards. Common players are valued at $2 in Near Mint condition; the complete set is $3,600.

1963 Topps (A.L. Batting Leaders)				
	2	25.00	12.50	7.50
* (with Hinton, Floyd Robinson, Runnels, Siebern)				
1963 Topps (Bomber's Best) 173		65.00	33.00	20.00
* (with Richardson, Tresh)				
1963 Topps	200	400.00	200.00	125.00

This 576-card set, one of the most popular of the 1960s, has a color photograph and colored circle with a black-and-white photo on the front. The player's name, team and position are in a colored band. The backs have career statistics, a cartoon and biographical information. This set is special, and derives most of its value, because it contains Pete Rose's rookie card, one of the most avidly-sought cards in history. Common cards numbered 1-283 are valued at $1.50 in Near Mint condition; commons 284-446 are $3; commons 447-506 are $10; commons 507-576 are $7. The complete set, standard size, is $5,000.

1964

1964 Bazooka (single)	1	200.00	100.00	60.00
(panel with Mantle/Groat/Barber)				
	1-2-3	250.00	125.00	75.00

This paneled set is identical in design and size to the 1963 set, but different photos are used. The 36-card set in complete panels is valued at $1,500 in Near Mint condition; a complete set in singles is $750. Common panels are $30; common singles are $5. Sheets of 10 full-color baseball stamps were also included inside of the box of Bazooka bubble gum.

1964 Topps	50	300.00	150.00	90.00
1964 Topps (A.L. Bombers)	331	90.00	45.00	27.00
* (with Cash, Kaline, Maris)				

This 587-card set features an innovative baseball quiz question on the back which required the rubbing of a white panel to reveal the answer. The cards are standard size. Commons numbered 1-370 are valued at $2 in Near Mint condition; commons 371-522 are $3; commons 523-587 are $7. The complete set is $3,000.

1964 Topps Giants	25	18.00	9.00	5.50

These 3 1/8-by-5 1/4-inch cards were Topps' first postcard-size issues. The fronts have a large color photograph surrounded by white borders with a white baseball containing the player's name, position and team. Card backs have another photo and a newspaper-style explanation of the depicted event. Seven of the 60 cards in the set, including Willie Mays and Sandy Koufax, were printed in fewer quantities than the rest and are scarcer. Common cards are 12 cents in Near Mint condition; the complete set is $110. Since the set has mainly stars, it offers an excellent means to get inexpensive cards of Hall of Famers.

1964 Topps Stand-Ups	—	400.00	200.00	120.00

These 2 1/2-by-3 1/2-inch cards were die cut, making it possible for a folded card to stand on display. The 77 unnumbered cards in the set feature color photographs of the player with yellow and green backgrounds. Directions for folding are on the yellow top background, and when folded only the green background remains. Of the 77, 55 were double-printed and 22 were single-printed, making them twice as scarce. Cards in this group include Warren Spahn, Willie McCovey, Juan Marichal, Carl Yastrzemski and Don Drysdale. Common stand-ups are $3.50 in Near Mint condition; the complete set is $2,400.

1964 Who Am I? scratch-off card				
	22	100.00	50.00	30.00

1965

1965 Bazooka (single)	1	200.00	100.00	60.00
(panel with Mantle/Jackson/Hinton)				
	1-2-3	225.00	115.00	70.00

This set is identical to the 1963 and 1964 sets. Different players were added each year, and different photos were used for those players included again. The 36-card paneled set is valued at $1,300 in Near Mint condition; the complete singles set is $700. Common panels are $25; common singles are $5.

1965 O-Pee-Chee (A.L. Home Run Leaders)				
	3	9.00	4.50	2.75
* (with Powell, Killebrew)				
1965 O-Pee-Chee (A.L. RBI Leaders)				
	5	9.00	4.50	2.75
* (with B. Robinson, Killebrew, Stuart)				
1965 O-Pee-Chee (Mantle's Clutch HR)				
	134	25.00	12.50	7.50

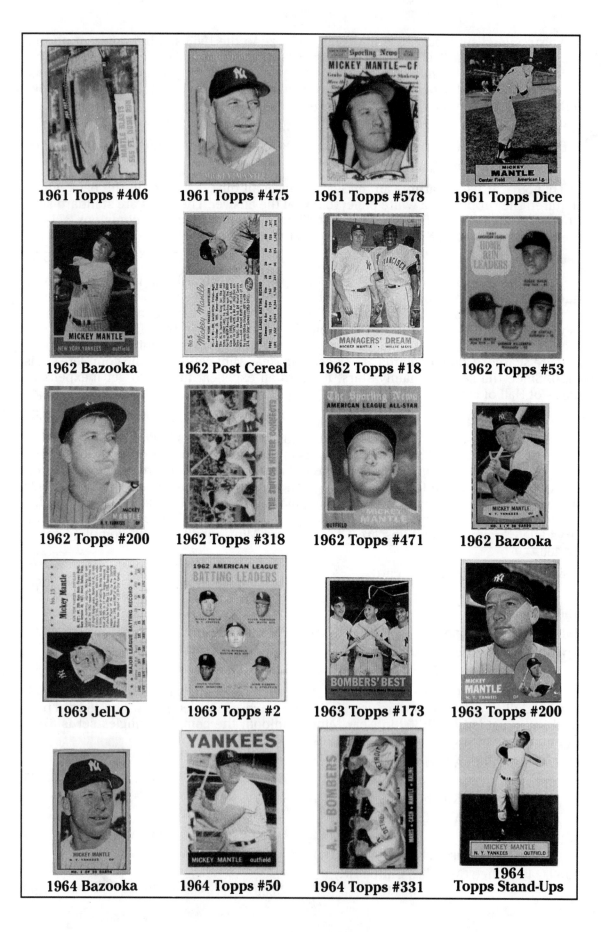

1961 Topps #406

1961 Topps #475

1961 Topps #578

1961 Topps Dice

1962 Bazooka

1962 Post Cereal

1962 Topps #18

1962 Topps #53

1962 Topps #200

1962 Topps #318

1962 Topps #471

1962 Bazooka

1963 Jell-O

1963 Topps #2

1963 Topps #173

1963 Topps #200

1964 Bazooka

1964 Topps #50

1964 Topps #331

1964
Topps Stand-Ups

Identical in design to the 1965 Topps set, this Canadian-issued set was printed on gray stock and has 283 cards which are the standard size. The words "Printed in Canada" appear along the bottom of the back of the cards. Common cards are valued at $3.50 in Near Mint condition; the complete set is $2,500.

1965 Topps (A.L. Home Run Leaders)				
	3	20.00	10.00	6.00
* (with Killebrew, Powell)				
1965 Topps (A.L. RBI Leaders)				
	5	20.00	10.00	6.00
* (with Killebrew, B. Robinson, Stuart)				
1965 Topps	350	450.00	225.00	135.00

This 598-card standard-sized set features a large color photograph of the player and a team pennant on each card front. Backs have statistics and, if space permits, a cartoon and headline about the player. Common players numbered 1-522 are valued at $2 in Near Mint condition; commons 523-598 are $5. The complete set is $3,500.

1965 Topps Embossed	11	15.00	7.50	4.50

These 2 1/8-by-3 1/2-inch cards were inserted into wax packs. The fronts feature an embossed profile on gold foil-like cardboard. The player's name, team and position are below the portrait, which is beneficial; most of the portraits are not recognizable. American Leaguers, 36 total, are framed in red; National Leaguers, 36, are in blue. Common players in Near Mint condition are 50 cents; the complete set is $100.

1966

1966 Bazooka (single)	7	200.00	100.00	60.00
(panel with Mantle/Wagner/Kranepool)				
	7-8-9	275.00	137.00	82.00

This set is similar to the 1965 set, except it has 48 cards in it, consisting of 16 three-player panels. Common panels are $25 in Near Mint condition; common singles are $5. A complete panel set is $1,750; a complete singles set is $1,000.

1947-66 Exhibits (portrait)	—	400.00	200.00	120.00
1947-66 Exhibit (batting, pinstripes)				
	—	100.00	50.00	30.00
1947-66 Exhibit (batting, no pinstripes)				
	—	75.00	38.00	23.00
* (name outlined in white)				
1947-66 Exhibit (batting, no pinstripes)				
	—	75.00	38.00	23.00
* (name not outlined)				

These unnumbered 3 3/8-by-5 3/8-inch cards are printed on heavy stock and were produced by the Exhibit Supply Co. of Chicago, Ill., during a 20-year span. The company issued a new set of black-and-white cards each year; many players were repeated year after year. Counting all the variations throughout the years, there are 305 cards total. Commons are $4 in Near Mint condition; the complete set is $5,000.

1966 O-Pee-Chee	50	200.00	100.00	60.00

These cards use the same design as the 1966 Topps set, except "Ptd. in Canada" appears along the bottom on the card backs. The standard-sized set contains 196 cards. Commons are valued at $2 in Near Mint condition; the complete set is $2,500.

1966 Topps	50	200.00	100.00	60.00

This standard-sized 598-card set includes statistical leaders and two runners-up on several cards. Most team managers have cards, too. A handful of cards lack a notice of the player's trade or sale to another team; cards without this notice bring higher prices. Common players numbered 1-110 are valued at $1 in Near Mint condition; commons 111-446 are $1.25; commons 447-522 are $5; common player single prints 523-598 are $20; common players 523-598 are $15. The complete set is $4,500

1967

1967 Bazooka (single)	7	200.00	100.00	60.00
(panel with Mantle/Wagner/Peters)				
	7-8-9	250.00	125.00	75.00

This set is identical in design to the previous Bazooka sets. The 48-card set in panels is valued at $1,600 in Near Mint condition; as singles a complete set is $900. Common panels are $25; common singles are $5.

1967 O-Pee-Chee (Checklist 2)				
	103	15.00	7.50	4.50
1967 O-Pee-Chee	150	200.00	100.00	60.00

Cards in this 196-card Canadian set are nearly identical to the 1966 O-Pee-Chee set, except the words "Printed in Canada" are found on the back in the lower right corner. The cards are standard size. Commons are valued at $2 in Near Mint condition; the complete set is $2,000.

1967 Topps (Checklist 2)	103	15.00	7.50	4.50
1967 Topps	150	200.00	80.00	50.00

This 609-card set marked Topps' largest set up to that time. The standard-sized cards feature a facsimile autograph on the front, except for card #254 (Milt Pappas). The backs are the first to be done vertically, although they still carried similar statistical and biographical information. The high numbers (534-609) are quite scarce. Common players numbered 1-110 are valued at $1 in Near Mint condition; commons 111-370 are $1.50; commons 371-457 are $1.25; commons 458-533 are $5; commons 534-609 are $12. The complete set is $5,000.

1967 Topps Stand-Ups	8	1,500.00	750.00	450.00

Never actually issued, no more than a handful of these rare test issues exist in the hobby market. Designed so the color photo of the player's head could be popped out of the black background, and the top folded over to create a stand-up display. Examples of these cards can be found either die-cut around the portrait or without the cutting. The 24 cards in the set are each 3 1/8-by-5 1/4 inches. They are numbered on the front at the bottom left. Common players are valued at $65 in Near Mint condition; the complete set is $6,750.

1968

1968 Bazooka (single)	(43)	150.00	75.00	45.00
(box 11, with Jim Lonborg pitching; has Curt Flood, Joel Horlen, Mantle, Jim Wynn)				
	(41-42-43-44)	$300.00	150.00	90.00

This set is radically different in design from previous efforts. The player cards are situated on the sides of the boxes, with the box back containing "Tipps From The Topps." Four unnumbered cards, measuring 1 1/4-by-3 1/8 inches, are featured on each box. The box back illustrates tips on various aspects of the game. The boxes are numbered 1-15 on the top panels. There are 56 different player cards in the set, with four cards (Tommie Agee, Don Drysdale, Pete Rose and Ron Santo) being used twice to round out the set of 15 different boxes. A complete box set is valued at $3,300 in Near Mint condition; a complete singles set is $2,000. Common boxes are $120; common single players are $5.

1968 Topps	280	200.00	100.00	60.00
1968 Topps (Super Stars)	490	100.00	50.00	30.00
* (with Killebrew, Mays)				

This 598-card set retained the vertical format for the backs, but the statistics are in the middle and a cartoon is at the bottom. The fronts feature color photographs on what appears to be a burlap fabric. Cards are standard size. Common players numbered 1-533 are valued at $1; commons 534-598 are $2.50. The complete set is $3,200.

1968 Topps Game	2	15.00	7.50	4.50

A throwback to the Red and Blue Back sets of 1951, the 33 cards in this set were inserted into wax packs or could be purchased as a complete boxed set, thus enabling the owner to play a game of baseball based on the situations on each card. The 2 1/4-by-3 1/4-inch cards have color photographs and the player's facsimile autograph. Common players are valued at 30 cents in Near Mint condition; the complete set is $70.

1968 Topps Giant Heads-Up test issue		
	8	800.00

1969

1969 Topps (Checklist)	412	7.00	3.50	2.00
1969 Topps (last name in white)				
	500a	475.00	190.00	119.00
1969 Topps (last name in yellow)				
	500b	175.00	87.00	52.00

This 664-card set was Topps' largest at the time. With a substantial number of variations, the number of possible cards is close to 700. Most significant among the variations are the white and yellow letter cards in the run of #s 440-511. The cards are standard size and returned to a horizontal format for the backs. The complete set, which does not include the scarcer, white-lettered variations, is valued at $2,500. Common players numbered 1-218, 328-512 and 513-664 are $1; commons 219-327 are $1.50.

1969 Topps Super	24	1,500.00	750.00	450.00

These 2 1/4-by-3 1/4-inch cards are dubbed not for their size but rather for their high-gloss finish which enhances the bright color photographs on the fronts. The fronts also have facsimile autographs. The backs have a box at the bottom which contains the player's name, team and position. A copyright and number are at the bottom. The cards have rounded corners. This set had a limited production, so supplies are tight. A complete set is valued at $6,000 in Near Mint condition; common players are $25.

1969 Transogram	27	125.00	62.00	37.00

Produced by the Transogram Toy Co., these 2 1/2-by-3 1/2-inch cards were printed on the bottom of toy baseball player statue boxes. The cards feature a color photo of the player surrounded by a rounded white border. Below the photo is the player's name in red; his team name and other personal details are printed in black. The overall background is yellow. The cards were designed to be cut off the box, but it is preferable to have the box intact, with the statue inside, if possible. The set is not too popular, but it is fairly scarce. Common players are valued at 80 cents in Near Mint condition; a complete set is $650.

1973

1973 Team Syracuse Chiefs	—	the set is $350 in Near Mint

This 30-card minor league set is in black-and-white. Cards measure 4-by-5 inches. Without a scarce, late-issue Mike Pazik card, the set is $200 in Near Mint condition.

1974

1974 Team Syracuse Chiefs	—	the set is $300 in Near Mint

1964 Topps Who Am I?

1965 Bazooka

1965 Topps #3

1965 Topps #5

1965 Topps #350

1965 Topps Embossed

1966 Bazooka

1947-66 Exhibits

1947-66 Exhibits

1966 Topps

1967 Topps #103

1967 Topps #150

1967 Topps Stand-Ups

1968 Bazooka

1968 Topps #280

1968 Topps #490

1968 Topps Game

1969 Topps #412

1969 Topps #500

This 30-card minor league set is in black-and-white and measures 4 7/8-by-3 7/8. There are no numbers on the cards. Without the late-issue, scarce Fred Frazier card the set is worth $185 in Near Mint condition.

1975

1975 Topps (MVP) * (1956/with Newcombe)	194	12.00	6.00	3.50
1975 Topps (MVP) * (1957/with Aaron)	195	12.00	6.00	3.50
1975 Topps (MVP) * (1962/with Wills)	200	12.00	6.00	3.50

This 660-card standard-sized set included 24 specialty cards on MVP winners since 1951. Each card shows the MVP winners for the year indicated, using the players Topps' cards from that year as photographs. Common players numbered 1-132 were printed in a somewhat shorter supply and are valued at 35 cents in Near Mint condition; commons 133-660 are 30 cents. The complete set is $900.

1975 Topps mini (MVP) * (1956/with Newcombe)	194	15.00	7.50	4.50
1975 Topps mini (MVP) * (1957/with Aaron)	195	17.00	8.50	5.00
1975 Topps mini (MVP) * (1962/with Wills)	200	15.00	7.50	4.50

This 660-card test issue is one of Topps' most popular sets from the 1970s. The cards are exactly the same as the regular issue, except they are 2 1/4-by-3 1/8 inches, 20 percent smaller. The cards were released mainly in Michigan and on the West Coast. Common cards are valued at 40 cents in Near Mint condition; the complete set is $1,400.

1978

1978 TCMA	262	20.00	10.00	6.00

This 293-card colored set, "The Sixties," was produced by TCMA, of Peekskill, N.Y. The numbered cards depict players from the 1960s. Numbers 43, 98, 127, 180, 235 and 248 were not issued. Numbers 27, 125, 165, 170, 231 and 249 had two cards printed for each number. Cards are 2 1/2-by-3 1/2 inches.

1979

1979 TCMA Baseball History Series				
	7	20.00	10.00	6.00

1981 and after prices are based on		**(MT)**	**(NR MT)**	**(EX)**
1981-82 Baseball Immortals	145	.25	.20	.10

This 199-card set was produced by Renata Galasso Inc. and TCMA with permission of Major League Baseball. The set, first issued in 1980, features players in the Hall of Fame. The cards, standard size, have color photos; most players who were active before 1950 have colored black-and-white photos. The fronts have the player's name, position an year of induction. The backs have a brief biography and a trivia question. The designation "first printing" appears on all cards issued in 1981 and after. The set has been updated each year since 1980 to include new inductees. Common players are valued at five cents each in Mint condition; the complete set is $18.

1982

1982 Cracker Jack	6	2.50	2.00	1.00

Topps produced this set to promote the first "Old-Timers Baseball Classic," held in Washington, D.C. Sixteen cards comprise the set, which was issued in two sheets of eight cards, plus an advertising card located in the center. The individual cards are 2 1/2-by-3 1/2 inches; the complete sheet is 7 1/2-by-10 1/2. Card #s 1-8 are American League players, while 9-16 are National Leaguers. The card fronts feature a full-color photo inside a Cracker Jack border. The backs contain the Cracker Jack logo plus a short player biography and his lifetime pitching or batting record. Complete sheets were available through a write-in offer. A complete panel set is valued at $10 in Mint condition; a complete singles set is $4. Common singles are five cents.

1982 K-Mart	1	.25	.20	.10

The theme of this set is Most Valuable Players and selected record-breaking performances from 1962-81. The design used miniature reproductions of Topps cards of the era, except in a few cases where designs had to be created because original cards were never issued (1962 Maury Wills, 1975 Fred Lynn). Cards were standard size. The 44-card boxed set usually sold for about $2 per box, but over-production and a lack of demand dropped set's value. Common players in Mint condition are valued at three cents; the complete set is $1. The box also has a picture of Mickey Mantle on it.

1983

1983 Donruss Hall Of Fame Heroes				
	7	1.00	.70	.40
1983 Donruss Hall Of Fame Heroes				
43 puzzle card		.09	.07	.04

The artwork of Dick Perez is featured in this 44-card set. The standard-size numbered cards were available in wax packs that contained eight cards and a Mickey Mantle puzzle piece card (three pieces on one card per pack). The backs, which display red and blue print on white stock, contain a short biographical sketch derived from the Hall of Fame yearbook. A checklist card was also made for the set. Common cards in Mint condition are valued at five cents; the complete set is $8.

1984

1984 Donruss Champions	50	1.00	.70	.40

This 60-card set includes 10 Hall of Famers, 49 current players and one numbered checklist. The cards are 3 1/2-by-5 inches. The 10 Hall of Famers cards (called Grand Champions) feature the artwork of Dick Perez. These cards represent hallmarks of excellence in various statistical categories. The remaining cards (called Champions) are color photographs. They show the leaders among active players in statistical categories. Duke Snider puzzle pieces were included with the cards. Common player cards are valued at seven cents in Mint condition; the complete set is $7.

1984 Renata Galasso	232	5.00	3.75	2.00
1984 R.T. Weiss/All-Time Greats				
	2	12.00	8.00	4.75
1984 The Mick promo card	—	.25	.17	.10
1984 Doug West/Sports Design				
	4	2.00	1.50	.80

1985

1985 Circle K	6	2.00	1.50	.80

Topps produced this 33-card set, titled "Baseball All-Time Home Run Kings" for Circle K stores. The standard-size cards are numbered on the back according to the player's position on the all-time career home run list. Joe DiMaggio, who ranked 31st, was not included in the set, so the set is skip-numbered from 30 to 32. The glossy card fronts contain the player's name in the lower left corner and feature a color photo, although black-and-white photos were used for some of the homer kings who played before 1960. The backs have blue and red print on white stock and contain the player's career batting statistics. The set was issued in a specially-designed box which pictures Mickey Mantle. Common cards are valued at 15 cents in Mint condition; the complete set is $8.

1985 Donruss Sluggers of the Hall of Fame

| | — | 3.00 | 2.25 | 1.25 |

In much the same manner as the first Bazooka cards were issued in 1959, this eight-player set from Donruss consists of cards which formed the bottom panel of a box of bubble gum. When cut off the box, the cards measure 3 1/2-by-6 1/2. The blank-backed cards feature paintings of players done by Dick Perez. Common cards are valued at 60 cents in Mint condition; the complete set is $12.

1985 Topps All-Time Record Holders

| | 023 | 1.00 | .70 | .40 |

Topps produced this 44-card set for the Woolworth chain stores. Many hobbyists refer to this set as the "Woolworth's" set, but that name does not appear anywhere on the cards. The standard-size cards feature a mix of black-and-white and color photos representing record holders from all eras. Backs, printed in blue and orange, give career details and personal data. Common cards are valued at five cents in Mint condition; the complete set is $5.

1986

1986 Big League Chew Home Run Legends

| | 6 | 1.25 | .90 | .50 |

This set, titled "Home Run Legends," consists of 12 cards featuring the players who have hit 500 or more career home runs. The standard-size cards were inserted in specially-marked packages of Big League Chew, the shredded bubble gum developed by former major leaguer Jim Bouton. The set was also available through a write-in offer on the package. Modern-day players are shown in color photos; older sluggers have black-and-white photos. Common cards are valued at 40 cents in Mint condition; the complete set is $6.

1986 Card Collectors Co. (10)	—	3.00 each		
1986 Ceramic set (7)	—	39.95 each		
1986 Sports Co. Living Legends 1		3.00	2.25	1.25
1986 Sportflics Decade Greats 26		3.50	2.75	1.50

This 75-card set, produced by Sportflics, features outstanding players, by position, from the 1930s to the 1980s, by decades. The cards are standard size and have fronts printed in sepia-toned photos or full color, with the Sportflics three-phase "Magic Motion" animation. Biographies appear on the card backs, which are printed in full color and are color coded by decade. The set, which contains 59 single player cards and 16 multi-player cards, was distributed only through hobby dealers. Common cards are valued at 15 cents in Mint condition; the complete set is $15.

In 1986-88 Bowman reprinted 1951 and 1952 Bowman sets. Mantle reprint cards usually sell for between $2-$3.

1987

| 1987 K-Mart Stars of the Decade 5 | 1.00 | .70 | .40 |

Topps produced this 33-card set to celebrate K-Mart's 25th anniversary. The set was issued in a special cardboard box with one stick of bubble gum. The standard-size card fronts feature a full-color photo set diagonally against a red background. The backs have career highlights plus pitching or batting statistics for the decade in which the

1969 Topps Super   **1969 Transogram**   **1974 Syracuse**   **1975 Topps #194**

1975 Topps #195   **1975 Topps #200**   **1981-82 Baseball Immortals**   **1982 K-Mart**

1983 Donruss Hall of Fame Heroes   **"The Mick" promo card**   **1985 Circle K**   **1985 Record Holders**

Card Collectors Co.   **Card Collectors Co.**   **1987 K-Mart**   **1987 Leaf Candy City Team**

1987 Nestle's   **1988 Pacific Trading Cards**   **1990 Baseball Wit**   **1991 Score**

player enjoyed his greatest success. Common cards in the set are valued at 10 cents in Mint condition; the complete set is $4.

1987 Leaf Candy City Team	1	1.00	.70	.40

As part of its endorsement for the Seventh International Special Olympics Summer Games, Leaf produced an 180-card set of trading cards. Twelve of the cards, numbered H1-H12, are baseball-related and feature Hall of Fame greats. The other six cards are numbered S1-S6 and feature Special Olympics champions. All cards feature artwork by Dick Perez. The cards were available through a mail-in offer advertised at special store displays. Common players are valued at 15 cents in Mint condition; the complete set is $4.

1987 Nestle	17	1.00	.70	.40

Nestle, in conjunction with Topps, produced this 33-card set. Three cards were inserted in specially-marked six-packs of various Nestle's candy bars. Two complete sets were available through a mail-in offer for $1.50 and three proof-of-purchase seals. Cards 1-11 feature black-and-white photos of players from the "Golden Era." Cards 12-22 feature color photos of American Leaguers from the "Modern Era," while cards 23-33 feature National Leaguers. The Bob Feller card (#20) isn't a photo, but rather a color rendering of his 1953 Topps card. The standard-size cards have all team emblems airbrushed away. Common players are available at 12 cents in Mint condition; the complete set is $9.

1988

1988 Pacific Trading Cards Baseball Legends

	7	1.00	.70	40

This card set features 110 players from the past 40 years who are (or were) members of the Major League Baseball Alumni Association. Fronts feature silver borders and large full-color photographs outlined in black against colorful banner-style inner borders of red, green, orange, blue or gold. The banners contain the player's name and position in white letters. The numbered card backs have biographical, personal and statistical information, and the Baseball Legends logo. The cards were sold in boxed sets (which feature Mickey Mantle on the box) via candy wholesalers, with emphasis in the Midwest and New England states. Complete collector sets in clear plastic boxes were made available via dealers or directly from Pacific Trading Cards. Common players are valued at six cents in Mint condition; the complete set is $12.

1988 Houston Show promo card

	9	1.50	1.00	.60
1988 O'Connell	150	3.00	2.25	1.25
(uncut sheet)	—	6.00	4.50	2.50

1989

1989 Collectors Marketing Corp.

(20 card set)		12.00	9.00	4.75

A 20-card set honoring Mickey Mantle is among the items found in this collecting kit produced by Collectors Marketing Corp. The cards were released along with a special album, a talking baseball card and a story about Mantle. The Yankee logo appears on the front and backs of the cards. Individual cards are 60 cents each in Mint condition.

1989 Kenner Starting Lineup Baseball Greats

	—	18.00	13.50	7.25

    * (package includes Joe DiMaggio)

This series of figurines features baseball greats of the past and were packaged two figurines and two collectors cards per package. The collector cards have original action pictures of the player done in a sepia-tone to enhance the historic nature of the set. The Starting Lineup logo and "Baseball Greats" heading appears at the top of the card. The player's name and a descriptive nickname, such as "Sultan of Swat," appear below the photo. The backs have a blue-and-white color scheme and include career stats. The value above reflects both cards and figurines. A complete set is valued at $200 in Mint condition; common packs are $15.

1990

1990 Baseball Wit	3	.40	.30	.15

This 108-card set was released in two printings. The first printing featured unnumbered cards and contained several errors. The second printing had corrections and numbered cards. The set, dedicated to Little League baseball, was available at several retail chain stores and features trivia questions on the card backs. Common cards are valued at six cents in Mint condition; the complete set is $8.

1991

1991 Score Mantle set
7 cards, $50 each; complete set $300, autographed $600

This seven-card set highlights Mantle's career with cards titled "The Rookie," "Triple Crown," "World Series," "Going-Going-Gone," "Speed and Grace," "True Yankee," and "Twilight." Randomly inserted in Score 1991 Series II baseball packs were 2,493 personally autographed and sequentially-numbered Mickey Mantle cards from the seven-card collection. Only 356 autographed sets of these seven cards were made available. Also inserted at random are 35,951 unsigned Mantle cards. Seven of the autographed cards, along with 49 unsigned cards, were to be awarded as prizes to collectors via a mail-in sweepstakes.

1991 Topps Archives	53-82	15.00	10.00	6.00

Miscellaneous Mickey Mantle items

1952 Rawlings 2x3		—	500.00-600.00	

This advertising and sales promotion is blank-backed with a bluish background. It features cards for 35 players and six poses for Stan Musial.

1952 Star Cal decal	70G	750.00	375.00	225.00

The Meyercord Co. of Chicago issued this set of decals consisting of 68 different major leaguers, each pictured on a 4 1/8-by-6 1/8-inch decal. The player's name and facsimile autograph are on the front, along with a decal number. The set is valued at $2,800 in Near Mint condition. Commons are $12.

1954 Louis Dormand postcards:

pose 1 (left-handed)	20.00-30.00
pose 2 (bat on shoulder)	75.00-125.00
pose 3 (6x9)	200.00-250.00
pose 4 (9x12)	300.00-400.00

These 3 1/2-by-5 3/8 inch postcards were issued in the New York area as a premium for Mason candy. They feature Yankees and Dodgers players. There are 44 cards, numbered from 101-140, in the set; four players, including Mickey Mantle, have two poses each. Numbers 131 and 137 were not issued. Mantle also has 6-by-9-inch and 9-by-12-inch cards.

1955 Don Wingfield postcard —   100.00

These postcards are 3 1/2-by-5 1/2 inches, black-and-white, and unnumbered. This set is divided into three groups — photo postcards (7), lithographs (36) and color (1, Harmon Killebrew). The photo postcards border with the player's name and have "Washington Nationals, Copyright 1955 — Don Wingfield, Griffith Stadium, Washington,

D.C.", at the bottom. The lithographs, which include Mantle, are black-and-white and have no player identification on the front; the player's identity is on the back.

1958 National Sports Council	A	150.00-225.00
1958 National Sports Council	B	150.00-225.00
1958 National Sports Council	C	150.00-225.00
1958 National Sports Council	D	40.00-50.00
1958 National Sports Council	E	200.00-250.00
1958 National Sports Council	F	250.00-325.00
1958 National Sports Council	G	40.00-50.00

(Note: Cards are from the National Sports Council's "Manly Art" course. They are titled as follows — A: "Self-Improvement"; B: "Live Like A Champion"; C: "Power Trigger"; D: Is an introductory letter from the NSC with a picture of Mantle; E: "Helping Hand"; F: "Glad To Be An American"; G: "Best Foot Forward.")

1959 Batting Cage decal	—	35.00	
1959 Holiday Inn of Joplin card	—	125.00-175.00	
1960 Topps Baseball Tattoos (autographed ball)			
	—	25.00	12.50	7.50
1960 Topps Tattoo	—	75.00	37.00	22.00

These tattoos were on the reverse of the wrappers for Topps' Tattoo Bubble Gum. The entire wrapper was 1 9/16-by-3 1/2 inches. Wrappers were applied to any wet spot on the skin to make one of 96 tattoos. There were 55 players depicted, 16 teams, 15 action shots and 10 autographed baseballs. Surviving specimens are very rare today. Commons are valued at $3 in Near Mint condition; the entire set is valued at $675.

1960s black-and-white key-chain insert	—	45.00		
1960s Mantle linen patch	—	250.00		
1961 Topps Stamps (green)	—	50.00	25.00	15.00

These 1 3/8-by-1 3/16-inch stamps were an added insert in 1961 Topps wax packs, two per pack. They were designed to be collected and placed in an album which could be bought for an additional 10 cents. There are 208 stamps featuring 207 different players; Al Kaline is featured twice. Half the players have brown stamps; the rest are green. Prices are low because there is relatively little interest in this non-card set. Common players are valued at 40 cents in Near Mint condition, while the complete set is $225 and the stamp album is $35.

1962 Topps Baseball Bucks	—	125.00	62.00	37.00

Issued in their own 1-cent packages, Baseball Bucks were 4 1/8-by-1 3/4 inches and looked somewhat like dollar bills. The center player portrait has a banner underneath with the player's name. His home park is on the right; biographical information is on the left. The back has a large denomination, with the team logo and player's league indicated. The 96-bill set is valued at $750 in Near Mint condition; commons are $2.

1962 Topps Stamps	—	45.00	22.00	13.50

These 1 3/8-by-1 7/8-inch stamps are an artistic improvement over the drab Topps issue from 1961. The stamps have color photographs on red or yellow backgrounds and were issued in two-stamp panels as an insert in Topps wax packs. The 201-stamp set includes team emblems and two Roy Sievers stamps; he was originally portrayed on the wrong team — the Athletics — but it was later corrected to the Phillies. The complete set is valued at $220 in Near Mint condition; commons are 25 cents. The stamp album is $35 in Near Mint condition.

1963 Topps Peel-Offs	—	50.00	25.00	15.00

These 1 1/4-by-2 3/4-inch peel-offs were an insert in Topps wax packs. There are 46 players in the unnumbered set, each pictured in a color photo inside an oval with the

1967 Topps Giant Stand-Ups

1960 Topps Baseball Tattoos

1967 Topps Punchout

1966 Topps Push-Pull

1962 Topps Baseball Bucks

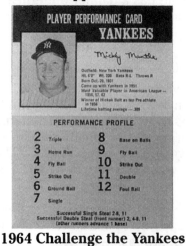

1964 Challenge the Yankees

1968 Topps Poster

player's name, team and position in a band below. The back is removable, making it a sticker. Thus, they are quite scarce, but, since they are a non-card issue, are not in great demand. Common players are $1 in Near Mint condition; the complete set is $175.

1964 Challenge The Yankees Game	—	200.00	100.00	60.00

These 4-by-5 3/8-inch cards were part of a baseball game which featured unnumbered cards for 25 Yankees and 25 All-Stars. The cards were blue and yellow and have a black-and-white photo of the player. Card fronts also have the player's name, position, statistics and game outcomes, as determined by rolling dice. Backs are blank.

1964 Mickey Mantle Game	—	200.00		
1964 Rawlings glove box (color)	—	200.00		
1964 Rawlings 8x10 photo	—	75.00-$100.00		
1964 Topps Photo Tattoos	—	100.00	45.00	27.00

These 1 9/16-by-3 1/2-inch tattoos feature 55 players and 20 team tattoos. The player tattoos have the player's face, name and team, while the team tattoos give the team logo and name. Common tattoos are valued at $3 in Near Mint condition; the complete set is $600.

1965 Challenge The Yankees	—	200.00	100.00	60.00

This set is similar to the 1964 set, except it had only 23 Yankees and 25 All-Stars.

1965 Philadelphia Cigar premium	—	175.00		
1965 Topps Transfers	—	60.00	30.00	18.00

Issued as strips of three players each as inserts in wax packs, the unnumbered transfers are 2-by-3 inches and have blue or red bands at the top (with the team name and position) and bottom (with the player's name). Commons are valued at 60 cents in Near Mint condition; the complete set is $225.

1966 Topps Rub-Offs	—	40.00	20.00	12.00

Returning to a concept used in 1961, Topps tried an expanded 120-rub-off set featuring 20 team pennants with a horizontal format and 100 players, in color, using a vertical format. Each unnumbered photo is 2 1/16-by-3 inches. Common players are valued 60 cents in Near Mint condition; the complete set is $225.

1966 Topps Push And Pull	6	400.00	200.00	125.00
1967 Coca-Cola Dexter Press	—	100.00		

(Note: There are at least two or three different sizes of this card.)

1967 Topps Punchout	—	250.00	125.00	75.00
1967 Topps Silver Paper	—	500.00	250.00	150.00
1967 Topps Stand-Ups	8	1,500.00	750.00	450.00

Never actually issued, no more than a handful of these rare test issues exist in the hobby market. Designed so the color photo of the player's head could be popped out of the black background, and the top folded over to create a stand-up display, examples of these cards can be found either die-cut around the portrait or without the cutting. There 24 cards in the set are each 3 1/8-by-5 1/4 inches. They are numbered on the front at the bottom left. Common players are valued at $65 in Near Mint condition; the complete set is $6,750.

1968 Topps Plaks	—	800.00	400.00	240.00
1968 Topps Baseball Plak checklist	—	250.00	125.00	75.00

Among the scarcest of the Topps test issues during the 1960s, these plaks were plastic busts of 24 stars of the era. They came packaged like model airplane parts. The busts had to be snapped off a sprue and could be inserted into a base which carried the player's name. Packed with the plastic plaks was one of two 2 1/8-by-4-inch checklist cards which featured six color photos per side. Common player plaks are valued at $20 in Near Mint condition; the complete set is $2,300.

1968 Topps Poster	18	50.00	25.00	15.00

These 9 3/4-by-18 1/8-inch posters were sold separately with a piece of gum, rather than as inserts. The 24 posters feature large color photographs with a star at the bottom containing the player's name, position and team. Each poster was folded several times to fit into its package. Common players are valued at $3 in Near Mint condition; the complete set is $325.

1968 Topps Poster (large)	—	50.00		
1968 Topps Poster box	—	45.00		
1968 Topps Action All-Star Sticker	7	300.00	150.00	90.00
* (with Carew/Gonzalez/Hargan/Mantle/McCovey/Monday/B. Williams)				
1968 Topps Action All-Star Sticker	10	100.00	50.00	30.00
* (with Aaron/Gibson/Harrelson/Hunter/Mantle/Peters/Pinson)				

These stickers were sold in strips of three, with bubble gum, for 10 cents. The strip is comprised of three 3 1/4-by-5 1/4 panels, perforated at the joints for separation. The central panel, which is numbered, contains a large color picture of a star player. The top and bottom panels contain smaller pictures of three players. While there are 16 numbered center panels, only 12 of them are different; panels 13-16 show players previously used. Similarly, the triple-player panels at the top and bottom of stickers 13-16 repeat panels from #s 1-4. Prices listed are for the stickers which have all three panels still joined. Individual panels are significantly lower. A complete set is valued at $1,300 in Near Mint condition.

1969 Topps Decals	—	75.00	38.00	23.00

These decals, included as insert in wax packs, are virtually identical in format to the 1969 cards. The 48 unnumbered decals are 1-by-2 1/2 inches, but are mounted on white paper backing which measures 1 3/4-by-2 1/8 inches.

Common players are valued at $4 in Near Mint condition; the complete set is $350.

1969 Topps Punchout	—	1,000.00
1969 Topps Punchout Wrapper	—	400.00

(Note: The punchout of Mantle comes in a wrapper that also pictures Mantle. This may or may not be a one-of-a-kind item. Do not confuse it with the 1967 punchout test issue.)

1969 Topps Team Posters	—	90.00	45.00	27.00
* (with Bahnsen, Clarke, Cox, Gibbs, Mantle, Pepitone, Peterson, Robinson, Stottlemyre, Tresh and White)				

These 24 posters are about 12-by-20 inches each and feature nine or 10 photos per team. A large team pennant is in the middle of the card front, surrounded by the player photos. Facsimile autographs are given for each player, too. The posters had to be folded to fit into their packages, so it's difficult to find ones without heavy creases. The common poster is valued at $17 in Near Mint condition; a complete set is $900.

1973 Batting Tips	—	40.00
1974 Yankee schedule	—	5.00
1975 SSPC promotional card	7	7.50
1975 SSPC promotional card	37	7.50
1981 MLBPA proof sticker	—	17.50
1981 Topps Thirst Break Sports Facts	12	15.00
1983 Donruss Hall of Fame Diamond King World Series promo sheet	—	7.50
1984 Donruss Champions wrapper/box	—	3.00
1984 National Convention ticket	—	5.00

1984 O'Connell	25	3.00
1984 O'Connell	140	3.00
1984 Pittman set (22)	—	125.00
1986 Sportflics disc (4 1/2")	—	7.50
1987 Fleer Mini Sticker (21)	—	10.00

(Note: These were Fleer Star Sticker premiums.)

More miscellaneous Mickey Mantle items
- 1952 Topps reprint card #311, $5.
- 1962 Exhibit on thin stock, black-and-white photo, 5 3/4x3 3/4, $10.
- 1965 Bazooka box with picture of Mantle, $18.
- 1966 Dexter Press photo 4x6 (same as 1967 Dexter Press photo, but smaller issue), $150.
- 1967 Dexter Press photo, 3 1/2x5 1/2, $4.
- 1968 K-Mart paper playing card, Ace of Spades, $20.
- Aug. 18, 1973, Waterbury Times Mickey Mantle Day 5x7 glossy photo, $35-$50.
- 1972 Laughlin Great Feats, #33, $4; Mantle die-cut used for card, $100.
- 1975 SSPC ad card #7, $8.
- 1975 SSPC #7, $8.
- 1975 Great Plains Great, #41, $7.50.
- 1977 Sportscaster card of Mickey Mantle and Roger Maris, $15.
- 1977 Rencontre S.A. sports broadcaster cards, Mickey Mantle and Roger Maris, "Home run Heroes," $12.50.
- 1980 Baskin-Robbins Ice Cream paper Baseball Hall Of Fame Collector's Series B#5, $15.
- 1980 Sertoma Star Card (yellow Dormand photo) Southside Indianapolis Sertoma Club, $6.50.
- 1980 Cramer Sports Legends, Series One #6, $5.
- 1980 Hall Of Fame issues, sepia, red, blue, $7.50.
- 1980 Baseball Greats of Hall Of Fame, blue, brown and green, $7.50
- 1980 Laughlin 300-400-500-club card #18, $3.
- 1981 San Diego Sports Convention, four different black-and-white cards: #10, Mantle, $5; #11, Mantle, $5; #12, Mantle/Mays, $5; #13, Mantle/Musial, $5.
- Superstar card set, series one, 1981: #6, #7, #10, #12, #30, #31, #32, #33; set is $15.
- 1981 Baseball Greats cartoon drawing #7, by Will Davis, $5.
- 1982 Mickey Mantle 72-card set: two varieties — #1 block-printed name, $17; #1 hand-autographed, $30.
- 1982 Topps K-Mart error cards with Mickey on front and Koufax on back, Koufax on front and Mickey on back and Mickey Mantle on front and Mickey Mantle on back, $7.50 each.
- 1982-83 Renata Galasso 1961 World Champion N.Y. Yankees, #7, $7.50.
- 1982-83 Renata Galasso 1961 World Champion N.Y. Yankees, #33, $7.50.
- 1983 Mactac reprint sticker of 1966 and 1967 Dexter glossies, $2.
- 1983 reprint of the Aug, 23, 1954, *Sports Illustrated* black-and-white card, $4.50.
- 1983 TCMA 50 Years of Yankee All-Stars, by Robert Stephen Simon: #1 Checklist with Mantle on front, $2; #26, Mickey Mantle, $2.
- 1983 National HOF metallic plaque card, $60.
- 1983 Hygrade Baseball All-Time Greats, unnumbered, $4.
- Mickey Mantle Stratomatic cards, all seasons exist, $5-$25.
- Cadaco Baseball game cards, several for different years, $5 each.
- APBA Baseball Cards, several for different years, $5 each.
- Yankee Photo Pack Cards: Many different black-and-white photos exist, produced by the Yankees and Big League Inc. 1968, however, is a colored photo. $15-$20 each.
- Baseball's Great Hall Of Fame exhibit card, $4.

- Mickey Mantle 8x10 black-and-white photo issue, by Sportspix, $30.
- National Baseball Hall of Fame and Museum plaque cards. Three different: 4EK-284 Curteichcolor 3-D color reproduction, dark gold color, $3; C34260 Mike Roberts color productions, light gold color, $3; DT-59549D Dexter Press, reddish-orange color, $1.
- Bazooka Baseball's All-Time Greats, postcard size and mini size, blue-and-white in color, $7.50 each.
- Alan Landsman Sports Deck playing cards, $5 each.
- Reserve Life Insurance Co., Dallas, Texas: Three different cards featuring Mantle, $15; promotional 8x10 black-and-white photo, $7.50; "How to Hit" booklet, $35.
- Mickey Mantle ceramic baseball cards, seven different, $50 each.
- Robert Stephen Simon superstar card set: #4, "Tribute to the Mick"; #7, "Mantle of Greatness"; #9, "Yanks of Yesteryear"; #11, "Mantle, 1952"; #18, "Stars in Stripes"; #23, "Mantle 4 Ways"; #24, "Mantle, 1956 World Series"; $2 each.
- 1970s Old Timer's Day at Dodger Stadium, with pictures of Mantle and Casey Stengel on a yellowish cardboard issue, $20.
- The Claridge Hotel and Casino has four different cards of Mantle and the Loma Linda Country Club has issued a promotional card with a Mantle portrait that promotes his annual golfing tournament. Claridge, $15; Loma Linda, $15.
- Bob Parker drawing of Mickey Mantle, $50-$75.
- Black-and-white old-timer's issues with Mantle's name printed horizontally: Two varieties — very thin paper stock or heavy cardboard stock, $7.50 each.
- Baseball's Great Hall of Fame, brown with vertical columns on both sides, 3 1/2x5 1/2, $10.

TCMA sets

Year/Set	No.	Value
All-Time New York Yankee postcard	—	7.00
All-Time Greats (3 1/2x5 1/2) (w/DiMaggio)	—	12.00
1970s Yankee team (3 1/2x5 1/2)	14	9.00
1973 All-Time Greats (w/1975 back)	—	9.00
1975 All-Time Yankee Team	—	7.00
1975 League Leaders 1950s	—	8.50
1977 Galasso Inc.	7	7.00
1978	262	7.00
1979	7	7.00
1979 Baseball History	7	11.50
1979-80 Yankees Of The '50s-'60s (postcard)	—	9.00
1980 All-Time Yankee team card	—	11.50
1981 The Sixties	303	7.00
	474	9.00
1982 Baseball's Greatest Sluggers	3	7.00
1982 '50s And '60s postcards (color)	—	12.00
1982 Yankees insert card	15	9.00
1983 Hank Aaron set	6	7.00
1983 Willie Mays set	3	7.00
1983 Joe DiMaggio set	9	8.50
	12	8.50
1983 50 Years Of Yankee All-Stars	1	2.00
	26	2.00
1984 Baseball Classic Postcards	—	7.00
	—	7.00
1985 Baseball Collector's Series	20	4.00
1985 Baseball's Greatest Hitters	—	4.00

TCMA

TCMA

TCMA

1969 Topps Team Poster

1977 Sportscaster

1968 Topps Action Stickers

1983 Hygrade

1952 Star-Cal Decals

1975 Great Plains Greats

153

Mantle completes 2,500 signatures for Score

Score has announced that baseball legend Mickey Mantle has completed his 2,500th signature for Score's blockbuster promotion and the company has begun shipping its Series II baseball product.

Randomly inserted in 1991 Series II baseball packs are 2,493 personally autographed and sequentially-numbered Mickey Mantle cards from the seven-card collection. Only 356 autographed sets of these seven cards will be available. Also inserted at random are 35,951 unsigned Mantle cards. Seven of the autographed cards, along with 49 unsigned cards, will be awarded as prizes to collectors via a mail-in sweepstakes. Instructions for ordering appear on specially-marked Series II wrappers.

"There's been a lot of anticipation for Score's Series II baseball," said Lou Costanzo of Champion Sports in California. "By far, Mickey Mantle is the most sought-after collectible. Anything he touches, people want. I imagine just one of his autographed Score cards will go for a minimum of $1,500, while the collection of seven could be close to $10,000."

Leading off the exclusive seven-card collection, which highlights the career of the most prodigious switch-hitting slugger in baseball history, is "The Rookie." This special card recounts Mantle's auspicious 1951 rookie year. Score's "Triple Crown" card tells of his 1956 season, when Mantle belted 52 homers, 130 RBI and had a .353 batting average. "World Series" takes a look at Mantle's 12 years of outstanding series performances, while "Going-Going-Gone" features the power hitter who won four home run titles in his career.

"Speed and Grace" highlights Mantle's outstanding defensive play and "True Yankee" portrays the man who left Oklahoma for the Big Apple, and led the Bronx Bombers to a dozen pennants. The final and seventh card, "Twilight," sums up a remarkable 18-year career that was shortened due to crippling injuries. Each card is distinctly designed by Score, and features authentic vintage photography accompanied by classic player profiles.

Score's Mickey Mantle Instant Win Promotion represents the first time a licensed card manufacturer has offered in-pack, instant-win prizes, featuring autographed cards of a current Hall-of-Famer. — *News brief, April 5, 1991*

Chapter 7

On this date in history

Mickey Mantle postcards

There are many different postcards that exist featuring Mickey Mantle. Some of the photographers include:

J.D. McCarthy: Five different Mantle postcards. Mantle is alone on three of them. The other two have Mantle with Roger Maris, and Mantle with Stan Musial ($7-$10). There is also a large 8x10 of Mantle and two 5x7s of Mantle ($25).

George Brace: 13 different black-and-whites of Mantle alone and with others ($10).

Jim Rowe: 12 black-and-white postcards of Mantle alone and with others ($7-$10 each).

Kimac Co.: Nearly 300 different postcards of Mantle alone and with others ($5).

Union Novelty of California: Two different sets of All-Time Yankee Greats; six different Mantles in each postcard set ($7-$10).

Holiday Inn of Joplin, Mo.: Three different Mantle issues, one with Mantle in the game room of the motel, one with two pictures of Mantle in his Yankee uniform and the third with just a picture of the motel with Mantle's name on the marquee ($20-$25).

Dormand, 1954: Four different issues with Mantle on them. Dormand has two different poses of Mantle in the standard postcard size and also two larger postcards issued in the 6x9 and 9x12 format. (The larger issues are very scarce and command prices up to $250).

Moss Photo Service: Fifteen sepia and black-and-white 4-by-6-inch Mickey Mantle postcards from the New York-based service. These are pictures of Mantle that were taken in his early years. They exist in sepia or black-and-white forms ($15-$25 each).

Sportflics: Promotional postcard with Mantle dressed in a coat and tie promoting the Sportflics set in 1986 ($7).

Perez-Steele postcards: Hall of Fame art postcard, autographed, 1981, yellow, $200; Perez-Steele Great Moments, 1987, unsigned, $50-$75; Perez-Steele Celebration, unsigned, $60-$75.

Perez-Steele Master Works set: Four tobacco card designs were used to create five-card sets for five players (Charlie Gehringer, Willie Mays, Mickey Mantle, Duke Snider and Warren Spahn.) In addition to a design created by artist Dick Perez, the other cards were modeled after the 1888 Goodwin Champions set, the 1908 Rose cards, the 1911 gold-bordered T205 set and the 1909 Ramly set. Each card sells for about $10.

Other issues
• 1970 New York Yankee Clinic Day postcards, Mantle and Joe DiMaggio ($20).
• 1971 New York Yankee Clinic Day postcards, Mickey Mantle (Dexter Press) ($15).
• Dallas, Texas, bowling alley postcards ($100).
• 1984 Way Back When postcard; title, "Mantle's 475 H.R." ($10).
• 1959 Dallas Wax Museum postcard of wax Mantle ($100).
• 1988 Willard Mullin postcard #7 ($5).

Mantle postcards/photos, clockwise, from top left: 1954 Dormand; contributor Kelly Eisenhauer's favorite Mantle photo; three by Jim Rowe; two by Robert Jennings; by Jim Rowe (with Joe DiMaggio); 1966 Dexter.

- "The Mick, Mickey Mantle the Legend," with Mantle stamp.
- Omaha Show Express, "Home Run Special #8"
- Babe Ruth, American Sports Series, Mantle, Ford, Martin, 7-6-83.
- Mantle Fiesta Cachet, 1969.
- New York Sports Collectibles Show, Mantle-Seaver-Garvey, 12-4-82.
- Superstar Convention, Atlantic City, N.J., 12-10-83.
- "Great Yankees" (Ruth/Mantle), 7-6-83.

Gateway Stamp Co.

This Florissant, Mo., company has been producing full-color "silk" commemorative cachets since 1977. The limited-edition envelopes are postmarked on historic dates by the United States Postal Service. The cachets feature gold borders, biographical information and full-color cachets, which are actual event photos, publicity photos or artists' renditions. They are designed to be autographed. Values are determined by condition (cleanliness, crispness of corners, centering, positioning of copy, clarity of postmarks) and autographs — quality and player represented.

GS23 Mickey Mantle: Postmarked June 12, 1979, Cooperstown, N.Y. Artwork by Phil Daigle. 2,000, autographed. $150.

GS304 Mantle/Maris: Postmarked Oct. 1, 1986, Bronx, the 25th anniversary of Roger Maris' 61st home run. He and Mickey Mantle set a record for teammates of 115. Bill Perry artwork. 1,500 issued, autographed by Mantle. $50.

GS418 Mickey, Willie & The Duke: Postmarked Jan. 14, 1989, Atlantic City, N.J. 700 issued bearing Mark Lewis artwork and autographed by Mickey Mantle, Willie Mays and Duke Snider, as three of the greatest center fielders to play in New York. Autographed $250.

Z Silk Cachets

Historic Limited Edition, Williston Park, N.Y., reproduces an artist's original painting of a ballplayer for its silk-cacheted philatelic covers. These silk cachets are then applied by hand to envelopes which have been stamped and postmarked by the post office in the corresponding city where the historic event occurred. Generally, the company creates 200-600 covers per event. Each is suitable for autographing.

New York Yankees Series 1 — Mickey Mantle Reinstated: Feb. 14, 1985, 600 issued, $8-$10; Mantle Throws First Ball: April 16, 1985, 600 issued, $8-$10.

New York Yankees Series 2 — Mickey Mantle Memorial Park: July 19, 1986, 600 issued, $30-$40; Mickey Mantle 7th National: July 25, 1986, 600 issued, $6-$8; Mickey Mantle Diamond Legends Show: Oct. 5, 1986, 600 issued $8-$10.

New York Yankees Series 3 — Mantle/Babe Ruth: July 6, 1983, 600 issued, $7-$10.

New York Yankees Series 4 — Mickey Mantle Second East Coast National: Aug. 18, 1989, 600 issued, $5-$7.50.

Gloria Rothstein Show covers — Second East Coast National: Aug. 18, 1989, 400 issued, $12-$15; Third East Coast National: Aug. 17, 1990, 300 issued, $8-$10; Fourth East Coast National: Aug. 17, 1991, 400 issued, $10-$12.50; Fourth East Coast National: Aug. 16, 1991, 400 issued (with Aaron, Mantle, Musial and Robinson), $8-$10; Raritan Center II: Oct. 27, 1990, 350 issued, $5-$7.50.

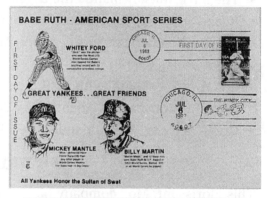

Clockwise, from left: by J.D. McCarthy; American Sports Series; two by Perez-Steele Galleries; by J.D. McCarthy (with Mickey Lolich); Z Silk Cachets.

MICKEY MANTLE

New York Yankees

Chapter 8

That classic signature

Mickey Mantle

Mickey Charles Mantle
(Oct. 20, 1931-)
"The Mick" is by far one of the most popular players to ever play the game of base-ball.

Mantle was known during his playing days for his legendary tape measure home runs, some of which carried 550 feet or more. Home runs were routine for Mantle, who blasted 536 and led the American League in round-trippers four times. A Triple Crown winner and three-time Most Valuable Player, Mantle smacked 18 home runs in 12 World Series contests.

Commonly signed "Mickey Mantle," his signature has varied significantly in charac-ter formation, slant and size. Mantle's signature breaks have also been inconsistent. Signatures originating during the 1950s exhibit breaks between the "M" and the "i," the "c" and the "k" in Mickey, and also between the first and second stroke of the letter "k" in Mickey.

His last name typically had just one break, which fell between the "M" and the "a" in Mantle. During the last two decades his signature was reduced to two consistent breaks, between the first and second stroke of the "k," and between the "M" and the "a" in Mantle. An occasional break also falls between the "M" and the "i" in Mickey.

The right slant of his signature has gradually been reduced with age, while the flam-boyance in his stroke has increased. Like DiMaggio and Dickey, the variations exhib-ited by his signature necessitate a character-by-character analysis.

Letter Variation

M Early examples (1950s) are traditional in character formation, with a heavier right slant. The beginning stroke, during the 1950s, began at the top of the letter with a small hook before the first loop. The stroke that formed the character began to incorporate loops which gradually increased in size and flamboyance.

By the 1960s, the character had become much rounder in appearance, with the opening stroke beginning to exhibit a large loop formation. The late 1960s saw the loop gradually beginning to dip below the signature's base line, and by the 1970s the forma-tion became established as a distinct characteristic of his autograph.

The opening of the loop now commonly extends below the base line and as far as the "i" in Mickey. The width of the descending loop is inconsistent and the "M" may or may not connect to the "i."

i The "i" has varied in width and may or may not connect to the "M." The "i" can be dotted with a circle instead of a dot. The beginning stroke leading to the character's formation can vary in length.

c The "c" may break with the "k," particularly in 1950s examples. The c's finishing stroke may form the stem of the "k" (circa 1960) or the letter's top arm (circa 1970 to present). The upward finishing stroke, exhibited by later signatures, may extend above the "e" in Mickey.

k During the 1950s the "k" could break with the "c" in Mickey. The k's formation has traditionally consisted of two strokes, a base (stem) stroke and a stroke for the letter's arm formation. Earlier examples may have the k's ascender extending to the height of the "M." The stem's stroke can be formed by the ending stroke of the "c," or may begin an entirely new stroke which then completes his first name. The stem's formation does vary, particularly if it is the beginning of an entirely new stroke. The top arm of the "k" can also vary in size.

e The "e" has remained relatively consistent in character formation.

y The "y" can vary in definition, with earlier examples showing greater attention paid to the character's formation. The descender of the "y" can extend well below the base line in earlier examples. However, later examples typically show a reduced descender, only extending as far as the bottom loop of the "M" in Mickey.

M The "M" is typically identical in formation to the "M" in Mickey, however, can vary slightly in size. The "M" commonly breaks with the "a" in Mantle. The opening loop of the letter typically is smaller than its predecessor's loop (The "M" in Mickey).

an The "an" has shown little variation.

t The "t" in earlier examples will have an ascender that can extend to or exceed the height of the "M" in Mantle. The ascender can also vary in width. Later examples show a simplified stem structure that has been reduced in size. The crossing of the "t" is typically a single stroke that extends the length of the character's space. The "t" may break with the "l" in earlier examples.

l Similar to the "t," its ascender has varied in size, becoming smaller and wider with age. Earlier examples will typically have the "l" extending well above any letter in his signature. The "l" can vary slightly in slant.

e The "e" has shown little variation, with the ending stroke typically being a simple ending to the letter. During the 1960s, on rare occasions, he may have added a flamboyant ending that doubled back above his signature to cross the "t."

Mantle has utilized the services of a ghost signer. These signatures, although challenging to recognize, typically are a bit larger with less attention paid to detail. The ghost signatures can adorn both black-and-white photographs and baseballs. Mantle facsimiles are also common, however are easily distinguished as such because of the identical appearance of each signature.

Like Babe Ruth, complicating the authentication of his signature are allegations of other New York Yankee personnel signing material on his behalf. Although these stories are just allegations, they remain a source of concern and discomfort to collectors.

Although mail requests typically go unanswered, Mantle has frequented the baseball card show circuit, allowing collectors easy access to his signature. Authentication of older material such as photographs or team baseballs may prove to be a challenge for the collector.

Availability: Plentiful
Demand: Average

Cut signature	$10
Single-signature baseball	$50-$70
3x5 index card	$20
Photograph/baseball card	$30
HOF plaque postcard	$35
Perez-Steele postcard	$250

- source: The Baseball Autograph Handbook, second edition, by Mark Allen Baker.

Mickey Mantle has diligently, flamboyantly signed his name throughout the years.

New York Yankee team baseballs

* means the player was traded during the season

1951 NEW YORK (AL) — Hank Bauer, Yogi Berra, Bobby Brown, Bob Cerv, Jerry Coleman, Joe Collins, Joe DiMaggio, Johnny Hopp, Jackie Jensen, Billy Johnson *, Jack Kramer *, Bob Kuzava *, Ed Lopat, Mickey Mantle, Cliff Mapes *, Billy Martin, Gil McDougald, Johnny Mize, Tom Morgan, Joe Ostrowski, Stubby Overmire *, Vic Raschi, Allie Reynolds, Phil Rizzuto, Fred Sanford *, Art Schallock, Spec Shea, Charlie Silvera, Casey Stengel (MANAGER), Gene Woodling

LESS THAN 10 GAMES: Jim Brideweser, Tommy Byrne *, Clint Courtney, Tom Ferrick *, Bobby Hogue *, Ralph Houk, Bob Muncrief, Ernie Nevel, Bob Porterfield *, Johnny Sain *, Bob Wiesler, Archie Wilson

NOTES: World Champions! Berra (MVP); McDougald (ROY); DiMaggio's final year.

KEY SIGNATURES: Stengel, Mize, Rizzuto, Brown, DiMaggio, Mantle, McDougald, Berra, Martin, Ford.

VALUE: $900-$1,000

Mantle's 1951 statistics — G: 96; AB: 341; R: 61; H: 91; 2B: 11; 3B: 5; HR: 13; RBI: 65; TB: 151; Ave: .267; SA: .443; SB: 8.

The Yankees were 98-56 in regular season play, finishing first in the American League. In the World Series, the Yankees defeated New York, 4-3.

Mantle's 1951 World Series statistics — AB: 5; R: 1; H: 1; 2B: 0; 3B: 0; HR: 0; RBI: 0; TB: 1; Ave: .200; SB: 0.

1952 NEW YORK (AL) — Loren Babe, Hank Bauer, Yogi Berra, Jim Brideweser, Bobby Brown, Andy Carey, Bob Cerv, Jerry Coleman, Joe Collins, Tom Gorman, Bobby Hogue *, Johnny Hopp *, Bob Kuzava, Ed Lopat, Mickey Mantle, Billy Martin, Jim McDonald, Gil McDougald, Bill Miller, Johnny Mize, Tom Morgan, Irv Noren *, Joe Ostrowski, Vic Raschi, Allie Reynolds, Phil Rizzuto, Johnny Sain, Kal Segrist, Charlie Silvera, Casey Stengel (MANAGER), Gene Woodling

LESS THAN 10 GAMES: Ewell Blackwell, Ralph Houk, Jackie Jensen *, Charlie Keller, Ray Scarborough *, Harry Schaeffer, Art Schallock, Johnny Schmitz *, Archie Wilson *

NOTES: World Champions!

KEY SIGNATURES: Stengel, Martin, Reynolds, Mantle, Berra, Raschi, Woodling, Brown, Mize, Rizzuto.

VALUE: $650-$725

Mantle's 1952 statistics — G: 142; AB: 549; R: 94; H: 171; 2B: 37; 3B: 7; HR: 23; RBI: 87; TB: 291 (2nd); Ave: .311 (3rd); SA: .530 (2nd); SB: 4.

The Yankees were 95-59 in regular season play, finishing first in the American League. In the World Series, the Yankees defeated Brooklyn, 4-3.

Mantle's 1952 World Series statistics — AB: 29; R: 5; H: 10; 2B: 1; 3B: 1; HR: 2; RBI: 3; TB: 19; Ave: .345; SB: 0.

1953 NEW YORK (AL) — Hank Bauer, Yogi Berra, Don Bollweg, Jim Brideweser, Andy Carey, Joe Collins, Whitey Ford, Tom Gorman, Bob Kuzava, Ed Lopat, Mickey Mantle, Billy Martin, Jim McDonald, Gil McDougald, Bill Miller, Willie Miranda *, Johnny Mize, Irv Noren, Vic Raschi, Bill Renna, Allie Reynolds, Phil Rizzuto, Johnny Sain, Ray Scarborough, Art Schult *, Charlie Silvera, Casey Stengel (MANAGER), Gus Triandos, Gene Woodling

LESS THAN 10 GAMES: Loren Babe *, Ewell Blackwell, Bob Cerv, Jerry Coleman, Ralph Houk, Steve Kraly, Art Schallock, Johnny Schmitz, Frank Verdi

NOTES: World Champions!

KEY SIGNATURES: Stengel, Martin, Rizzuto, Mantle, Berra, Mize, Ford.

VALUE: $675-$750

Mantle's 1953 statistics — G: 127; AB: 461; R: 105; H: 136; 2B: 24; 3B: 3; HR: 21; RBI: 92; TB: 229; Ave: .295; SA: .497; SB: 8.

The Yankees were 99-52 in regular season play, finishing first in the American League. In the World Series, the Yankees defeated Brooklyn, 4-2.

Mantle's 1953 World Series statistics — AB: 24; R: 3; H: 5; 2B: 0; 3B: 0; HR: 2; RBI: 7; TB: 11; Ave: .208; SB: 0.

1954 NEW YORK (AL) — Hank Bauer, Yogi Berra, Bobby Brown, Harry Byrd, Andy Carey, Bob Cerv, Jerry Coleman, Joe Collins, Whitey Ford, Tom Gorman, Bob Grim, Bob

Kuzeva *, Frank Leja, Ed Lopat, Mickey Mantle, Jim McDonald, Gil McDougald, Willie Miranda, Tom Morgan, Irv Noren, Allie Reynolds, Phil Rizzuto, Eddie Robinson, Johnny Sain, Charlie Silvera, Bill Skowron, Enos Slaughter, Casey Stengel (MANAGER), Marlin Stuart *, Gene Woodling

LESS THAN 10 GAMES: Lou Berberet, Ralph Branca *, Tommy Byrne, Woodie Held, Ralph Houk, Jim Konstanty *, Bill Miller, Art Schallock, Gus Triandos, Bob Wiesler

NOTES: Berra (MVP); Grim (ROY).

KEY SIGNATURES: Stengel, Rizzuto, Mantle, Berra, Slaughter, Grim, Ford.

VALUE: $575-$650

Mantle's 1954 statistics — G: 146; AB: 543; R: 129; H: 163; 2B: 17; 3B: 12; HR: 27 (3rd); RBI: 102; TB: 285 (3rd); Ave: .300; SA: .525 (3rd); SB: 5.

The Yankees were 103-51 in regular season play, finishing second in the American League.

1955 NEW YORK (AL) — Hank Bauer, Yogi Berra, Tommy Byrne, Andy Carey, Tommy Carroll, Bob Cerv, Jerry Coleman, Rip Coleman, Joe Collins, Whitey Ford, Bob Grim, Elston Howard, Billy Hunter, Jim Konstanty, Johnny Kucks, Don Larsen, Ed Lopat *, Mickey Mantle, Billy Martin, Gil McDougald, Tom Morgan, Irv Noren, Bobby Richardson, Phil Rizzuto, Eddie Robinson, Charlie Silvera, Bill Skowron, Enos Slaughter *, Casey Stengel (MANAGER), Tom Sturdivant, Bob Turley, Bob Wiesler

LESS THAN 10 GAMES: Lou Berberet, Johnny Blanchard, Ted Gray *, Frank Leja, Johnny Sain *, Art Schallock *, Gerry Staley *, Dick Tettelbach, Marv Throneberry

NOTES: Berra (MVP).

KEY SIGNATURES: Stengel, Mantle, Slaughter, Howard, Martin, Berra, Rizzuto, Ford, Larsen.

VALUE: $725-$775

Mantle's 1955 statistics — G: 147; AB: 517; R: 121; H: 158; 2B: 25; 3B: 11; HR: 37; RBI: 99; TB: 316; Ave: .306; SA: .611; SB: 8.

The Yankees were 96-58 in regular season play, finishing first in the American League. In the World Series, Brooklyn defeated the Yankees, 4-3.

Mantle's 1955 World Series statistics — AB: 10; R: 1; H: 2; 2B: 0; 3B: 0; HR: 1; RBI: 1; TB: 5; Ave: .200; SB: 0.

1956 NEW YORK (AL) — Hank Bauer, Yogi Berra, Tommy Byrne, Andy Carey, Tommy Carroll, Bob Cerv, Jerry Coleman, Rip Coleman, Joe Collins, Whitey Ford, Bob Grim, Elston Howard, Billy Hunter, Johnny Kucks, Don Larsen, Jerry Lumpe, Mickey Mantle, Billy Martin, Mickey McDermott, Gil McDougald, Tom Morgan, Irv Noren, Phil Rizzuto, Eddie Robinson *, Norm Siebern, Bill Skowron, Enos Slaughter *, Casey Stengel (MANAGER), Tom Sturdivant, Bob Turley, Ted Wilson *

LESS THAN 10 GAMES: Jim Coates, Sonny Dixon, Jim Konstanty *, Bobby Richardson, Charlie Silvera, Lou Skizas *, Gerry Staley *, Ralph Terry

NOTES: World Champions! Mantle won the Triple Crown and MVP.

KEY SIGNATURES: Stengel, Martin, Mantle, Howard, Rizzuto, Slaughter, Berra, Bauer, Ford.

VALUE: $800-$1,000

Mantle's 1956 statistics — G: 150; AB: 533; R: 132 (1st); H: 188; 2B: 22; 3B: 5; HR: 52 (1st); RBI: 130 (1st); TB: 376 (1st); SA: .705; Ave: .353 (1st); SA: .705 (1st); SB: 10.

The Yankees were 97-57 in regular season play, finishing first in the American League. In the World Series, the Yankees defeated Brooklyn, 4-3.

Mantle's 1956 World Series statistics — AB: 24; R: 6; H: 6; 2B: 1; 3B: 0; HR: 3; RBI: 4; TB: 16; Ave: .250; SB: 1.

A 1955 New York Yankees team ball.

1957 NEW YORK (AL) — Hank Bauer, Yogi Berra, Tommy Byrne, Andy Carey, Al Cicotte, Jerry Coleman, Joe Collins, Art Ditmar, Whitey Ford, Bob Grim, Elston Howard, Darrell Johnson, Tony Kubek, Johnny Kucks, Don Larsen, Jerry Lumpe, Mickey Mantle, Billy Martin *, Gil McDougald, Bobby Richardson, Bobby Shantz, Harry Simpson *, Bill Skowron, Enos Slaughter, Tom Sturdivant, Bob Turley

LESS THAN 10 GAMES: Zeke Bella, Bobby Del Greco *, Woodie Held *, Sal Maglie *, Casey Stengel (MANAGER), Ralph Terry *

NOTES: Mantle (MVP); Kubek (ROY).

KEY SIGNATURES: Stengel, Slaughter, Berra, Howard, Sturdivant, Ford.

VALUE: $575-$625

Mantle's 1957 statistics — G: 144; AB: 474; R: 121 (1st); H: 173; 2B: 28; 3B: 6; HR: 34 (3rd); RBI: 94; TB: 315 (2nd); Ave: .365 (2nd); SA: .665 (2nd); SB: 16 (4th).

The Yankees were 98-56 in the regular season, finishing first in the American League. In the World Series, Milwaukee defeated the Yankees, 4-3.

Mantle's 1957 World Series statistics — AB: 19; R: 3; H: 5; 2B: 0; 3B: 0; HR: 1; RBI: 2; TB: 8; Ave: .263; SB: 0.

1958 NEW YORK (AL) — Hank Bauer, Yogi Berra, Andy Carey, Bobby Del Greco, Art Ditmar, Ryne Duren, Whitey Ford, Bob Grim *, Elston Howard, Tony Kubek, Johnny Kucks, Don Larsen, Jerry Lumpe, Duke Maas *, Mickey Mantle, Gil McDougald, Zack Monroe, Bobby Richardson, Bobby Shantz, Norm Siebern, Harry Simpson *, Bill Skowron, Enos Slaughter, Tom Sturdivant, Marv Throneberry, Virgil Trucks *, Bob Turley

LESS THAN 10 GAMES: Fritzie Brickell, Murry Dickson *, Johnny James, Darrell Johnson, Sal Maglie *, Casey Stengel (MANAGER)

NOTES: World Champions! Turley (Cy Young).

KEY SIGNATURES: Kubek, Mantle, Berra, Howard, Slaughter, Turley, Ford, Larsen.

VALUE: $600-$650

Mantle's 1958 statistics — G: 150; AB: 519; R: 127 (1st); H: 158; 2B: 21; 3B: 1; HR: 42 (1st); RBI: 97 (5th); TB: 307 (1st); Ave: .304; SA: .592 (3rd); SB: 18 (4th).

The Yankees were 92-62 in the regular season, finishing first in the American League. In the World Series, the Yankees defeated Milwaukee, 4-3.

Mantle's 1958 World Series statistics — AB: 24; R: 4; H: 6; 2B: 0; 3B: 1; HR: 2; RBI: 3; TB: 14; Ave: .250; SB: 0.

1959 NEW YORK (AL) — Hank Bauer, Yogi Berra, Johnny Blanchard, Gary Blaylock *, Clete Boyer, Fritzie Brickell, Jim Bronstad, Andy Carey, Jim Coates, Art Ditmar, Ryne Duren, Whitey Ford, Eli Grba, Elston Howard, Tony Kubek, Don Larsen, Hector Lopez *, Jerry Lumpe *, Duke Maas, Mickey Mantle, Gil McDougald, Jim Pisoni *, Bobby Richardson, Bobby Shantz, Norm Siebern, Bill Skowron, Enos Slaughter *, Ralph Terry *, Marv Throneberry, Bob Turley

LESS THAN 10 GAMES: Mark Freeman *, John Gabler, Ken Hunt, Johnny Kucks *, Zack Monroe, Casey Stengel (MANAGER), Tom Sturdivant *, Gordon Windhorn

KEY SIGNATURES: Stengel, Kubek, Mantle, Berra, Howard, Slaughter, Ford, Larsen.

VALUE: $475-$525

Mantle's 1959 statistics — G: 144; AB: 541; R: 104 (2nd); H: 154; 2B: 23; 3B: 4; HR: 31 (5th); RBI: 75; TB: 278 (4th); Ave: .285; SA: .514 (3rd); SB: 21 (2nd).

The Yankees were 79-75 in the regular season, finishing third in the American League.

1960 NEW YORK (AL) — Luis Arroyo, Yogi Berra, Johnny Blanchard, Clete Boyer, Bob Cerv *, Jim Coates, Joe DeMaestri, Art Ditmar, Ryne Duren, Whitey Ford, John Gabler, Eli Grba, Kent Hadley, Elston Howard, Ken Hunt, Johnny James, Tony Kubek, Dale Long *, Hector Lopez, Duke Maas, Mickey Mantle, Roger Maris, Gil McDougald, Jim Pisoni, Bobby Richardson, Bobby Shantz, Bill Short, Bill Skowron, Bill Stafford, Casey Stengel (MANAGER), Ralph Terry, Bob Turley

LESS THAN 10 GAMES: Andy Carey, Jesse Gonder, Deron Johnson, Fred Kipp, Billy Shantz, Hal Stowe, Elmer Valo *

NOTES: Stengel's final year with the Yankees; Maris (MVP).

KEY SIGNATURES: Stengel, Kubek, Maris, Mantle, Howard, Berra, Ford.

VALUE: $625-$725

Mantle's 1960 statistics — G: 153; AB: 527; R: 119 (1st); H: 145; 2B: 17; 3B: 6; HR: 40 (1st); RBI: 94; TB: 294 (1st); Ave: .275; SA: .558 (2nd); SB: 14.

The Yankees were 97-57 in the regular season, finishing first in the American League. In the World Series, Pittsburgh defeated the Yankees, 4-3.

Mantle's 1960 World Series statistics — AB: 25; R: 8; H: 10; 2B: 1; 3B: 0; HR: 3; RBI: 11; TB: 20; Ave: .400; SB: 0.

1961 NEW YORK (AL) — Luis Arroyo, Yogi Berra, Johnny Blanchard, Clete Boyer, Bob Cerv *, Tex Clevenger *, Jim Coates, Bud Daley *, Joe DeMaestri, Art Ditmar *, Whitey Ford, Billy Gardner *, Jesse Gonder, Bob Hale *, Ralph Houk (MANAGER), Elston Howard, Deron Johnson *, Tony Kubek, Hector Lopez, Mickey Mantle, Roger Maris, Jack Reed, Hal Reniff, Bobby Richardson, Rollie Sheldon, Bill Skowron, Bill Stafford, Ralph Terry, Earl Torgeson *, Tom Tresh, Bob Turley

LESS THAN 10 GAMES: Al Downing, Ryne Duren *, Johnny James *, Duke Maas, Danny McDevitt *, Lee Thomas *

NOTES: World Champions! Maris won the MVP and set the single-season home run record; "M&M" Boys (Mantle/Maris); Ford (Cy Young)

KEY SIGNATURES: Kubek, Maris, Mantle, Berra, Howard, Tresh, Ford.

VALUE: $1,250-$1,600

Mantle's 1961 statistics — G: 153; AB: 514; R: 132 (1st); H: 163; 2B: 16; 3B: 6; HR: 54 (2nd); RBI: 128 (5th); TB: 353 (3rd); Ave: .317 (4th); SA: .687 (1st); SB: 12.

The Yankees were 109-53 in the regular season, finishing first in the American League. In the World Series, the Yankees defeated Cincinnati, 4-1.

Mantle's 1961 World Series statistics — AB: 6; R: 0; H: 1; 2B: 0; 3B: 0; HR: 0; RBI: 0; TB: 1; Ave: .167; SB: 0.

1962 NEW YORK (AL) — Luis Arroyo, Yogi Berra, Johnny Blanchard, Jim Bouton, Clete Boyer, Marshall Bridges, Bob Cerv *, Tex Clevenger, Jim Coates, Bud Daley,

Whitey Ford, Ralph Houk (MANAGER), Elston Howard, Tony Kubek, Phil Linz, Dale Long *, Hector Lopez, Mickey Mantle, Roger Maris, Joe Pepitone, Jack Reed, Bobby Richardson, Rollie Sheldon, Bill Skowron, Bill Stafford, Ralph Terry, Tom Tresh, Bob Turley

LESS THAN 10 GAMES: Hal Brown *, Jack Cullen, Al Downing, Billy Gardner *, Jake Gibbs, Hal Reniff

NOTES: World Champions! Mantle (MVP), Tresh (ROY).

KEY SIGNATURES: Tresh, Maris, Mantle, Howard, Berra, Kubek, Terry, Ford.

VALUE: $575-$625

Mantle's 1962 statistics — G: 123; AB: 377; R: 96; H: 121; 2B: 15; 3B: 1; HR: 30; RBI: 89; TB: 228; Ave: .321; SA: .605; SB: 9.

The Yankees were 96-66 in the regular season, finishing first in the American League. In the World Series, the Yankees defeated San Francisco, 4-3.

Mantle's 1962 World Series statistics — AB: 25; R: 2; H: 3; 2B: 1; 3B: 0; HR: 0; RBI: 0; TB: 4; Ave: .120; SB: 2.

1963 NEW YORK (AL) — Yogi Berra, Johnny Blanchard, Jim Bouton, Clete Boyer, Marshall Bridges, Harry Bright *, Al Downing, Whitey Ford, Pedro Gonzalez, Steve Hamilton *, Ralph Houk (MANAGER), Elston Howard, Tony Kubek, Bill Kunkel, Phil Linz, Dale Long, Hector Lopez, Mickey Mantle, Roger Maris, Joe Pepitone, Jack Reed, Hal Reniff, Bobby Richardson, Bill Stafford, Ralph Terry, Tom Tresh, Stan Williams

LESS THAN 10 GAMES: Luis Arroyo, Bud Daley, Jake Gibbs, Tom Metcalf

NOTES: Howard (MVP).

KEY SIGNATURES: Maris, Howard, Mantle, Berra, Ford.

VALUE: $475-$500

Mantle's 1963 statistics — G: 65; AB: 172; R: 40; H: 54; 2B: 8; 3B: 0; HR: 15; RBI: 35; TB: 107; Ave: .314; SA: .622; SB: 2.

The Yankees were 104-57 in regular season play, finishing first in the American League. In the World Series, Los Angeles defeated the Yankees, 4-0.

Mantle's 1963 World Series statistics — AB: 15; R: 1; H: 2; 2B: 0; 3B: 0; HR: 1; RBI: 1; TB: 5; Ave: .133; SB: 0.

1964 NEW YORK (AL) — Yogi Berra (MANAGER), Johnny Blanchard, Jim Bouton, Clete Boyer, Bud Daley, Al Downing, Whitey Ford, Pedro Gonzalez, Steve Hamilton, Elston Howard, Tony Kubek, Phil Linz, Hector Lopez, Mickey Mantle, Roger Maris, Pete Mikkelsen, Archie Moore, Joe Pepitone, Pedro Ramos *, Hal Reniff, Roger Repoz, Bobby Richardson, Rollie Sheldon, Bill Stafford, Mel Stottlemyre, Ralph Terry, Tom Tresh, Stan Williams

LESS THAN 10 GAMES: Harry Bright, Jake Gibbs, Mike Hegan, Elvio Jimenez, Bob Meyer *

KEY SIGNATURES: Berra, Maris, Mantle, Howard, Ford, Stottlemyre.

VALUE: $400-$450

Mantle's 1964 statistics — G: 143; AB: 465; R: 92; H: 141; 2B: 25; 3B: 2; HR: 35 (3rd); RBI: 111 (3rd); TB: 275; Ave: .303 (4th); SA: .591 (2nd); SB: 6.

The Yankees were 99-63 in the regular season, finishing first in the American League. In the World Series, St. Louis defeated the Yankees, 4-3.

Mantle's 1964 World Series statistics — AB: 24; R: 8; H: 8; 2B: 2; 3B: 0; HR: 3; RBI: 8; TB: 19; Ave: .333; SB: 0.

1965 NEW YORK (AL) — Ray Barker *, Johnny Blanchard *, Gil Blanco, Jim Bouton, Clete Boyer, Horace Clarke, Jack Cullen, Al Downing, Doc Edwards *, Whitey Ford, Jake Gibbs, Steve Hamilton, Elston Howard, Johnny Keane (MANAGER), Tony Kubek, Phil Linz, Art Lopez, Hector Lopez, Mickey Mantle, Roger Maris, Pete Mikkelsen, Ross Moschitto, Bobby Murcer, Joe Pepitone, Pedro Ramos, Hal Reniff, Roger Repoz, Bobby

Richardson, Bob Schmidt, Bill Stafford, Mel Stottlemyre, Bobby Tiefenauer *, Tom Tresh, Roy White

LESS THAN 10 GAMES: Rick Beck, Jim Brenneman, Duke Carmel, Pedro Gonzalez *, Mike Jurewicz, Archie Moore, Rollie Sheldon *

KEY SIGNATURES: Mantle, Howard, Maris, Murcer, Stottlemyre, Ford.

VALUE: $325-$375

Mantle's 1965 statistics — G: 122; AB: 361; R: 44; H: 92; 2B: 12; 3B: 1; HR: 19; RBI: 46; TB: 163; Ave: .255; SA: .452; SB: 4.

The Yankees were 77-85 in the regular season, finishing sixth in the American League.

1966 NEW YORK (AL) — Ruben Amaro, Ray Barker, Jim Bouton, Clete Boyer, Bill Bryan *, Horace Clarke, Lu Clinton, Al Downing, Mike Ferraro, Whitey Ford, Bob Friend *, Jake Gibbs, Steve Hamilton, Mike Hegan, Ralph Houk (MANAGER), Elston Howard, Johnny Keane (MANAGER), Hector Lopez, Mickey Mantle, Roger Maris, Bobby Murcer, Joe Pepitone, Fritz Peterson, Pedro Ramos, Hal Reniff, Roger Repoz *, Bobby Richardson, Dick Schofield *, Mel Stottlemyre, Fred Talbot *, Tom Tresh, Steve Whitaker, Roy White, Dooley Womack

LESS THAN 10 GAMES: Stan Bahnsen, Jack Cullen, Bill Henry, John Miller

KEY SIGNATURES: Maris, Mantle, Howard, Stottlemyre, Ford.

VALUE: $350-475

Mantle's 1966 statistics — G: 108; AB: 333; R: 40; H: 96; 2B: 12; 3B: 1; HR: 23; RBI: 56; TB: 179; Ave: .288; SA: .538; SB: 1.

The Yankees were 70-89 in the regular season, finishing last in the American League.

1967 NEW YORK (AL) — Ruben Amaro, Steve Barber *, Ray Barker, Jim Bouton, Billy Bryan, Horace Clarke, Al Downing, Jake Gibbs, Steve Hamilton, Mike Hegan, Ralph Houk (MANAGER), Elston Howard *, Dick Howser, John Kennedy, Jerry Kenney, Mickey Mantle, Bill Monbouquette *, Ross Moschitto, Joe Pepitone, Fritz Peterson, Hal Reniff *, Bill Robinson, Charley Smith, Mel Stottlemyre, Fred Talbot, Bob Tillman *, Thad Tillotson, Tom Tresh, Joe Verbanic, Steve Whitaker, Roy White, Dooley Womack

LESS THAN 10 GAMES: Lu Clinton, Frank Fernandez, Whitey Ford, Cecil Perkins, Dale Roberts, Charlie Sands, Tom Shopay, Frank Tepedino

KEY SIGNATURES: Mantle, Howard, Stottlemyre, Ford.

VALUE: $275-$325

Mantle's 1967 statistics — G: 144; AB: 440; R: 63; H: 108; 2B: 17; 3B: 0; HR: 22; RBI: 55; TB: 191; Ave: .245; SA: .434; SB: 1.

The Yankees were 72-90 in the regular season, finishing ninth in the American League.

1968 NEW YORK (AL) — Ruben Amaro, Stan Bahnsen, Steve Barber, Jim Bouton, Horace Clarke, Rocky Colavito *, Bobby Cox, Al Downing, Frank Fernandez, Mike Ferraro, Jake Gibbs, Steve Hamilton, Ralph Houk (MANAGER), Dick Howser, Andy Kosco, Mickey Mantle, Lindy McDaniel *, Gene Michael, Bill Monbouquette *, Joe Pepitone, Fritz Peterson, Bill Robinson, Charley Smith, Mel Stottlemyre, Fred Talbot, Tom Tresh, Joe Verbanic, Steve Whitaker, Roy White, Dooley Womack

LESS THAN 10 GAMES: John Cumberland, Gene Michael, Ellie Rodriguez, Tony Solaita, Thad Tillotson, John Wyatt *

NOTES: Bahnsen (ROY); Mantle's final season.

VALUE: $225-$275

Mantle's 1968 statistics — G: 144; AB: 435; R: 57; H: 103; 2B: 14; 3B: 1; HR: 18; RBI: 54; TB: 173; Ave: .237; SA: .398; SB: 6.

The Yankees were 83-79 in the regular season, finishing fifth in the American League.

A 1959 New York Yankees team ball.

American League All-Stars team baseballs

1952 AMERICAN LEAGUE ALL-STAR TEAM — Bobby Avila, Hank Bauer, Yogi Berra, Tony Cuccinello (COACH), Dom DiMaggio, Larry Doby, Ferris Fain, Nellie Fox, Mike Garcia, Jim Hegan, Jackie Jensen, Eddie Joost, Bob Lemon, Al Lopez (COACH), Mickey Mantle, Gil McDougald, Minnie Minoso, Dale Mitchell, Satchel Paige, Vic Raschi, Allie Reynolds, Phil Rizzuto, Eddie Robinson, Al Rosen, Bobby Shantz, Casey Stengel (MANAGER), Vic Wertz, Eddie Yost

   PLAYERS WHO WERE REPLACED: George Kell

   NOTES: 7 HOFers. Mantle did not play in the American League's 3-2 loss.

   KEY SIGNATURES: Mantle, Paige.

   VALUE: $950-$1,100

1953 AMERICAN LEAGUE ALL-STAR TEAM — Hank Bauer, Yogi Berra, Lou Boudreau (COACH), Chico Carrasquel, Larry Doby, Ferris Fain, Nellie Fox, Mike Garcia, Billy Goodman, Billy Hunter, George Kell, Harvey Kuenn, Bob Lemon, Mickey Mantle, Minnie Minoso, Johnny Mize, Satchel Paige, Billy Pierce, Allie Reynolds, Phil Rizzuto, Eddie Robinson, Al Rosen, Johnny Sain, Casey Stengel (MANAGER), Jim Turner (COACH), Mickey Vernon, Sammy White, Ted Williams, Gus Zernial

   NOTES: 9 HOFers; includes Williams, who was an honorary member. Mantle was 0-2 in the American League's 5-1 loss.

   KEY SIGNATURES: Mantle, Williams, Paige.

   VALUE: $600-$700

1954 AMERICAN LEAGUE ALL-STAR TEAM — Bob Avila, Hank Bauer, Yogi Berra, Ray Boone, Chico Carrasquel, Sandy Consuegra, Larry Doby, Jim Finigan, Whitey Ford, Nelson Fox, Fred Hutchinson (COACH), Bob Keegan, Harvey Kuenn, Bob Lemon, Sherm Lollar, Mickey Mantle, Marty Marion (COACH), Orestes Minoso, Irv Noren, Jim Piersall, Bob Porterfield, Al Rosen, Casey Stengel (MANAGER), Dean Stone, Virgil Trucks, Bob Turley, Mickey Vernon, Ted Williams

   PLAYERS WHO WERE REPLACED: Ferris Fain, Mike Garcia, George Kell, Allie Reynolds

NOTES: 6 HOFers. Mantle was 2-5, with one run scored in the American League's 11-9 win.

KEY SIGNATURES: Williams, Mantle.

VALUE: $550-$625

1955 AMERICAN LEAGUE ALL-STAR TEAM — Bobby Avila, Yogi Berra, Chico Carrasquel, Tony Cuccinello (COACH), Larry Doby, Dick Donovan, Jim Finigan, Whitey Ford, Nellie Fox, Don Gutteridge (COACH), Billy Hoeft, Jackie Jensen, Al Kaline, Harvey Kuenn, Sherm Lollar, Al Lopez (MANAGER), Mickey Mantle, Billy Pierce, Vic Power, Al Rosen, Herb Score, Al Smith, Frank Sullivan, Bob Turley, Mickey Vernon, Ted Williams, Jim Wilson, Early Wynn

NOTES: 7 HOFers. Mantle was 2-6, with one run scored and a three-run home run in the American League's 6-5 loss.

KEY SIGNATURES: Williams, Mantle.

VALUE: $500-$600

1956 AMERICAN LEAGUE ALL-STAR TEAM — Yogi Berra, Ray Boone, Tom Brewer, Chuck Dressen (COACH), Whitey Ford, Nellie Fox, Al Kaline, George Kell, Johnny Kucks, Harvey Kuenn, Sherm Lollar, Mickey Mantle, Billy Martin, Charlie Maxwell, Gil McDougald, Billy Pierce, Jimmy Piersall, Vic Power, Herb Score, Roy Sievers, Harry Simpson, Casey Stengel (MANAGER), Frank Sullivan, Jim Turner (COACH), Mickey Vernon, Ted Williams, Jim Wilson, Early Wynn

PLAYERS WHO WERE REPLACED: Ray Narleski

NOTES: 8 HOFers. Mantle homered in one at bat, with one run scored and one RBI in the American League's 7-3 loss.

KEY SIGNATURES: Williams, Mantle — "Yogi, Billy, Whitey & Mickey."

VALUE: $550-$650

1957 AMERICAN LEAGUE ALL-STAR TEAM — Yogi Berra, Jim Bunning, Frankie Crosetti (COACH), Joe DeMaestri, Nellie Fox, Bob Grim, Elston Howard, Al Kaline, George Kell, Harvey Kuenn, Billy Loes, Frank Malzone, Mickey Mantle, Charlie Maxwell, Gil McDougald, Minnie Minoso, Don Mossi, Bill Pierce, Bobby Richardson, Bobby Shantz, Roy Sievers, Bill Skowron, Casey Stengel (MANAGER), Gus Triandos, Jim Turner (COACH), Vic Wertz, Ted Williams, Early Wynn

NOTES: 7 HOFers. Mantle was 1-4, with one run scored in the American League's 6-5 win.

KEY SIGNATURES: Williams, Mantle.

VALUE: $475-$575

1958 AMERICAN LEAGUE ALL-STAR TEAM — Luis Aparicio, Yogi Berra, Rocky Bridges, Bob Cerv, Ryne Duren, Whitey Ford, Nellie Fox, Lum Harris (COACH), Elston Howard, Jackie Jensen, Al Kaline, Tony Kubek, Harvey Kuenn, Sherm Lollar, Frank Malzone, Mickey Mantle, Gil McDougald, Ray Narleski, Billy O'Dell, Billy Pierce, Bill Skowron, Casey Stengel (MANAGER), Gus Triandos, Bob Turley, Jim Turner (COACH), Mickey Vernon, Ted Williams, Early Wynn

NOTES: 8 HOFers. Mantle was 1-2 in the American League's 4-3 win.

KEY SIGNATURES: Williams, Mantle — "Yogi, Whitey & Mickey."

VALUE: $475-$525

1959 AMERICAN LEAGUE ALL-STAR TEAM — Luis Aparicio, Yogi Berra, Jim Bunning, Rocky Colavito, Harry Craft (COACH), Tony Cuccinello (COACH), Buddy Daley, Ryne Duren, Whitey Ford, Nellie Fox, Al Kaline, Harmon Killebrew, Harvey Kuenn, Sherm Lollar, Frank Malzone, Mickey Mantle, Gil McDougald, Minnie Minoso, Billy Pierce, Vic Power, Pete Runnels, Roy Sievers, Bill Skowron, Casey Stengel (MANAGER), Gus Triandos, Hoyt Wilhelm, Ted Williams, Early Wynn

NOTES: 10 HOFers. Mantle pinch ran in the American League's 5-4 loss.

VALUE: $500-$600

1959 AMERICAN LEAGUE 2ND GAME ALL-STARS — Bobby Allison, Luis Aparicio, Yogi Berra, Rocky Colavito, Frank Crosetti (COACH), Buddy Daley, Ryne Duren, Nellie Fox, Elston Howard, Al Kaline, Harmon Killebrew, Tony Kubek, Harry Lavagetto (COACH), Sherm Lollar, Frank Malzone, Mickey Mantle, Roger Maris, Cal McLish, Minnie Minoso, William O'Dell, Vic Power, Pedro Ramos, Bobby Richardson, Pete Runnels, Roy Sievers, Casey Stengel (MANAGER), Gus Triandos, Jerry Walker, Hoyt Wilhelm, Ted Williams, Eugene Woodling, Early Wynn

  PLAYERS WHO WERE REPLACED: Camilio Pascual

  NOTES: 9 HOFers. Mantle was 1-3 in the American League's 5-3 win.

  KEY SIGNATURES: Mantle, Maris, Williams.

  VALUE: $575-$650

1960 AMERICAN LEAGUE ALL-STAR TEAM — Luis Aparicio, Gary Bell, Yogi Berra, Jim Coates, Tony Cuccinello (COACH), Buddy Daley, Chuck Estrada, Whitey Ford, Nellie Fox, Jim Gentile, Don Gutteridge (COACH), Ron Hansen, Elston Howard, Al Kaline, Harvey Kuenn, Frank Lary, Jim Lemon, Sherm Lollar, Al Lopez (MANAGER), Frank Malzone, Mickey Mantle, Roger Maris, Minnie Minoso, Bill Monbouquette, Camilo Pascual, Vic Power, Brooks Robinson, Pete Runnels, Bill Skowron, Al Smith, Gerald Staley, Dick Stigman, Ted Williams, Early Wynn

  NOTES: 9 HOFers; There were no roster changes for the second all-star game played in the 1960 season. Mantle walked twice and scored a run in the American League's 5-3 loss in the first game. He was 1-4 in the second game, a 6-0 loss.

  KEY SIGNATURES: Mantle, Maris.

  VALUE: $575-$650

1961 AMERICAN LEAGUE ALL-STAR TEAM — Yogi Berra, John Brandt, Jim Bunning, Norm Cash, Rocky Colavito, Frank Crosetti (COACH), Dick Donovan, Ryne Duren, Whitey Ford, Miguel Fornieles, Nellie Fox, Jim Gentile, Elston Howard, Dick Howser, Al Kaline, Harmon Killebrew, Tony Kubek, Frank Lary, Mickey Mantle, Roger Maris, Jim Perry, Billy Pierce, Paul Richards (MANAGER), Brooks Robinson, John Romano, John Temple, James Vernon (COACH), Hoyt Wilhelm

  NOTES: 7 HOFers. Mantle was 0-3 in the American League's 5-4 loss.

  KEY SIGNATURES: Mantle, Maris.

  VALUE: $600-$675

1961 AMERICAN LEAGUE 2ND GAME ALL-STARS — James Adair (COACH), Luis Aparicio, Luis Arroyo, Yogi Berra, John Brandt, Jim Bunning, Norm Cash, Rocky Colavito, Dick Donovan, Whitey Ford, Nellie Fox, Tito Francona, Jim Gentile, Mike Higgins (COACH), Elston Howard, Dick Howser, Al Kaline, Harmon Killebrew, Tony Kubek, Barry Latman, Mickey Mantle, Roger Maris, Ken McBride, Camilo Pascual, Paul Richards (MANAGER), Brooks Robinson, John Romano, Don Schwall, Roy Sievers, Bill Skowron, Johnny Temple, Hoyt Wilhelm

  NOTES: 8 HOFers. Mantle was 0-3 in the 1-1 tie game.

  KEY SIGNATURES: Mantle, Maris.

  VALUE: $600-$675

1962 AMERICAN LEAGUE ALL-STAR TEAM — Hank Aguirre, Luis Aparicio, Earl Battey, Jim Bunning, Rocky Colavito, Dick Donovan, Jim Gentile, Billy Hitchcock (COACH), Ralph Houk (MANAGER), Elston Howard, Jim Landis, Mickey Mantle, Roger Maris, Bill Monbouquette, Billy Moran, Milt Pappas, Camilo Pascual, Bobby Richardson, Brooks Robinson, Richard Rollins, John Romano, Norm Siebern, David Stenhouse, Ralph Terry, LeRoy Thomas, Tom Tresh, Mickey Vernon (COACH), Leon Wagner, Hoyt Wilhelm

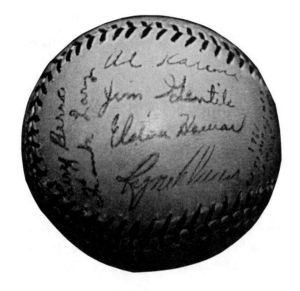

A team ball for the 1961 American League All-Stars is worth $600. Players signing this ball, from the first 1961 game, include Mickey Mantle, Al Kaline, Jim Gentile, Elston Howard, Ryne Duren, Yogi Berra and Frank Lary.

NOTES: 4 HOFers. Mantle was 0-1 in the American League's 3-1 loss.

KEY SIGNATURES: Mantle, Maris.

VALUE: $500-$550

1962 AMERICAN LEAGUE 2ND GAME ALL-STARS — Hank Aguirre, Luis Aparicio, Earl Battey, Hank Bauer (COACH), Yogi Berra, Jim Bunning, Rocky Colavito, Dick Donovan, Jim Gentile, Ray Herbert, Ralph Houk (MANAGER), Elston Howard, Jim Kaat, Al Kaline, Mickey Mantle, Roger Maris, Billy Moran, Camilo Pascual, Bobby Richardson, Bill Rigney (COACH), Brooks Robinson, Rich Rollins, John Romano, Pete Runnels, Norm Siebern, David Stenhouse, Ralph Terry, Leroy Thomas, Tom Tresh, Leon Wagner, Hoyt Wilhelm

PLAYERS WHO WERE REPLACED: Ken McBride

NOTES: Mantle did not play in the American League's 9-4 win.

KEY SIGNATURES: Mantle, Maris.

VALUE: $525-$600

1963 AMERICAN LEAGUE ALL-STAR TEAM — Bob Allison, Luis Aparicio, Earl Battey, Jim Bouton, Jim Bunning, Nellie Fox, Jim Grant, Ralph Houk (MANAGER), Elston Howard, Al Kaline, Harmon Killebrew, Don Leppert, Frank Malzone, Ken McBride, Sam Mele (COACH), Bill Monbouquette, Albie Pearson, Joe Pepitone, Johnny Pesky (COACH), Juan Pizarro, Dick Radatz, Bobby Richardson, Brooks Robinson, Norm Siebern, Tom Tresh, Zoilo Versalles, Leon Wagner, Carl Yastrzemski

PLAYERS WHO WERE REPLACED: Steve Barber, Mickey Mantle

NOTES: 5 HOFers. Mantle did not play in the American League's 5-3 loss.

VALUE: $350-$425

1964 AMERICAN LEAGUE ALL-STAR TEAM — Bobby Allison, Ed Bressoud, Dean Chance, Rocky Colavito, Tony Cuccinello (COACH), Whitey Ford, Bill Freehan, Jim Fregosi, Jimmie Hall, Chuck Hinton, Gil Hodges (COACH), Elston Howard, Harmon Killebrew, John Kralick, Al Lopez (MANAGER), Jerry Lumpe, Frank Malzone, Mickey Mantle, Tony Oliva, Camilo Pascual, Joe Pepitone, Gary Peters, Juan Pizarro, Dick Radatz, Bobby Richardson, Brooks Robinson, Norm Siebern, John Wyatt

PLAYERS WHO WERE REPLACED: Luis Aparicio, Al Kaline

NOTES: 5 HOFers. Mantle was 1-4 in the American League's 7-4 loss.

KEY SIGNATURES: Mantle.

VALUE: $375-$450

1965 AMERICAN LEAGUE ALL-STAR TEAM — Max Alvis, Earl Battey, Rocky Colavito, Vic Davalillo, Eddie Fisher, Bill Freehan, Jim Grant, Don Gutteridge (COACH), Jimmie Hall, Willie Horton, Elston Howard, Al Kaline, Harmon Killebrew, Bob Lee, Al Lopez (MANAGER), Felix Mantilla, Dick McAuliffe, Sam McDowell, Sam Mele (COACH), John O'Donoghue, Tony Oliva, Milt Pappas, Joe Pepitone, Bobby Richardson, Pete Richert, Brooks Robinson, Mel Stottlemyre, Zoilo Versalles

PLAYERS WHO WERE REPLACED: Mickey Mantle, Bill Skowron, Carl Yastrzemski

NOTES: 4 HOFers. Mantle did not play in the American League's 6-5 loss.

VALUE: $350-$425

1967 AMERICAN LEAGUE ALL-STAR TEAM — Tommie Agee, Max Alvis, Hank Bauer (MANAGER), Ken Berry, Rod Carew, Paul Casanova, Dean Chance, Tony Conigliaro, Al Downing, Andy Etchebarren, Bill Freehan, Jim Fregosi, Steve Hargan, Joel Horlen, Jim Hunter, Harmon Killebrew, Jim Lonborg, Mickey Mantle, Dick McAuliffe, Jim McGlothlin, Don Mincher, Tony Oliva, Gary Peters, Rico Petrocelli, Bill Rigney (COACH), Brooks Robinson, Eddie Stanky (COACH), Carl Yastrzemski

PLAYERS WHO WERE REPLACED: Al Kaline, Frank Robinson

NOTES: 6 HOFers. Mantle was 0-1 in the American League's 2-1 loss.

KEY SIGNATURES: Mantle.

VALUE: $450-$525

1968 AMERICAN LEAGUE ALL-STAR TEAM — Jose Azcue, Gary Bell, Bert Campaneris, Rod Carew, Cal Ermer (COACH), Bill Freehan, Jim Fregosi, Ken Harrelson, Willie Horton, Frank Howard, Tommy John, Dave Johnson, Duane Josephson, Harmon Killebrew, Mickey Mantle, Sam McDowell, Denny McLain, Rick Monday, Blue Moon Odom, Tony Oliva, Boog Powell, Brooks Robinson, Mayo Smith (COACH), Mel Stottlemyre, Luis Tiant, Don Wert, Dick Williams (MANAGER), Carl Yastrzemski

PLAYERS WHO WERE REPLACED: Jose Santiago

NOTES: 5 HOFers. Mantle was 0-1 in the American League's 1-0 loss.

KEY SIGNATURES: Mantle.

VALUE: $425-$475

Chapter 9

The tools of the trade

Mickey Mantle equipment

This is a sample of what the price ranges are on various pieces of Mickey Mantle equipment. Most of the items were offered for sale in memorabilia auctions.

Mickey Mantle game-used bat: This 35-inch Louisville Slugger Mickey Mantle 125 model has a minor crack on the handle and "P104" on the knob. It dates from 1965-68. $7,000-$8,000.

Mickey Mantle game-used bat: This Louisville 125 bat with a D113 knob is from 1963-64. $8,000-$10,000.

Mickey Mantle 1958 All-Star Game used bat: This Louisville 125 model is stamped "All-Star Mickey Mantle Baltimore 1958." $14,000-$16,000.

Mickey Mantle's last All-Star Game bat: Mantle used this Adirondack bat for his pinch-hit appearance during the 1967 game. The bat is 35 inches long, has "Mantle" written on the knob and "Mantle, 1967 All Stars" stamped on the barrel. $15,000-$20,000.

Mickey Mantle's 1964 World Series bat: Used in Game 7 to hit his record-setting 18th World Series home run. The batboy retrieved this Adirondack bat, which is cracked and has "1964 World Series Adirondack MANTLE" burned in the barrel. $23,000-$26,000.

Mickey Mantle coach's bat: A genuine K55 from 1977-79, this bat has #7 on the knob in black marker and shows wear. $500-$600.

Mickey Mantle signed bat: Hillerich & Bradsby M110 Mickey Mantle signature model, a new bat with a bold blue Sharpie "Mickey Mantle No. 7" autograph. $1,000-$1,500.

Mickey Mantle signed bat: Louisville Slugger 125 replica bat signed in gold pen. $1,000-$1,300.

500 Home Run Club signed bat: A Rawlings Adirondack bat autographed by each of the 11 living members of the 500 Home Run Club. The bat has a commemorative gold plaque attached to the barrel. Mantle, Hank Aaron, Willie Mays, Frank Robinson, Reggie Jackson, Mike Schmidt, Harmon Killebrew, Ted Williams, Willie McCovey, Eddie Mathews and Ernie Banks have each signed in blue ink. $1,200-$1,500.

Triple Crown winners autographed bat: Rawlings Adirondack Big Stick bat autographed in blue Sharpie by Mantle, Ted Williams, Frank Robinson and Carl Yastrzemski, the only living Triple Crown winners. $1,500-$2,000.

Mantle equipment, clockwise from above: Mantle's 1960 World Series uniform uniform (sold in an auction for $77,000); Mantle's retired uniform number; the brass plaque from Mantle's locker; Mantle's 1967 MacGregor road jersey.

1955 New York Yankees black bat (American League Champions): $600-$800.

1957 New York Yankees black bat (American League Champions): $600-$800.

1961 New York Yankees black bat (World Champions): $500-$700.

1964 New York Yankees black bat (American League Champions): $400-$500.

Mickey Mantle autographed replica black bat, with handpainted art: This Louisville Slugger 125 is signed in gold on the barrel next to a bust pose of Mantle in his Yankee uniform. An American flag is in the background. $1,500-$1,800.

1974 Louisville Slugger Hall of Fame bat: Gold lettering was used to engrave these players' names in the bat barrel — Mantle, Cool Papa Bell, Jim Bottomley, Jocko Conlan, Whitey Ford and Sam Thompson. $300-$400.

500 Home Run Club autographed baseball: Signed by the 11 living members of the 500 Home Run Club. $500-$600.

Mickey Mantle/Roger Maris autographed baseball: On an official American League baseball, Maris is on the sweet spot, Mantle is on the side panel. $1,000-$1,200.

Mickey Mantle signed baseball, with artwork: This official American League baseball has Mantle's signature, plus "The Commerce Comet." One panel has an original artwork bust pose of Mantle in his Yankee uniform. $400-$500.

Mickey Mantle signed official NBA basketball. Signed on the sweet spot. $400-$500.

Mickey Mantle signed official NFL football. Signed on the side panel. $400-$500.

Official Wilson NFL football, with original artwork, autographed by Mickey Mantle: This football has a silver signature and handpainted artwork of Mantle in a bust pose and in a fielding shot. $350-$450.

Mickey Mantle autographed baseball glove: Black Rawlings Super Size, signed "Mickey Mantle NO. 7" on the top in silver. $300-$400.

Mickey Mantle autographed baseball glove: All-Pro Little Leaguer model, circa 1970s, signed "Mickey Mantle N.Y. Yankees" on the inside. $150-$250.

Mickey Mantle model Rawlings baseball glove: Model No. MM8, with original box. $700-$800.

Mickey Mantle Revelation store model glove: Junior size. $100-$125.

Mickey Mantle 1957 Triple Crown Rawlings: Store model glove honors his Triple Crown accomplishment in 1957. $125-$150.

Mickey Mantle game-used cap: This Tim McAuliffe hat is autographed and has the #7 in its brim. The band is separated. $3,000-$4,000.

Mickey Mantle autographed Yankees replica cap: Autographed on the top of the brim "Mickey Mantle #7" in silver Sharpie. $200-$300.

Mickey Mantle game-used batting helmet: Uncracked but well worn, in 1960 or 1961, this size 7 1/2 helmet has the hand-painted NY logo still visible, plus a tape marker which says "7 Mantle." An American Baseball Cap sticker and leather band are still inside, too. $4,000-$5,000.

1967 Mickey Mantle MacGregor road flannel: This grey flannel, with "NEW YORK" across the chest, has #7 inside the collar and the infamous #7 on the back. $70,000-$75,000.

Autographed replic Mickey Mantle jersey: Pinstriped home jersey made by Mitchell and Ness for the Cooperstown Collection. Signed under the #7 on the back in blue ink. $500-$700.

Mickey Mantle's autograph has appeared on all sorts of memorabilia, including baseballs, player model gloves, game-used bats and even NFL footballs.

Mickey Mantle retired number: This pinstripe uniform #7 was taken from a game-worn Mantle jersey and was displayed in Yankee Stadium before its renovation. Mantle autographed the jersey next to the number. Also included is the brass name plaque which hung on Mantle's locker. $10,000-$15,000.

Mickey Mantle Yankee jacket: A 1960s MacGregor, size 46, this navy blue wool with leather pocket trim has the #7 written in marker on a tag in the neck, along with a faded typed name tag inside the waist. $12,000-$15,000.

Mickey Mantle autographed Starter Yankee jacket: Never-worn child-sized jacket has been signed "Mickey Mantle No. 7" on the front under the NY logo. $400-$500.

Clockwise from top left: Mantle's 1960-61 batting helmet; an unused, autographed Starter New York Yankees jacket; a game-used cap; Mantle's 1960 team jacket; a signed replica Yankees cap.

Chapter 10

Baseball's legacy continues

The Mick raps out another one
Mickey Mantle: My Favorite Summer 1956

By Robert Grayson

If you write it, they will come. And come they did!

Fans and celebrities packed into Mickey Mantle's Restaurant on Central Park South in New York City recently to help launch the Mick's new book "My Favorite Summer 1956."

The star-studded event was believed to be the biggest ever held to launch a new sports book and, like the tome itself, those who attended the book bash were full of stories about the days when the Bronx Bombers reigned over the national pastime.

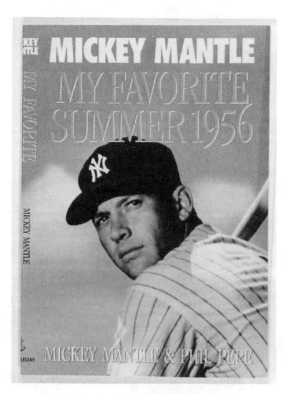

In this book, Mantle recalls his 1956 Triple Crown season.

"I remember waiting by the gate at the players' parking lot at the stadium, hours before game time," one middle-aged fan said. "The players always stopped to sign autographs and sometimes they would let you carry their bags to the players' entrance at the ballpark. When you got there, they would give you a free ticket to the game," he said.

Many of Mantle's old teammates were on hand and so were notables such as sportscasters Howard Cosell and Bob Costas.

National League President Bill White, another well-wisher, quipped, when asked if he was reading Mantle's new book, "No, I'm reading that new one on Nancy Reagan."

The gathering spawned a lot of good-natured ribbing of Mantle, who recaptured in his new book many of the good times he and his Yankee teammates had during his Triple Crown year in 1956.

As at any event Mantle attends, there were a number of autograph requests from fans who strolled by the Mick's New York restaurant and dropped in on the celebration. All the fans carried copies of Mantle's latest literary endeavor, and that must have thrilled Doubleday, the book's publisher.

But Mantle has been giving his publishers a host of thrills in recent days. Soon after the release of "My Favorite Summer 1956," Mantle held a signing at a local bookstore in New York City. More than 650 copies of the book whizzed by busy cashiers in an hour, as fans lined the streets around the bookstore to get a copy of the book and the Mick's famous John Hancock.

Mantle coauthored the book with noted New York sportswriter Phil Pepe, who has covered baseball for more than 30 years. "My Favorite Summer 1956," Pepe's 24th book, continues what seems to be a trend in sports books recently — focusing on one particular season, as David Halberstam did in the very popular "Summer of '49," a bestseller several years ago.

Actor Vincent Gardenia, most recently seen in several episodes of television's "L.A. Law," came to the debut for the new Mantle book to exchange stories with some of his contemporaries about the glory days of baseball. Most baseball fans vividly recall Gardenia's portrayal of New York Mammoths Manager Dutch Schnell in the 1973 film "Bang the Drum Slowly."

"This is what baseball means to me — the old Yankees, the Brooklyn Dodgers, the New York Giants. That's what I think of when I think of baseball, and some of those guys are here today," the veteran actor said.

Yogi Berra was not only a teammate of Mantle's, he also managed the Yankee great for one season, in 1964. Asked what it was like to manage Mantle, a close personal friend and a superstar, Berra chuckled, "It was good. He (Mantle) did all right for me. We won." The Yankees won the American League pennant in 1964 but lost the World Series to the St. Louis Cardinals.

Mantle's sensational year in 1956 didn't surprise teammate Berra.

"We all knew he had the talent. Everybody knew he would be great. It's tough to win the Triple Crown but if any guy had the talent to do it, Mickey did. That 1956 — what a great year it was for him!" the Hall of Fame catcher remembered.

Mantle called 1956 a turning point in his career. Up to that point, Mantle had been playing well but not performing up to his full potential. He used to worry that he might never achieve the pinnacle of success that Yankee manager Casey Stengel had predicted for him.

In his new book, Mantle details the drive to the Triple Crown and the American League Most Valuable Player award in 1956. Not only did Mantle challenge Babe Ruth's record for home runs in a single season, he also battled the legendary Ted Williams for the batting title and just edged out another young phenom, Al Kaline, for the RBI total.

In 1956 Mantle belted 52 homers, batted .353 and amassed 130 RBI, becoming, at age 25, a baseball hero.

Mantle, of course, again flirted with the Babe's season home run record in 1961 when he slammed 54 round trippers and vied all season long with teammate Roger Maris for the American League home run crown. But interestingly, Mantle endured greater pressure in 1956 than in 1961.

"Everybody was saying I was the next Babe Ruth, the next Lou Gehrig, the next Joe DiMaggio — all three rolled into one — but I hadn't shown that. I didn't want people down on me. So I felt pressure all year to keep up the pace, to prove I could do it. Once that season was over, I felt like a weight had been lifted off me. I had finally lived up to the predictions."

According to Mantle, in 1961 there was more pressure on Roger Maris. "No doubt about that, he had the greater burden that year."

In his new book Mantle talks extensively about the 1956 World Series between the New York Yankees and the Brooklyn Dodgers. He pointed out that while he was pursuing the Triple Crown in 1956, his teammates were focused on getting into the World Series and wrestling the World Championship from the Dodgers.

Only a year earlier the Dodgers had fulfilled their dream of beating the Yankees and winning the World Championship. But even though the Yankees had won a number of world championships, including five in a row from 1949 to 1953, losing to the rival Dodgers in 1955 grated on them and the Bronx Bombers were anxious for a rematch.

In fact, regaining the World Championship meant so much that Mantle said his Triple Crown "would have meant nothing if we didn't beat the Dodgers in the World Series. Beating the Dodgers was something everybody on the Yankees was determined to do," Mantle said.

Of his sensational 1956 season, Mantle recalled, one thing that stands out the most in his mind is Don Larsen's perfect game in the World Series. A great catch by Mantle in the fifth inning helped save the World Series gem.

"I was aware of it (the perfect game). You start to realize those things in the fourth or fifth inning. I knew this could be a very important play," Mantle said of his pivotal catch.

Looking back on the play today, Mantle calls his catch during Larsen's perfect game in the 1956 World Series the greatest catch he ever made. "Some may disagree, but I believe that," the former center fielder said.

The play actually showcased many of Mantle's talents, one of which he holds very dearly — his speed, before injuries took their toll.

Mantle remembers that Gil Hodges was at the plate with one out in Game 5 of the 1956 World Series. Out of respect for Hodges, Mantle was playing deep and over to the left against the powerful Brooklyn Dodger first baseman.

"He got hold of one and drove it to left center. I just took off. I didn't know if I was going to get there," Mantle said.

But the speedy Yankee center fielder did catch up with Hodges' screamer just as it began to drop. Mantle had to reach across his body to make the grab. "The ball dropped in my glove," he noted modestly.

Though the book focuses on 1956, other highlights of the Yankee outfielder's career are included to set the story of the season in historical perspective. Mantle writes about his early days in New York City and being asked by veteran Yankee Hank Bauer to room with him. At the time, Bauer had another roommate, Johnny Hopp.

Bauer, who attended the book launching, remembered watching a young Mantle putting a charge in the ball back in 1951. "He could really hit the ball, even as a kid. You could tell he had talent," Bauer said.

Knowing that Mantle was just a kid from Oklahoma, Bauer took the young rookie under his wing, so he could have a friend in the big city.

"In those days I had an apartment over the Stage Deli in Manhattan. The food was great. When Mickey started to live with us in the beginning of the season he weighed 170 pounds, but he was 190 by October," said Bauer.

Joe Pepitone chuckled while feasting on some hors d'oeuvres and listening as Mantle recalled one of their first encounters. In Mantle's playing days, most young players were established stars, at least until youngsters made it through their rookie season.

When Pepi first came up to the Bronx Bombers in 1962, Mantle remembers sitting in the clubhouse after a game and asking the rookie to get him a beer. The brash Pepi just looked up at the veteran slugger and responded, "Get it yourself...and bring me one while you're there." The two have laughed at that story many times since.

Also on hand for the gala book reception was Mantle's close friend Moose Skowron. Of all the Yankees, Mantle has known Moose the longest — since 1950. In September of that year, Mantle had just finished his second year of pro ball, and Skowron had just signed with the Yankees.

The big club had wanted to take a good look at both youngsters so Mantle and Skowron traveled with the team for a couple of weeks at the end of the 1950 season. Mantle and Skowron roomed together and it was Moose who introduced the kid from Commerce, Okla., to pizza.

Skowron said he loved playing on the power-laden Yankees and still misses the fabled M-O-O-O-O-S-E calls in Yankee Stadium that the fans used to bellow out each time he made a big play.

"And I knew the difference between M-O-O-O-O-S-E and boos. Strike out twice in a row and you learn the difference," he said.

Though fans laughed and chimed as Mantle held court during the book launching at his New York restaurant, the story that caught most by surprise was his tale of salary woes.

Mantle recalled that after winning the Most Valuable Player award again in 1957 on the heels of his Triple Crown and MVP season in 1956, the Yankees sent him a contract with a salary reduction for 1958.

The Yankee general manager at the time, George Weiss, had a succinct explanation for the salary cut, according to Mantle. "I didn't have as good a season in 1957 as I did in 1956 so I deserved the pay cut."

Weiss was offering a contract for the 1958 season calling for a $10,000 pay cut.

But the Yankee owners, Dan Topping and Del Web, interceded on Mantle's behalf and signed the superstar to a $75,000 a year contract — a $10,000 raise over his 1957 annual paycheck.

Mantle recalled that Skowron hit over .300 for three consecutive years and didn't get a raise. But Moose chimed in, "I didn't care. I just wanted to play baseball." — *Robert Grayson, Sports Collectors Digest, May 31, 1991*

* * *

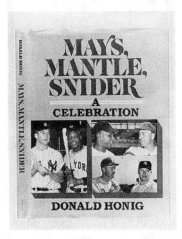 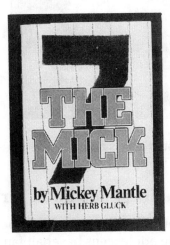 

There aren't too many scarce Mantle books.

Although Mickey Mantle is a magic name in the baseball card market, there is no scarce Mantle biography. Thus, much harder-to-find biographies of lesser players, such as Rocky Colavito's "Don't Knock the Rock", are considered more valuable than any Mantle biography.

In general, however, book prices as a whole are rising, based on four factors — scarcity (there must be a demand to have any value), desirabilty, condition (with the dust jacket intact) and edition (first editions are more valuable). Because there's no guarantee that books will appreciate dramatically, a collector is advised to buy books he enjoys for his own sake.

Top sources to find books through include card shows, library sales, garage sales, used books stores, antique shops, mail order catalogs and hobby periodicals.

Books about Mickey Mantle include:
- "Mays, Mantle, Snider": hardcover, by Donald Honig.
- "Mick, An American Hero": paperback, $4.99.
- "The Mick": by Mantle with Herb Gluck; autographed copies sell for between $65-$85.
- "Five O'Clock Lightning": by Tommy Henrich with Bill Gilbert; 1992; hardcover; 298 pages about the Yankees' glory days, as told by outfielder Henrich; $19.95.
- "The Bronx Bombers, Memories and Memorabilia of the New York Yankees": by Bruce Chadwick and David M. Spindel; 1992; hardcover; 140 pages; $24.95.
- "My Favorite Summer, 1956": by Mantle with Phil Pepe; 1991; hardcover; 246 pages; $18.95; paperback, 1992, is 323 pages, $5.99. A three-hour audiocassette, narrated by Pepe, was also produced and sells for about $15.95.
- "Five O'Clock Lightning": 1982, by William L. DeAndrea, paperback, New York, St. Martin's Press; this fictional mystery has McCarthy-era extremists who are implicated for threats made against Mickey Mantle.

 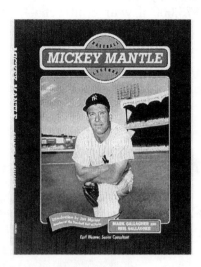 

Book prices have steadily risen, but there's no guarantee they'll appreciate dramatically.

Baseball Legends book series

The Baseball Legends series of 33 books, including a book devoted to Mickey Mantle, is specifically written with the adolescent baseball fan in mind; the biographies of Hall of Famers are designed to encourage youngsters to read.

Chelsa House, of New York and Philadelphia, hired veteran baseball writers and began publishing the books in 1990, available for sale at $14.95 each. Each 64-page book is presented in a straight-forward, uncomplicated style long on narration and fact, but short on speculation and opinion.

The player's life and career are covered, with special emphasis on the star's childhood to help the reader identify with the player; most of the subjects had to overcome some type of obstacle or adversity while growing up. The introduction, which is the same for each book, discusses how one can succeed not only in baseball, but in life, too.

Each book has 20-25 photos, including one of the player's Hall of Fame plaque. A one-page chronolgy, a bibliography and statistical information are also given. The full-color laminated cover of each book is designed with a baseball card style, featuring paintings done by Dan O'Leary.

In addition to Mantle, the others selected for the series are: Grover Cleveland Alexander, Joe DiMaggio, Bob Feller, Willie Mays, Johnny Bench, Jimmie Foxx, Brooks Robinson, Jackie Robinson, Hank Aaron, Ernie Banks, Yogi Berra, Roy Campanella, Roberto Clemente, Ty Cobb, Dizzy Dean, Lou Gehrig, Bob Gibson, Rogers Hornsby, Walter Johnson, Sandy Koufax, Christy Mathewson, Stan Musial, Satchel Paige, Frank Robinson, Babe Ruth, Duke Snider, Warren Spahn, Willie Stargell, Honus Wagner, Ted Williams, Carl Yastrzemski and Cy Young.

Mickey Mantle poetry

Mantle, 1985: by William Heyen, published in The Morrow Anthology of Younger American Poets, New York, Quill/William Morrow and Co.

The Mantle/Mays Controversy Solved, 1982: paperback by Mike Shannon, Kent, Ohio, Cathcer Press; contains 27 baseball-related poems.

Most magazines with Mantle on the cover are between $10-$40.

Mickey Mantle periodical covers

There are hundreds of different magazines that have had the picture of Mickey Mantle on their front cover. Most magazines are valued from $10-$40.

These non-sport magazines feature some of the best Mantle covers: Life, June 25, 1956; Life, July 30, 1965; and Boys Life, June 1969 ("My Father and I"). Others featuring

Mantle on the cover include 1983 *The National Pastime*; 1987 *Pinstripes* magazine, the premier edition with Joe DiMaggio on the front cover also; 1987 *Yankee* magazine and the May 14, 1987, *USA Today* newspaper with Mantle on the front page.

Sporting News Baseball Guides

1957 Mickey Mantle	$55-$60

American League Red Book

1962 Mantle, Maris, home run leaders	$30

Sports Illustrated

June 18, 1956: Mickey Mantle	$40
July 9, 1956: Mays, Mantle, All-Stars	$35
Oct. 1, 1956: World Series/Mantle	$35
July 7, 1958: Musial/Mantle/Mays	$15
July 2, 1962: Mickey Mantle	$22
June 21, 1965: Mickey Mantle	$22
May 8, 1967: Mickey Mantle/Ken Berry	$25
March 25, 1985: Mantle/Mays/Peter Ueberroth	$7

Dell Publishing Baseball Annual

1957 Mickey Mantle	$40

Dell Publishing *Baseball Stars*

1956 Mickey Mantle	$35
1964 Mantle/Koufax	$15

Dell Publishing *Who's Who in the Big Leagues*

1959 Mickey Mantle	$30

Who's Who in Baseball, by *Baseball Magazine*

1957 Mickey Mantle	$25

Sport Magazine

April 1953: Mickey Mantle	$35
October 1956: Mickey Mantle	$30
March 1957: Mickey Mantle	$27.50
June 1959: Mantle/Williams	$25
August 1959: Mickey Mantle	$20
August 1960: Mickey Mantle	$20
September 1961: Mantle/DiMaggio	$27.50
July 1962: Mickey Mantle	$20
May 1963: Mantle/Berra	$22.50
October 1963: Mickey Mantle	$18
September 1964: Mickey Mantle	$16.50
August 1965: Mickey Mantle	$15
July 1966: Mickey Mantle	$15
May 1967: Mickey Mantle	$15
April 1969: Mickey Mantle	$20

Street and Smith's Baseball Yearbooks

1953 Mickey Mantle	$87.50
1956 Mantle/Snider	$80
1957 Mantle/Larsen/Berra	$75
1964 Mantle	$45

Baseball Digest

April 1953: Mantle/Musial	$18.50
July 1956: Mickey Mantle	$16
Oct./Nov. 1961: Koufax/Robinson/Maris/Mantle	$15
June 1962: Mickey Mantle	$15
February 1969: Mickey Mantle	$16

The Sporting News
- Jan. 31, 1951
- April 4, 1951
- April 25, 1951 ($125)
- Nov. 12, 1952
- April 29, 1953
- June 17, 1953
- July 1, 1953
- June 13, 1956
- Oct. 10, 1956
- Nov. 14, 1956
- Jan. 2, 1957
- Jan. 23, 1957
- March 29, 1961
- June 28, 1961
- Sept. 6, 1961
- Sept. 27, 1961
- April 6, 1968

This is just one of many magazines to have pictured Mickey Mantle.

Miscellaneous magazines

Baseball Stars of 1957; The Thrilling True Story of the Baseball Yankees; 1981 Family Weekly; My Greatest Thrills in Baseball (comic book, by Mission of California); Great Moments in Sports; Home-Run Hitters; Baseball Yearbook 1963; Inside Baseball; Baseball Review; Great Hitters I've Known (comic book).

Newsweek Magazine

June 25, 1956: Mickey Mantle	$40

Life Magazine

June 25, 1956: Mickey Mantle	$90
Aug. 18 1961: Mantle/Maris	$75
July 30, 1965: Mickey Mantle	$30

New York Yankee yearbooks

1967 Mickey Mantle	$60
1968 Mantle, Stottlemyre, others	$45
1969 Mantle, Stottlemyre, others	$45
1973 Ruth, DiMaggio, Mantle, Gehrig	$30
1985 Maris, Mantle, Ruth, Gehrig	$9
1987 Gehrig, Mattingly, Mantle	$9

New York Yankee media guides

1974 Mantle, Ford	$15

Collector's books
- 1987 Surf Yankee book with all of Mantle's cards ($30).
- 1988 Surf Yankee book with all of Mantle's cards ($30).

News story

Mickey Mantle collectors should be aware that some of the "Mickey Mantle Day" programs currently circulating in the hobby are actually nothing more than photocopies of the real thing.

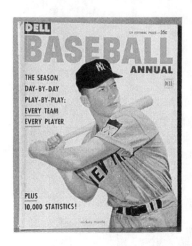
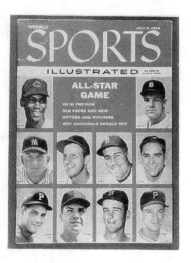
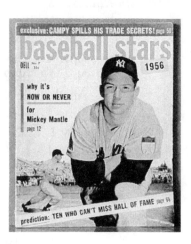

Mantle has been on hundreds of different magazine covers.

The program was an official souvenir of "Mickey Mantle Day," held at Yankee Stadium on Sept. 18, 1965. The four-page programs were given to fans attending the game. (They are worth $35)

It's very easy to tell the photocopies from the genuine program, but if you've never seen the real thing, you could be fooled.

Most important, the genuine program was printed on a glossy enameled paper and had a full-color portrait of Mantle on the cover. The reproductions were done on "photocopy" paper and have a different black-and-white photo of Mantle (holding a bat over his right shoulder) on the front. The reason for changing the photo isn't clear, but apparently the color portrait did not reproduce enough on the photocopies.

The program measures 8 1/2". The inside of both programs is printed in black-and-white. The origin of the photocopied programs is not known, but they are apparently circulating at shows and hobby shops in various parts of the country. *SCD* advises collectors who recently purchased a photocopy to contact the person they bought it from. — *News brief, July 17, 1987*

The 500 Home Run Club
Video spotlights elite long ball hitters

By David Craft

Officially, there is no "inner circle" of greats enshrined in the National Baseball Hall of Fame. A man is either in or he isn't.

Besides, it would be difficult, if not impossible, to go about defining who merits such extra special recognition. What parameters would be used? Who would make the selection?

But among the game's hitters we can say there exists, if not an inner circle, at least a unique subset. Out of the many ballplayers considered sluggers, only 14 in the history of the game have socked 500 or more home runs lifetime.

Highlights from the careers of these men are shown in an ingratiating video tribute titled, appropriately enough, "The 500 Home Run Club." The 55-minute program is hosted by NBC sports announcer and talk show host Bob Costas, along with Hall of Famer Mickey Mantle. "The Mick" offers personal recollections of some of his own exploits, as well as on some of his fellow "club members." Costas, as always, is excellent as interviewer and narrator.

The teaming of Costas and Mantle is perfect for this production. Their banter is smooth when it needs to be, funny when it should be, and insightful when it can be. The video is also enjoyable for its liberal use of filmed highlights, still shots and appropriate stats covering each player's legendary career.

Some of the 14 players profiled here were contemporaries of one another; the careers of other players overlapped. But the video manages to present these men in something of a chronological view: Babe Ruth; Jimmie Foxx; Mel Ott; Ted Williams; Mickey Mantle; Willie Mays; Eddie Mathews; Ernie Banks; Hank Aaron; Frank Robinson; Harmon Killebrew; Willie McCovey; Reggie Jackson; Mike Schmidt.

Some of the footage used in this video may not be that familiar to fans. This writer, for one, was pleased to see some brief clips of Foxx, Ott and Ruth (in his last season) that seemed fresh.

In several cases actual play-by-play sound bites accompany the footage — for example, Milo Hamilton's call of Aaron's record-setting 715th home run. Nothing like a little audio adrenaline to add to one's enjoyment of historical moments.

At a suggested retail price of only $19.95, "The 500 Home Run Club" is worth seeking out if you're a fan of the long ball, or if you simply enjoy a good show. While it covers familiar territory, it is fun to watch, even after repeated viewings.

The video is from Cabin Fever Entertainment Inc. It may be available through your local video store, so check there first. It has been advertised in various major sports periodicals, and is also available by mail through Sports Books Etc., the Virginia-based firm headed up by Paul Haas. — *David Craft, Tale of the Tape, May 18, 1990* (This video can currently be purchased for about $10).

Film and television memorabilia

It's My Turn — Columbia Pictures, 1980, color, 91 minutes: A modern-day romance between a former ballplayer and a career woman. Mantle, Elston Howard, Roger Maris and Bob Feller play themselves.

Safe At Home! — Columbia Pictures, 1962, black-and-white, 83 minutes: Roger Maris and Mickey Mantle are committed to appear at a Little League banquet by a 10-year-old boy who falsely says he knows them. Mantle, Maris, Ralph Houk and Whitey Ford play themselves. Memorabilia from the movie includes a large 28-by-41-inch movie poster ($800-$1,000); eight different lobby cards (five have Mantle on them; $175-$225 each); and a Mantle/Maris 8mm film and box from the movie.

That Touch of Mink — Universal-International, 1962, color, 99 minutes: New York Yankees Mantle, Roger Maris and Yogi Berra appear in this film when a suitor tries to impress his lady friend by introducing them to her. Two different lobby cards were made for the movie, which starred Doris Day and Cary Grant.

Mantle and Roger Maris appeared in the 1962 movie "Safe at Home."

Mickey Mantle's Baseball Tips for Kids of All Ages — CBS-Fox, 1986, color, 90 minutes: Whitey Ford, Phil Rizzuto and Mantle are featured in this instructional film.

Mickey Mantle: The American Dream Comes To Life, $19.95.

The Life of Mickey Mantle — Kraft Television Theatre, aired on NBC Oct. 3, 1956, 60 minutes: A dramatization of Mantle's career up to that point. It focused on Mantle's relationship with his father. James Olson starred as Mantle.

Second Base Steele — MTM Enterprises Inc., aired on NBC's Remington Steele show on Oct. 23, 1984, 60 minutes: Mantle and Whitey Ford play themselves as Remington Steele solves a murder at a fantasy baseball camp.

The Dick Cavett Show — PBS, June 19-20-21, 1979, 30 minutes each night: Tom Gorman, Hank Aaron, Leo Durocher and Mantle appeared on a 90-minute panel devoted to baseball.

A Comedy Salute to Baseball — OCC Productions, aired on NBC July 15, 1985, 60 minutes: Mantle, Tom Lasorda, Reggie Jackson, Steve Garvey, Dwight Gooden, George Steinbrenner, Bob Uecker and Billy Crystal make fun of themselves.

The Late T.C. — Hanna-Barbera Productions, ABC, aired Feb. 21, 1962, 30 minutes: Top Cat is hit on the head by a home run hit by Mickey Mantle.

Pinstripe Power, The Story of the 1961 New York Yankees

Radio

The Game of Baseball, 1953 — CBS, aired Sept. 25, 1953, 60 minutes: includes interviews with Mantle, Warren Spahn, Yogi Berra, Pee Wee Reese, Stan Musial, Phil Rizzuto, Gil Hodges and more.

Theater

Mickey Mantle Ruined My Life — Premiered in the Ensemble Studio in Los Angeles, Calif., from June 30, 1984-July 15, 1984: A one-act comedy about a male dancer who hates baseball.

That Holler Guy! and A Day To Remember are two records which feature Mickey Mantle.

Recorded music and song

The Bambino, the Clipper and the Mick — 1982, by Terry Cashman, Lifesong (45): "Talkin' Baseball" tribute to the New York Yankees.

I Love Mickey — 1956, by Teresa Brewer, Coral Records (45): Mantle and Brewer are featured on the cover of this record tribute to Mantle. A record, sheet music and pin are available.

Seasons in the Sun — 1985, by Terry Cashman, Metrostar (45): A musical tribute to Mickey Mantle. The reverse has "The Bambino, the Clipper and the Mick."

When you were Mickey Mantle and I was Stan the Man — by Ken Carlysle, Inglewood (45).

Willie, Mickey and the Duke (Talkin' Baseball) — by Terry Cashman, Lifesong (45): A tribute to New York's three stars and others from the 1950s. Memorabilia includes a signed, limited-edition album; sheet music and a large poster of the three.

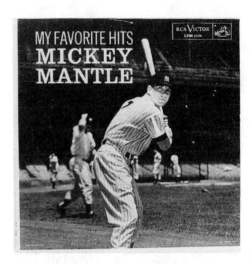

Mickey picks his favorite songs.

Baseball — An Action History, 1958 — (with booklet of Mantle): Columbia Masterworks (33), narrated by Buddy Blattner.

My Favorite Hits, Mickey Mantle — RCA Victor (33): Mantle selects a collection of non-baseball-related songs.

The Mick — 1985, Newman Communications Corp.: The book, by Mantle and Herb Gluck, is read by Bob Askey and is two cassettes.

Mickey Mantle of the Yankees — 1958, American Printing House: Two-record set of Gene Schoor's book, read by Milton Metz.

That Holler Guy! — 1958, 33 record by Joe Garagiola, United Artists.

There Goes Another One — Mickey Mantle and Roger Maris ($75).

Yankee Stadium: The Sounds Of A Half Century, Fleetwood Records ($15).

Baseball in the Great Yankee Tradition

Mickey Mantle story record — by Auravision in 1962-1964, Sports Champion Inc. There are two versions, a 33 rpm and a 33 1/3 rpm.

Mickey Mantle A Day To Remember — Columbia Records, June 8, 1969, record album and jacket sleeve.

Auravision released these Mantle story records in 1962-64.

Chapter 11
Strike a pose

Mickey Mantle advertising pieces

There are hundreds of advertisements that featured Mickey Mantle. Most appeared in the mid-1950s to the late 1960s, but there are a few companies that still use him for their advertising. Most ad pieces are valued at $10-$20.

Some of the companies that have used Mantle in their advertisements include: AMF; Bantron; Batter-Up Pancakes; Big Yank Clothing; Bloomingdale's; Brookfield Sports-coats (three different); Cable Vision; Camel Cigarettes (two different); Claridge Casino; Employment Office; Florida Citrus Commission; Haggar Slacks (10 different); Junior Sales Club of America; Karo Syrup; Kodak (with the Mantle family); Kretschmer Wheat Germ (with Pancho Gonzales); Kretschmer Wheat Germ (with John Unitas); La-Z-Boy Chairs; Lee Jeans; Lifebouy Soap; Loma Linda Country Club;

Mantle Manors; Mantle Men and Namath Girls; Master Card; Mayo Spruce Underwear; Mission Orange Drink; Natural Light Beer; Phillies Cigars; Rawlings; Red Heart Dog Food; Reserve Life Insurance Co.; Sports Illustrated (1958); Timex (two different); Topps; Universal Thermos; Van Heusen Shirts; Viceroy Cigarettes; Wheaties Home Run Sweepstakes; Wheaties Cereal (three different); Yoo-Hoo.

Mickey Mantle art prints

• Baseball Superstars of the 20th Century/Mantle action portrait drawing.
• Art Brownell, Baseball's Great Seasons, "Mantle 1956."
• Joseph Catalano has done two different lithographs, distributed by Tom Catal, Lou Avon.
• Joseph Catalano has done "Yankee Tradition" (Mantle and Mattingly), Sports Impressions.
• Cope Enterprises in 1985, Mirror Art.
• The Decathlon Corp., Sports Prints Series, 1988.
• David Dellarte, Diamond Legends, Wilkes-Barre, Pa.
• 1982 #55 Diamond Classic (10x12) print.
• Terrence Fogarty, print of the M&M boys, Mantle and Maris.
• Bill Gallo, A Look Back series, "The Mick," "The Center Fielders," and "The Mick Parks One."
• Jerry Hirsh, Mantle stationery, with box.
• Jerry Hirsh has done two original art pieces.
• 1981 John Jodauga Productions 1981 limited-edition art print.
• Andy Jurinko, "Yankee Stadium Panorama," lithograph, Bill Goff Inc.
• Jack Lane, "The Triple Crown," Sports Art, (8x10).
• Ron Lewis, "Living Triple Crown Winners," Sports Impressions.

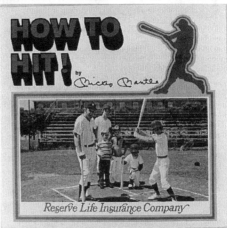

Mantle's appearances in advertisements, clockwise from upper left: Yoo-Hoo drink; Natural Light beer; Reserve Life Insurance Co.; Rawlings Sporting Goods; Mantle Men & Namath Girls Inc.

• Ron Lewis, "Willie, Mickey and the Duke."

• Ron Lewis, Living Legends series includes Mickey Mantle portrait.

• George Loh, Mickey Mantle art print, Equitable Life Assurance Society of the United States ad.

• Louella, "#7 — The Mick," by Louella, 1987, (18x24).

• David Marc Millman, "Willie, Mickey and the Duke."

• LeRoy Neiman, "Mantle at Home," poster, Mantle sliding into home plate.

• LeRoy Neiman, "Warm Up Swings," photo etchings of Mantle warming up, 1972.

• O'Connell and Son Ink, Mickey Mantle pen and ink drawing card 4 1/2x6 (1983); Superstar Gallery 8x10 (1984); 1952 Topps reproduction 8x10 (1984).

• Christopher Paluso has done two prints, one large, one mini, in 1984.

• P.M. Antiques and Collectibles, 1983 Baseball Collector's Print Series.

• Bill Purdom, "Long Gone Griffith," lithograph, Bill Goff Inc.

• Prestige Collectibles, 1952 Topps Mickey Mantle lithograph.

• Robert Riger, *Sports Illustrated* The Champions Mickey Mantle print.

• Sue Rini, "Mantle-Ford-Martin," Historic Limited Editions.

• Mark Rucker, Mantle switch art print.

• Irene D. Schadetan has done two different color portraits.

• Mary Jo Schwalbach, "Mickey Mantle," mixed media, fielding pose, 1972.

• Kendall Shaw, "Four at Bat," Mantle/Maris/Ruth/Gehrig, acrylic on canvas, four-panel silhouette, 1964.

• Robert Stephen Simon has done "Mickey at Night;" "All-Star;" "Triple Crown;" "Hall Of Fame;" "World Series;" "Greatest Switch Hitter;" "Rookie Edition;" "Mickey, Willie and the Duke;" "Yankee Tradition;" and "Triple Crown Winnerss;" all (8x10).

• Don Sprague, "Maris, Ford, Martin and Mantle" print.

• Sports Print, signed or unsigned print.

• Jim Williams, Mickey Mantle woodburning, Hot Iron Originals.

• Art Prints by Wolf: Mantle/Mays/Snider, Mantle/DiMaggio/Mattingly, Mantle (8x10).

Many of these art prints have been made into 8x10s, posters and lithographs. Most 8x10s and posters are usually between $10-$20. The lithographs are usually between $100-$200.

Mickey Mantle collector plates

• Mickey Mantle limited-edition plate: "Mickey," painting done by Pablo Carreno, 1984.

• Mickey Mantle Braniff Golf Fiesta pewter plate: West End Grand Bahamas, 1975.

Sports Impressions has done several plates on Mantle: 1) "Switch Hitter" mini plate, 4 1/4" diameter, porcelain, Joseph Catalano. 2) "The Life of a Legend," collectoval, gold plate, porcelain/gold, 12" diameter, limited edition of 1,968, Terrence Fogarty. 3) "Mickey 7" gold edition plate, porcelain/gold, 10 1/4" diameter, limited edition of 1,500. 4) "Golden Years" mini plate, 4 1/4" diameter, porcelain, Mike Petronella.

5) "Golden Years" plate, 8 1/2" diameter, limited edition of 5,000, Mike Petronella. 6) "Golden Years" collectoval, featuring Willie Mays, Duke Snider and Mantle, porcelain/gold, limited edition of 1,000, 12" diameter, Mike Petronella. 7) "The Greatest Center-fielders," mini plate, (Mays/Snider/Mantle), 4 1/4" diameter, porcelain, Ron Lewis. 8) "The Greatest Centerfielders," porcelain/gold, 10 1/4" diameter, limited edition of 3,500, Ron Lewis.

9) "Mickey, Willie, & Duke," mini plate, porcelain, 4 1/4" diameter, R. Simon. 10) "Mickey, Willie & Duke," regular plate, porcelain, 10 1/4" diameter, limited edition of

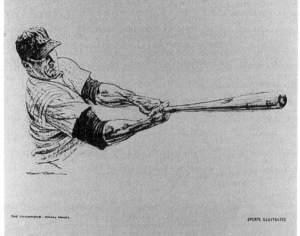

THE CHAMPIONS - Mickey Mantle

SPORTS ILLUSTRATED

Artistic pieces, clockwise, from upper left: Equitable Life Assurance Society of the U.S.; Sports Illustrated's "Champions" art print; Ron Lewis artwork (Willie, Mickey and the Duke); Yankee Stadium Panorama, by Andy Jurinko; Robert Simon porcelain plate.

3,500, R. Simon. 11) "Mickey, Willie & Duke," gold plate, porcelain, 10 1/4" diameter, limited edition of 1,500, R. Simon. 12) "Living Triple Crown," mini plate, 4 1/4" diameter, features Mantle, Ted Williams, Frank Robinson and Carl Yastrzemski, artist Ron Lewis.

13) "Living Triple Crown," regular plate, 10 1/4" diameter, limited edition of 10,000, Ron Lewis. 14) "Living Triple Crown," gold edition plate, gold/porcelain, 10 1/4" diameter, limited edition of 1,000, Ron Lewis. 15) "Yankee Tradition," features Mantle and Don Mattingly, porcelain bisque/wood, 7 1/2" diameter, limited edition of 900, Joseph Catalano. 16) "Yankee Tradition," mini plate, 4 1/2" diameter, Joseph Catalano.

17) "Yankee Tradition," regular plate, porcelain, 10 1/4" diamater, limited edition of 10,000, Joseph Catalano. 18) "Yankee Tradition," artist proof, 7 1/2" diameter, porcelain bisque/wood, limited edition of 90.

Above, Mantle signs a lithograph of his 1952 Bowman card. Below left, Terrence Fogarty artwork of Mantle and Maris. Below right, Ron Lewis artwork.

Chapter 12

Coins & Pins

Above are a 1967 Coca-Cola bottle cap insert and a 1960 Armour Franks coin.

Mickey Mantle coins

Year/Set	No.	Value NM	EX	VG
1955 Armour Franks (spelled Mantel)	—	150.00	75.00	45.00
(spelled Mantle)	—	400.00	200.00	125.00

In 1955 Armour inserted 1 1/2" plastic coins in its packages of hot dogs. The front has a raised portrait, player's name and full team name. The back has the player's name, position, birthplace and date, batting and throwing preference, and 1954 hitting or pitching record. The coins are unnumbered and come in a variety of different colors. The complete set of 24 different players, plus variations for Mickey Mantle and Harvey Kuenn, is worth $1,000 in Near Mint condition. Commons are $12.

1960 Armour Franks	—	100.00	50.00	30.00

These 20 coins are similar to those issued in 1955, but do not contain as much information on the back. The birthplace and date, team and batting or throwing preference have been omitted. The fronts include the player's name, but only the team nickname is given. The set price of $1,200 in Near Mint condition does not include three variations in the set. Commons are $7.

1962 Salada-Junket Dessert	41	125.00	62.00	37.00

These 1 3/8" plastic coins were issued in packages of Salada Tea and Junket Pudding mix. There are 221 players available, with variations bringing the total to 261. Each coin has a paper color photo inserted in the front, along with the player's name, position and coin number. The plastic rims are color-coded according to the player's team. (Mantle's is light blue). The set, without variations, is valued at $2,500 in Near Mint, and $6,250 with the variations. Commons are $2.

1962 Shirriff Potato Chips	41	75.00	37.00	22.00

This set features plastic coins for 221 players. The set, marketed in Canada by Shirriff Potato Chips, is similar to the Salada sets, except the printing on the back is different and they are scarcer. Each coin is 1 3/8 inches in diameter and is either light blue, dark blue, black, orange, red or white. A color portrait is printed on paper inserted into the obverse surface. The set is worth $1,500 in Near Mint. Commons are between $3-$4.

1963 Salada-Junket Dessert	56	125.00	62.00	37.00

In 1963, Salada-Junket issued a set of 63 1 1/2" metal coins. The set, called "All-Star Baseball Coins," featured top American League (blue rims) and National League (red rims) players. The fronts have no printing, but have full-color pictures. The backs have the coin number, player's name, team, position, brief statistics and sponsors' logos. In Near Mint condition, the set is valued at $750. Commons are $3.

1964 Topps	120	40.00	20.00	10.00
1964 Topps (left-handed/All-Star)	131	45.00	23.00	13.50
(right-handed/All-Star)	131	45.00	23.00	13.50

The 164 1 1/2" metal coins in this set were included inside Topps wax packs. There are 120 regular coins, featuring a full-color background on the front, and 44 All-Star coins, featuring red or blue backgrounds. The backs include the player's name, coin number, and a brief summary of the player's career. Mickey Mantle is one of three players with variations in the set. The set is valued at $700 in Near Mint. Commons are $1.

1965 Old London	—	125.00	62.00	37.00

Old London included these 1 1/2" metal coins in its snack food packages. There are 40 coins in the set; two players per team are featured, except there's only one for the Mets and three for the Cardinals. The fronts have a color photo and the player's name. The silver backs have brief biographies and the Old London logo. The set is valued at $550 in Near Mint condition. Commons are $3.

1967 Coca-Cola cap inserts (Coke)	—	30.00
(Tab)	—	30.00
(Fresca)	—	30.00

There were 409 caps of baseball players issued on bottles caps for Coke, Tab King Size Coke, Fresca, Sprite and Fanta. Each cap had a baseball on the front and a player photo inside. Most photos were protected by a thin plastic liner, but some were buried under cork. Team emblems were airbrushed from the players' hats, but the player's name, position, team and a set number were given. All major league teams except the St. Louis Cardinals were represented by 18 players, and two subsets of All-Stars were created, too. Commons are generally $1-$3; stars are $5-$7.50; superstars are as much as $30; All-Star subsets are $30-$50; complete team sets are $20-$40.

Mickey Mantle pins

1983 MLBPA Pins	—	3.00	2.25	1.25

This set is apparently a reprinted set of the 60-pin set issued by the Major League Baseball Players Association in 1969. The 1983 unnumbered set patterns itself after the

1969 set, except it has 36 players — 18 from each league. Each pin features a black-and-white photo. American League players have a red border; National Leaguers have blue borders. The player's name is at the top; the team name is at the bottom. Also at the bottom is a line which says "c MLBPA MFG. in USA." The complete set is worth $15 in Near Mint condition, while commons are 25 cents.

PM10 Stadium pins 1 3/4"

These pins, generally black-and-white, were sold at the stadiums during several seasons and were produced in three basic diameters — 1 3/4" (approximately 205 pin variations), 2" or 2 1/4" (approximately 44 pins). A complete set of the 1 3/4" pins is about $9,000 in Near Mint condition; a common player is about $7.50. The set of 2 1/4" pins is about $2,000 in Near Mint condition; commons are $30. Sometimes the pins were sold with ribbons or chains with miniature plastic bats, gloves or balls attached.

The 1 3/4" pins have seven Mantle variations: 1) NY on cap, white background, name in white border, eyes nearly closed, $125-$150; 2) NY on cap, blue background, right ear missing, $100-$125; 3) NY on cap, stitched baseball, right ear missing, head and shoulders, $75-$100; 4) NY on cap, blue background, batting right-handed, left hand is not visible, name starts at the wrist, $75-$100; 5) NY on cap, white background, batting right-handed, left hand is not visible, name starts at the elbow, $50-$75; 6) I Love Mickey, no cap, with Teresa Brewer, they are both holding a bat, $20-$35; 7) NY on cap, white background, batting right handed, both hands visible, $15-$30. A 2" diameter Mantle pin ($175-$225) exists, too. It shows NY on the cap, with the name at the top on a light gray background.

The 1956 PM15 Yellow Basepath Pins   —   400.00   200.00   120.00

The sponsor of this 32-pin set is not identified. They are commonly called "Yellow Basepaths" because the black-and-white player photo is set inside a green infield with yellow basepaths. The unnumbered pins are 7/8" in diameter. Commons are $25; the complete set is $2,000 in Near Mint condition.

Mickey Mantle 3 1/2" pin with a yellow background, $75-$100.

Mickey Mantle 3" Baseball Hall of Fame, 1981, $5-$10.

Mickey Mantle 3" Dormand 6x9 photo for pin, $5-$10.

TCMA Collectors black-and-white pin, 1970s era, $15-$20.

"Shooting for 61 in 1961," Mantle/Maris/Ruth, $300-400.

Mantle Lee Jeans, Gayfer's promo pin; two sizes, $15-$20 each.

Mantle "Day To Remember" pin, dated 6-8-69, $15-$20.

Mickey Mantle collector's club pins by Tom Catal, different, $15-$20 each.

Yankee Team pin from 1953, a 3 1/2-inch pin with Mantle, $150-$200.

Mickey Mantle has appeared on several pins.

Chapter 13

Commerce Comet collectibles

Card-related items

• Mickey Mantle's 1951 Bowman card contract: His first with any baseball card company, and the basis for his 1951 Bowman card. $10,000-$15,000.

• Mickey Mantle's 1951 Bowman addendum contract: This additional piece states Mantle's gift reimbursement for his exclusive signing. $5,000.

• Mickey Mantle's 1952 Topps contract: His first with the Topps Chewing Gum Co., it authorizes the use of his picture and biographical sketch for his 1952 card. $10,000.

• Mickey Mantle autographed baseball card kit: Contains a blue vinyl folder with 20 autographed baseball cards depicting Mantle's life. The inside covers are autographed, too, as is the vinyl front cover, which is signed "Mickey Mantle, The Commerce Comet." The kit includes a talking baseball card which explains how Mantle was influenced by his father and grandfather to become a switch-hitter. There are 24 autographs in all. $1,000-$1,500.

Autographed items

• Mickey Mantle signed food bill: A $23.05 food bill from El Torito restaurant, for an order of Willy's beans, cheese, mud pie and four margaritas. Folded twice, matted and framed. $150-$250.

• 1973 Mickey Mantle New York Yankees payroll check: This cancelled check, dated May 26, 1973, is for $306.74 and is endorsed. $650-$750.

• 1978 Mickey Mantle New York Yankees paycheck: Dated Feb. 24, 1978, made out for $339.50, and endorsed by Mantle. It was most likely given to Mantle for his services as a spring training consultant. $500-$700.

• A Mickey Mantle autographed restaurant menu: $50-$75.

• 1984 Mickey Mantle fan club hand-signed letter: $50-$75.

Toys/games

• Mickey Mantle/Willie Mays 1963 Transogram 30" bat, ball and helmet set: Includes three balls, a brown plastic bat and a cardboard insert of Mantle and Mays. $250.

• Mickey Mantle's Official Zoom Ball: Throw it and it automatically returns. Toplay Products Inc., New York, N.Y., 1960s $150.

• Willie Mays and Mickey Mantle's pitch-up device, Champion's Choice with Mantle/Mays pictures on cardboard, circa 1964 $100.

• Mickey Mantle "On-Deck" bat: From 1962, this plastic weighted bat includes the original cardboard with a facsimile autograph. $225.

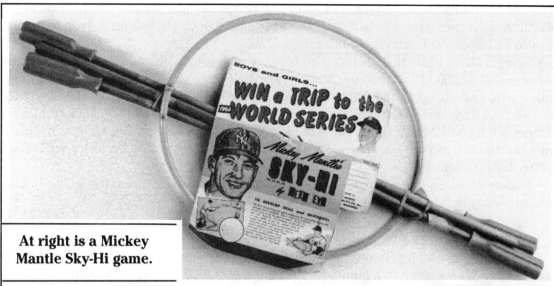

At right is a Mickey
Mantle Sky-Hi game.

Mantle has endorsed many practice games,
and canvas shoes, too.

• Mickey Mantle's Sky-Hi Game: Players use two wooden sticks to catch or propel a plastic ring to themselves or another player. Includes four sticks and a flyer, featuring Mantle's likeness, still attached to the ring. $150.

• Several Mickey Mantle baseball games have been issued, currently ranging in value between $175-$250. They include: Mickey Mantle's Baseball Game, 1957, by Gardner, with cards and autographed photo; Mickey Mantle's Backyard Baseball Game, 1960s, by the L.C. Toy Division, with paper insert, game, bat, ball, photo; Mickey Mantle Kohner's Baseball Action Game No. 425 (1960s); Mickey Mantle's Big League Baseball with photo and record, Gardner (1960s); and Mickey Mantle's All American Baseball Game, 1987, (about $50).

• Mickey Mantle's Backyard 4 Bagger Bean Bag Game can be found for $250-$300, as can a 1960s "Pitch to Mickey" game board.

Photographs/postcards

• Mickey Mantle high school graduation photograph: This postcard with a matching postcard back was given to a family friend by the Mantle clan. $1,500-$2,000.

• Mickey Mantle sophomore and senior year high school yearbooks: Commerce High School 1946-47 "Bengal Tales" and a 1949 edition. $2,000-$2,500.

• Mickey Mantle Sports Illustrated poster: 1968, available through ads in the magazine at that time. $150-$225.

• Dormand photo collection 1954-55: This complete set of 42 cards includes two Mantle cards and is mostly Yankees (34), including Yogi Berra, Johnny Mize, Whitey Ford, Pee Wee Reese, Enos Slaughter, Casey Stengel and Roy Campanella. $2,000-$2,500.

Advertisements

• 1953 Mickey Mantle Vitalis agreement: This one-page agreement says Vitalis can use Mantle's name and likeness on radio and television. $350-$500.

• Louisville Slugger advertising banner (42x29): This silken banner with the logo "Louisville Slugger Bats" shows a Mickey Mantle Hillerich & Bradsby model 125 bat with the slogan "Performance Makes Them Famous." $300-$400.

• "I Love Mickey" promotional 8x10: This is an original promo photo, signed by Mantle, for the record sung by Teresa Brewer. $100-$150.

• Mantle and Maris Home Run Derby sign: This 1961 promotional package from Louisville Slugger allows sporting goods stores to track the September home run duel between the M&M Boys. Three pieces: 1) Original envelope reading "Will There Be A New Champion?" 2) Advertising poster which pictures them and compares them to Babe Ruth and Lou Gehrig. 3) A home run scoreboard to track their progress against Ruth's 60. $250-$325.

• Mickey Mantle's Joplin Holiday Inn matchbook, two different, $85 each. Matches and menus from Mantle's Sports Bar Restaurant in New York also exist.

• Mickey Mantle Monument (24x18): This 43-pound bronze slab with a three-dimensional bust of Mantle reads, in part, "Mickey Mantle, New York Yankees 1951-69, A Magnificent Yankee, 536 Home Runs." Joe DiMaggio presented this plaque to Mantle on Mickey Mantle Day at Yankee Stadium on June 8, 1969. A similar plaque is in Yankee Stadium's Monument Park and a smaller version is outside Mickey Mantle's Restaurant in New York City. $28,000-$32,000.

• Mickey Mantle special premium Wheaties box: This box, autographed on the front in blue Sharpie, is encased in a specially-made lucite holder. It was available only directly from Wheaties. $400-$500.

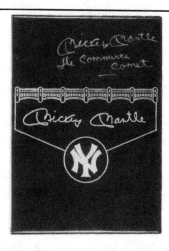

Mickey Mantle's autographed baseball card kit.

At left is Mantle's 1952 Topps contract; above is an autographed $23.05 food bill from El Torito restaurant; below, a 1978 Yankees paycheck endorsed by Mantle.

Above is a Mickey Mantle Holiday Inn matchbook; at right, a Louisville Slugger bat ad for the 16-inch model.

• Louisville Slugger has had Mantle endorse several advertising pieces, including an 11x17 poster in 1965, a miniature 16-inch bat ($15), a plastic bank bat ($15), a wooden bats pen-and-pencil set, and 115 limited-edition Louisville Slugger bats marking the 115 homers he and Roger Maris hit in 1961.

• Mickey Mantle *Boy's Life* ad: Two pages, 13x20, from the mid 1960s, features a Mantle portrait, offers prizes for selling greeting cards. $20-$30.

• Big Yank clothing tag picturing Roger Maris, Whitey Ford and Mantle: This early 1960s large-size advertising clothing tag from Big Yank Boys Clothing features head shots of the players, with a hole at the top for a string to connect to the clothing. The reverse has a mail-in offer for an autographed baseball. $500-$600.

• Mantle has appeared on several advertising posters during the 1980s, including efforts for Budweiser (1987 All-Star Game); R.B. Rice (1986 8x10 picture); Hall of Fame Baseball Star Tru-Value premium poster (1981-82); and Kool-Aid (1987 poster). He's also been featured on a 1985 Play Cable Vision brochure and a Hyatt Regency flyer for a Jan. 19, 1987, show and banquet.

• Mickey Mantle/Whitey Ford Fantasy Baseball Camp memorabilia includes letterhead and brochure ($10-$20) and camp hats, which, autographed, are $100.

• Mickey Mantle Rawlings promotional piece: 11x8 1/2, black-and-white, 1950s, features the first Rawlings glove to be endorsed by Mantle, plus two other models, and an offer for a Mantle baseball. $150-$200.

• Budweiser Natural Light advertising pieces from 1983 include table tents ($50), keychains, billboards and 18x24 posters.

Programs

• Mantle has appeared on several programs, including the "A Day To Remember" program from June 8, 1969; the 1969 Baseball Writers Association Dinner program, with a full page devoted to Mantle; and a Sept. 21, 1968, Fan Appreciation Day, program, with a team photo and two Mantle pictures.

• Booklets have also featured Mantle, including those issued by Carvel Ice Cream (1970s "Great Hitters I've Known"), 1956 Lifebuoy ("How I Hit") and Brylcreem's 1976-77 Mickey Mantle's "Official World Series Fact Book."

• Golf programs also exist from the Loma Linda Country Club for an annual tournament held in Joplin, Mo., and for a Nov. 2, 1987, Gateway Sports celebrity golfing tournament in Broken Arrow, Okla.

Newspapers

Here are examples which Box Seat Collectibles, Halesite, N.Y., has advertised in *Sports Collectors Digest* (in Excellent condition unless stated):

• 1951: "Yank Youth Program Paces Entire League!" From the *New York Daily News*. Mantle, Martin, Jensen and McDougald lead the way. $85

• 1956: "Yanks Win, 10-4! Mantle Slams 2 (HRs)!" From the *New York Daily News*. Mantle hits 485-foot and 438-foot home runs at Griffith Park during the Yankees' 1956 season opener. $75.

• 1957: "Yanks Rip Braves, 12-3 (in World Series)! Mantle Clouts 4-Bagger!" From the *New York Herald Tribune*. $40.

• 1961: "Mick Hits 3, Now at 43!" From the *New York Mirror*. Mantle surpasses Roger Maris by two in their chase for Babe Ruth's record of 60.

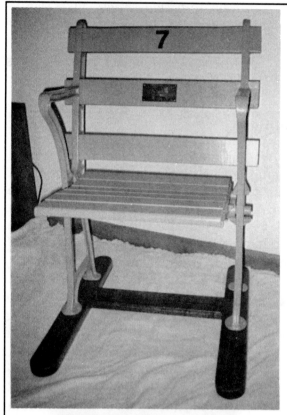

Above is Mantle's 1956 World Series ring; at left is a #7 box seat from Yankee Stadium. Below is an autographed, hand-painted Mantle golf bag.

Above is a Big Yank clothing tag featuring Mantle, Roger Maris and Whitey Ford. Below is a 1964 Phillies Cigar Mickey Mantle premium glove made by Rawlings.

• 1961: "Mantle Signs $82,000 Pact!" From the *New York Daily News* (VG). Mantle, coming off his best season ever, with a .317 batting average, 54 home runs and 128 RBI, signs the biggest contract of his career.

• 1964: "Mantle's 500-Foot Homer Jars Sox." From *The Des Moines Register.* Yankees win 7-3, as Mantle hits two homers in rookie Mel Stottlemyre's first major league win. $150.

Miscellaneous

• Mickey Mantle's 1956 New York Yankees World Series ring: Mantle capped this Triple Crown season with a trip to the World Series against the Brooklyn Dodgers. He hit three home runs during the series, including one during Don Larsen's perfect game. The 14K ring, made by Balfour Co., has a two carat diamond on its face and is framed by "New York Yankees World Champions." "1956" is raised and embossed on each side, with "Mickey C. Mantle" engraved inside the shank. Pre-auction estimate was $250,000.

• New York Yankee Stadium seat: #7 is on the slat on the seat, an homage to Mickey Mantle. The paint has been restored. $700-$900.

• Dairy Queen statue set of 18: Each white, plastic three-inch statue features a player in action. The player's name is engraved on the bottom of the base. Other players besides Mantle include Yogi Berra, Roy Campanella, Gil Hodges, Stan Musial, Duke Snider and Willie Mays. $600-$800 for the set.

• Mickey Mantle Hartland statue and box: Hartland Plastics Co. primarily sold these eight-inch statues of 18 baseball stars, including Mantle, in retail stores and at ballparks from 1960-63. Up to 15,000 Mantle statues were made; it is one of the more common of the 18 and can be found with or without a magnet. Having the cardboard box and hang tag for the statue adds to the value. A white Mantle statue is $300-$400, with lower off-whites starting at about 50 percent less of the white figure.

• Mickey Mantle bobbing head doll and box: Mickey Mantle bobbing head dolls were created in 1961-62. Each has either an embossed "N.Y." or "Yankee" decal on the chest. The doll was originally issued with a box, which is worth $100-$150. The Mantle doll is worth $400-$550.

• 1989 Kenner Baseball Greats: Mantle and Joe DiMaggio were packaged together, with cards for each player, too. $25-$35.

• Sports Impressions has featured Mantle on various sizes of plates (up to $200) and figurines (up to $400).

• Salvino Inc., of Corona, Calif., has created autographed porcelain figurines of Mantle hitting and fielding ($350-$450 each) and batting with uniform #6 or #7 ($700 each).

• Autographed Mickey Mantle golf bag, hand painted: Dark blue vinyl golf bag made by Ron Miller Associates. A color 8-by-10-inch autographed photo is affixed to the side inside a clear plastic covering. The bag is signed "Mickey Mantle #7," below the photo, and above a hand-painted image of Mantle in a batting stance and in a bust pose. Several zippers on the bag have attached "M" charms. $1,200-$1,500.

• Mickey Mantle 1964 Phillies Cigar premium glove: Signature model made by Rawlings, offered as a mail-in premium only. Includes the original mailing box, postmarked August 1964, with a "Phillies Mickey Mantle Special" return address label and original Rawlings plastic bag. $500-$600.

• Mickey Mantle's Isometric Minute A Day Gym: 1960s, by Beacon. "Invest 1 minute a day and have the muscles and physique of an athlete...without strain, without sweat, without exhaustive exercises." ($175).

Above is a Mickey Mantle Hartland statue, with original tag and box.

Above is a Mickey Mantle bobbing head doll from the early 1960s.

The Mantle statue above is by Sports, Accessories & Memorabilia.

Sports Impressions has offered a Mickey Mantle Collectors' Club.

- Mickey Mantle pencil set: Made by World Pencil, includes picture and two unsharpened pencils; $75 for the pair of pencils. The box has a picture of Mantle on it and can be had for up to $200.
- Mickey Mantle original Hartland lamp: This lamp has a Mantle statue standing on a wood base. The shade has two bats and a ball sewn on in brown and white felt. The bat is not the original. $550.
- Mickey Mantle game-used glove lamp: This lamp uses a Mantle game-used glove as its base. $1,500.
- Mickey Mantle and Roger Maris 1960s electric Stellar clock radio: With a bat and baseball on the dial and raised plastic ballplayers over the speaker. $700.
- Mickey Mantle 7-Eleven cups: Given away in 1972-1973, these cups featured 60 players in 1972 and 20 Hall of Famers in 1973. Each has a portrait and a brief biography, and can usually be found for less than $10 each.
- Mantle's Country Cookin five-piece dish set: Early 1970s Shenango China U.S.A., it includes two bowls, two plates and a dish. $150.
- Budweiser "Part Of A City's Proud Tradition," limited-edition collector's series (Mickey Mantle and Roger Maris). $7-$10.
- 1958 tin framed novelty watch with Mantle and Hank Aaron. $175.
- 1957 red plastic swinging mobile with large picture of Mickey Mantle, insert states, "Year of the Slugger." $150.
- Mickey Mantle and Roger Maris baseball caps: A blue cap has a large patch on the front and two different patches on back. $75-$100. A red hat, the "Home Run Twins," has a large photo linen patch of them. $100-$125.
- Mickey Mantle wristwatch and alarm clock from the 1960s. $100-$150.
- A June 8, 1969, red felt pennant from Mickey Mantle Day at Yankee Stadium. $15.
- A 1968 Winners Circle game piece. $35.
- Mickey Mantle and Roger Maris photo premium with rounded top corners and straight bottom corners, producer unknown. $20.
- 1974 Syracuse Chiefs scorecard inserts, two different: A glossy photo is $15; a black-and-white baseball card is $30.
- 1976-77 Shakey's Pizza Hall of Fame Series #145. $15.
- 1971 Sunnydale Farms plaques. $150.
- 1964 Meadow Gold Dairy. $125.
- 1956 Big League statue with back package card. $250-$300.
- Mickey Mantle paint-by-numbers paint set: Consists of painting and a picture of Mickey on the box. $125-$175.
- 1970s Mickey Mantle Sports Stix, brown circular sticker without Yankee emblem. $25.
- Mantle 3-D photos cut out on wooden plaques, several different. $15-$20 each.
- 1970s Play It Safe/Dairy Lee reflector sticker. $150-$175.
- 1964 Rawlings eight-page trade digest. $35-$50.
- Mantle Loma Linda Country Club golf hat with emblem and Mantle's name on a patch. $35.
- 1974 National Baseball Hall of Fame pewter plate. $75-$125.
- Mantle/Maris 16x24 paper issue from 1962. $25.
- Mickey Mantle shortbread sticker, $7, shortbread canister. $10.
- Mantle Sports Legend tape with Mantle on box, $15.
- Mantle/Mays Sports Legends tape with pictures of Mantle and Mays on the box. $25.
- Mantle pewter coaster MVP set from the Yankee Clubhouse Catalog. $75-$100 set.

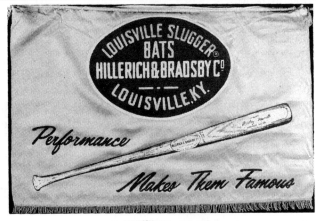

Mickey Mantle has been featured on Louisville Slugger banners, Hall of Fame plaques, keychains, pen/pencil sets, Lee Jeans buttons, Slurpee cups and pencil sets.

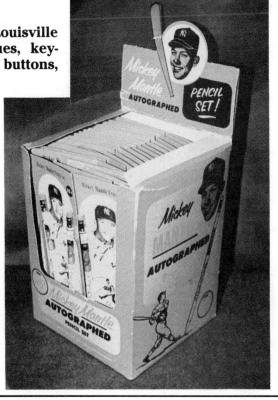

• 1962 Hoffman ginger ale label with Mantle/Maris. $125.

• 1963 Topps wrapper premium, 3-D plastic mask. $750.

• 1960s Star Jack book cover with Mantle. $75.

• 1952 Mantle bicycle decal with signature, yellow and blue. $200.

• 1960s exhibit telescope with Mantle, $150-$200; and a 1960s exhibit television with Mantle on the screen. $250-$300.

• 1987 New York Yankees field-box tickets with pictures of DiMaggio/Mantle. $7-$10.

• 1960s Mantle Manors form letter and travel voucher check with pics of Mantle, letter, $10-$15, voucher. $50-$75.

• 1988 Mickey Mantle National Baseball Hall of Fame gallery collection of mini plaques, bronze, $50, silver. $125.

• 1986 Mickey Mantle's Baseball Tips for Kids of All Ages video tape, by CBS Fox, $25; poster board, $25; display. $25.

• 1983 Mantle Time Saver, VISA-MasterCharge card application. $7.

• 1987 Fuji film advertisements and Mantle game. $3.

• 1987 Fuji film baseball premium, two different baseballs with facsimile autographs. $10 each.

• 1986 "7 Views Of Genius," reprints on cards from *Sports Illustrated* magazine. $25.

• Mickey Mantle Hero Medal, Arizona. $50.

• 1990 National Baseball Hall of Fame silver proof commemorative coin with collectors tin (Legends of Baseball). $10.

• 1986 Bronze replica of 1952 Topps #311. $25.

• 1991 Nobody Beats the Wiz promotional posters, two. $15 each.

• 1991 Baseball Flipp Tipps (Legends), Switch Hitting H.R. Swings. $10.

• Mickey Mantle baseball with 1952 Topps card picture. $15.

• 1989 Grenada stamp. $5.

• Sooner Pride Committee Inc. 1989 9-inch bronze replica sculpture, $500; 20-inch sculpture, $5,000; Ted Watts art print. $150-$200.

• Mickey Mantle Hartland statue reproduction, 1989-90. $25.

• Mickey Mantle caricature T-shirts from the Baseball Hall of Fame. $15.